Dear Sister

Medieval Women and the Epistolary Genre

edited by

KAREN CHEREWATUK and
ULRIKE WIETHAUS

University of Pennsylvania Press
Philadelphia

Library of Congress Cataloging-in-Publication Data
Dear sister : medieval women and the epistolary genre / edited by
   Karen Cherewatuk and Ulrike Wiethaus.
      p.   cm. — (Middle Ages series)
   Includes bibliographical references and index.
   ISBN 0-8122-3170-8 (cloth). — ISBN 0-8122-1437-4 (pbk.)
      1. Letters—Women authors—History and criticism.   2. Literature,
Medieval—Women authors—History and criticism.   3. Women—History—
Middle Ages, 500–1500—Historiography.   I. Cherewatuk, Karen.
II. Wiethaus, Ulrike.   III. Series.
PN6131.D4   1993
809.6'0082—dc20   93-20024
                                                           CIP

PN
6131
.D4
1993

To our sisters, in the spirit and in the flesh,
and especially to Kathryn, Christine,
Katharina, Doris, Ursula, and Renate

Contents

Acknowledgments

Many people helped make *Dear Sister* a rich experience for us. We are grateful to our contributors, who invariably revised with energy and good cheer; to our readers, Barbara Newman and Elizabeth Alvilda Petroff, for their incisive and practical reports; to E. Ann Matter, for her continued support and helpful comments; to Jean Parker, ever resourceful behind the reference desk; to Ruth Hamilton of the Newberry Library for finding the cover illustration; to the administrations of St. Olaf College and Wake Forest University for generously supporting this project; to our editor, Jerome E. Singerman, whose integrity we admire and whose encouragement helped; and to Richard J. DuRocher, who first suggested that we do a book together and whose enthusiasm never waned.

K.C. and U.W.

Karen Cherewatuk and Ulrike Wiethaus

Introduction: Women Writing Letters in the Middle Ages

Letters are remarkably suited for self-expression and communication. Unlike learned treatises, letters have long been accessible to women because of the directness with which they convey ideas and emotions and because of the immediate availability of audience. Through letters, women who desired to write could bypass the need for formal education, literary patronage, editors, and publishers, and they often thus circumvented the censorship of a patriarchal literary industry.

We are not the first students of the genre to note its appeal to women in Western European culture. Elizabeth C. Goldsmith has recently stated that "since the sixteenth century, when the familiar letter was first thought of as a literary form, male commentators have noted that the epistolary genre seemed particularly suited to the female voice. Newly educated women could easily learn to write letters, and as epistolary theory became more adapted to worldly culture, women's letters began to be considered the best models of the genre."[1] From our perspective, Goldsmith's claim begins too late in the history of letter writing. By the Renaissance, male humanists had already noted the achievements of medieval women correspondents: Anton Francesco Doni, for example, named Catherine of Siena's *epistolario* in his catalogue of ancient works to revere. John Stevens included Christine de Pizan's *Epistre a la Reine* in his formulary as a model letter.[2] The essays in this volume explore the distinctive contributions to letter writing in Western Europe made by these and other medieval women from the sixth to the sixteenth centuries. The primary texts discussed here, however, do not represent a comprehensive survey of the genre. As editors we attempted to include instead epistolary examples from each of the areas in which medieval women excelled as letter writers. Our first three essays treat learned women who wrote in Latin. In "Radegund and the Epistolary Tradition," Karen Cherewatuk explores how St. Radegund joined classical poetic tradition, in particular the rhetoric of Ovid's *Epistulae Herodium*, with the form of Germanic lament to illustrate her own personal and political needs. In Gillian T. W. Ahlgren's "Visions and Rhetorical Strategy in the Letters of Hildegard of Bingen," Hildegard emerges as a rhetorician who is as self-conscious as Radegund, but whereas Radegund is concerned to imitate poetic precursors, Hildegard forges her own sophisticated strategy for expressing her visions. Ahlgren documents how the literary formulae Hildegard chooses depend upon her addressees' gender and socio-religious status. In "'Wholly Guilty, Wholly Innocent': Self-Definition in Héloïse's Letters to Abélard," Glenda McLeod traces Héloïse's epistolary experimentation in self-definition which took place in "a unique open-ended dialectic with her *dominus*."[3] Moving from a study of Héloïse's choice of pronouns (the singular "I" representing Héloïse's private role as Abélard's wife, and the plural "We" representing Héloïse's public role as abbess) to her use of a letter's salutation as a stage for ensuing argument, McLeod traces the conflict between personal self and public persona.

The remaining essays in the book treat vernacular letters. In "'*Io Caterina*': Ecclesiastical Politics and Oral Culture in the Letters of Catherine of Siena," Karen Scott analyzes Catherine's *epistolario* in light of oral tradition. Scott argues (contra Catherine's confessor and biographer, Raymond of Capua) that the saint's correspondence was not a gift from God but part of her active apostolate—which for Catherine involved "ordinary speech and oral communication, and not prophetic or supernatural speech."[4] The illiterate Catherine's technique directly contrasts with that of Hildegard. Whereas Hildegard carefully chooses literary formulae to express her visions, in her *epistolario* Catherine tailors individual sermons to fit particular audiences but without relying on and scarcely referring to the visionary mode. The influence of oral tradition in medieval women's epistolary style emerges again in Diane Watt's essay, "'No Writing for Writing's Sake': The Language of Service and Household Rhetoric in the Letters of the Paston Women." Like Catherine, Margaret Paston wrote for an immediate purpose in a colloquial style that displays the features of oral narrative, but Margaret's concerns are very much tied to her family. She is busy seeking educational opportunities and appropriate spouses for her children, supervising servants, organizing provisions, and maintaining family property. Whatever the status of her formal education, Margaret's letters show her understanding of law and court politics and depict her as a formidable player in the social and political affairs of the family. Illiteracy as defined by the male canon does not appear to have barred Margaret Paston from exerting power. Christine de Pizan's topics, as reflected in Earl Jeffrey Richards's "*'Seulette a part'*—The 'Little Woman on the Sidelines' Takes Up Her Pen: The Letters of Christine de Pizan," expand beyond the household concerns of the Paston women to embrace the question of women's nature and social status. Throughout her literary career Christine experimented with the epistolary genre, synthesizing courtly verse epistles, Latin dictamenal instruction, and humanist epistolography. Christine's epistolary experiments illustrate her lifelong commitment to exploding clerical myths about women's nature and to calling for education open to both men and women. Through her letters, Christine de Pizan moves from her self-proclaimed position as "little woman on the sidelines" to the center of the humanist debate on learning. In contrast to Christine's unified appeal, the correspondence of the Beguine Maria de Hout presents multiple and fractured personae.

In "'If I had an Iron Body': Femininity and Religion in the Letters of Maria de Hout," Ulrike Wiethaus reads the Beguine's correspondence against the gendered hierarchy of the post-Reformation Church. Wiethaus discovers that different personae emerge depending on audience: when addressing fellow Beguines, Maria is confident and articulate; when writing to her Carthusian and Jesuit supporters, Maria is a maternal guide who strives to balance humility with authority; when corresponding with her confessor, who most fully represents ecclesiastical power, Maria is obedient to the point of self-abnegation. The voice of Maria's correspondence vacillates between life-affirming optimism and morose dejection, an indication of a holy woman's difficulties in carving out a niche for herself at the close of the Middle Ages.

In the Middle Ages the letter was a genre that appealed both to women who were formally attached to the church through vows and those who were not. Our interest in the medieval epistle springs from the genre's unusual flexibility in regard to authors, topics and audiences. Women could use it to teach, as when Hildegard von Bingen preaches church reform; to influence politics, as when Christine de Pizan writes to the queen of France; to maintain familial ties, as when Radegund poetically recreates the fall of Thuringia for her cousin; to explore innermost emotions, as when Héloïse examines her matrimonial and religious vows; or to convey a simple message, as when Margaret Paston asks her husband to buy her almonds, sugar, cloth, and crossbows. In an age when most letters were dictated, the epistle enabled women to transcend not only gender but also educational barriers, as when the illiterate Catherine of Siena excoriates the government of

Rome. To dictate a letter, however, does not imply the low status of the sender.

In an essentially oral culture such as the Middle Ages, the written word conferred great authority on both sender and recipient. Indeed, letters in the Middle Ages often were read aloud to a community or circulated publicly. They served as legal documents as well as means of personal communication. As Giles Constable notes in his introduction to the genre, "in the Middle Ages letters were for the most part self-conscious, quasi-public literary documents, often written with an eye to future collection and publication."[5] The personal letter comes into being only with the rise of the vernacular, and even then a writer sometimes seems conscious of an audience beyond the immediate one. The Paston family, for example, saved their voluminous correspondence as potential evidence for future legal disputes.[6] The historian of the medieval epistle must therefore become sensitive to double strategies employed by the writer who says as much through implication as through direct statement.

In *Epistolarity: Approaches to a Form* Janet Gurkin Altman develops a model which captures the complex strategies employed by the author to engage her or his audience.[7] Because of the intensely dialogical nature of the genre, the addressee (Altman's "implied reader") is omnipresent in the text and to a large degree determines its form, its content, and the representation of the author's self. Thus disclosures about the author may be a mask or an honest portrait; shared information can be significant either as bridge between two parties or as a consciously erected barrier. Furthermore, the letter's meaning is derived as much from the use or neglect of already existing epistolary conventions as from the content of the letter itself.

Medieval letters composed by women call for certain modifications of Altman's criteria, however, because the letter's public dimension by far outweighed its use within a private, intimate context. Our modern notion of correspondence, with an assumed exchange of letters between two persons, does not always apply to epistles written by medieval women. Concomitantly, the presence or absence of status-oriented rules on form and style played a significantly larger role in negotiating the relationship between addressee and author in the medieval period than today. When we add a gender-sensitive perspective, this emphasis on status and form becomes even more important. In our collection, perhaps no letters demonstrate this point more poignantly than those by Maria de Hout, whose style and presentation of self seem to depend exclusively upon her audience.[8]

As Altman points out, "literary genres and subgenres develop the greatest cohesion and complexity when they evolve within a limited socio-historical context."[9] For medieval women, the cohesiveness of formalized epistolary rules was determined by medieval patriarchy. In this "limited sociohistorical context," women constituted what anthropologists call a "muted group." Given asymmetrical power relations, women were at a disadvantage in formulating their ideas, concerns, and experiences, because rules for public and semi-public communication were controlled by the dominant group.[10] Therefore medieval women letter writers could either choose to break into the privileged epistolary precinct reserved for men as primary definers or opt to ignore it and create their own system. In the end, however, neither option allowed women to exert the same influence as cultural primary definers. We need to remind ourselves that medieval women always wrote at the margins of a realm staked out by male authors. Our thesis is that although such marginalization reflects women's subordination it also left us a testimony of women's tremendous strength to swim against the current, of their creativity, inventiveness, and intelligence. Although barred from the centers of cultural and economic power, women did not remain silent. Their epistolary legacy testifies to that.

Historians of medieval culture generally cite the *ars dictaminis* or *ars dictandi*, the rhetorical study and practise of epistolary compositions, as a "major achievement of medieval civilization."[11] This field of rhetoric has its roots in Italy where the professional teacher of epistolography, the *dictator*, first appeared. The dictamenal manual of Alberic of Monte Cassino, the earliest handbook to survive, lists the five parts of the letter which became standard in medieval Europe: the *salutatio* or epistolary greeting, which carefully articulates the recipient's social position; the *benevolentiae captatio*, which usually consists of a proverb or quotation from scripture intended to secure the recipient's good will; the *narratio* or statement of particular purpose; the *petitio* in the form of an argument deduced from premises established earlier in the letter; and the *conclusio*.[12] The format is derived from the divisions of classical oration, with the letter adding a formal salutation. Formularies or *dictamina*, books of sample letters, survive from all parts of medieval Europe, indicating the popularity of the *ars dictaminis* at cathedral schools and universities. By the thirteenth century treatises began to appear in Italian dialects, and by the fourteenth and fifteenth centuries they were found in many vernacular languages such as French, German, Czech, and Polish. Several of the women writers who appear in this volume modeled their letters on the conventions of the formularies. The Franco-Italian Christine de Pizan clearly knew the dictamenal tradition and consciously manipulated it to serve her own purposes. In her *Livre des Trois Vertus* or *Book of the Three Virtues* (also known as *The Treasure of the City of Ladies*), Christine offers a model letter for women counseling younger women. In her *Epistre a la Reine* or *Epistle to the Queen*, Christine adjures Isabeau de Bavière to sue for peace, weaving into the letter Hebrew, classical, and Christian exempla, thus marrying humanist scholarship and dictamenal tradition.[13]

Since women were excluded from the schools at which the *ars dictaminis* was taught, it is not surprising that most authors follow the models in only a rudimentary way, primarily in salutations and closings.[14] The long sequences of conventional phrases which appear at the opening of the letters by women writers of fifteenth-century Germany and England testify to the way in which the lessons of the *dictatores* eventually influenced even middle class writers. As Norman Davis pointed out, so familiar are these stock phrases that Margaret Brews in her "Valentine" to John Paston III in 1477 playfully inverts the expected conventions.[15] Whether they were ignorant or well versed in *dictamen*, women throughout the Middle Ages wrote letters that speak eloquently of their times.

In the following pages, we will briefly explore how medieval women responded to epistolary tradition from the sixth to the sixteenth century.

Early Middle Ages

The material that survives from the early Middle Ages seemingly contradicts our modern sense of a letter. These epistles are not often personal; they lack spontaneity; they are composed exclusively in Latin. What these epistles lack in familiarity for the modern reader, they compensate for in exploration of form. The term *epistula* encompassed a wide variety of works, almost any written document with a salutation attached to it. Among the earliest works by medieval women which we might classify as a letter is the travelogue by the pilgrim Egeria from the first half of the fifth century. She was a member of a religious community in Galicia who wrote an epistolary travelogue addressed to "my sisters, my light" and "ladies dear to me."[16] On the basis of this formidable work, she is credited with helping to forge a united Christian identity by establishing "a new spiritual geography of a second homeland of which all members of this Christian empire can be citizens."[17] Radegund's verse epistles recreate the fall of her homeland in language reminiscent not only of Vergil and Ovid but also of the anonymous Anglo-Saxon elegists. The ninth-century Carolingian noble woman Dhuoda combines verse and prose in her *speculum* or mirror for princes. The acrostic greeting toward the beginning of the treatise suggests that this work too might be classified as a letter: "DHUODA SENDS GREET-INGS TO HER BELOVED SON, WILLIAM. READ!" ("DHUODA DILECTO FILIO UUILEHLMO SALUTEM LEGE").[18] Epistles in the more familiar sense of correspondence also survive from as early as the eighth century. Included among the correspondence of Boniface (672–754), for example, are letters written by his circle of women supporters: letters by Abbess Eadburg, by Abbess Eangyth and her daughter Heaburg, by Leoba, and by Abbess Cyneburg.[19]

In the early Middle Ages, the distinction between religious and secular women authors is somewhat artificial. For noble women, the only female authors of extant letters from this period, the boundaries between family and religious community were still very permeable. Just as the playwright Hrotsvit, a canoness, traveled between the Ottonian court and her abbey at Gandersheim, St. Radegund deserted her husband, King Lothar I, for the monastery and yet remained involved in royal politics.[20]

The epistles surviving from this early period show a high degree of literary accomplishment and attest to the remarkable level of education these noble women attained. Their letters have often been preserved either because of the important status of the recipient or of the writer herself. For example, four *epistulae* by the Gothic queen Amalasuntha survive in the *Variae* of Cassiodorus, a twelve-book collection of letters written while Cassiodorus served her and her husband Theodoric, a man of dubious reputation. Amalasuntha's letters are addressed to the Roman senate, the Emperor Justinian, and the Empress Theodora. Queen Brunhilda likewise wrote to the royal house in Byzantium. In 566, Brunhilda pleads with the Empress Anastasia for the return of her orphaned and ransomed infant grandson; the letter is referred to in Gregory of Tours' *History of the Franks*. Also fearing for a loved one, Herchenefreda in 630 writes with practical and spiritual advice and maternal longing to her son Desiderius; her three letters are now preserved in the *vita* of that saint. In the 770s the nun Berhtgyth describes her situation while in Thuringia, where she had gone to teach with Boniface. Preserved in Boniface's correspondence are three letters in which she begs a visit from her brother Balthard, her only surviv-ing relative in her native England. Gisela, Charlemagne's sister, and Ro-trud, his daughter, correspond with a clergyman of high stature. Their exchange of letters with Alcuin dates from 800. In the correspondence, he seeks their criticism on his commentary on John's Gospel and they ask him to gloss select passages from St. Augustine.[21]

These epistles, in which a woman communicates on equal or near equal terms with a man, indicate not only the noble status of the author but also flexible roles for the sexes. Sharply increasing gender dichotomy in the high Middle Ages leads to women's achievements in two other aspects of epistolography: use of the visionary mode and the rise of the personal vernacular letter.[22]

The Later Middle Ages

In comparison to the noble women authors of the early Middle Ages, the identity of a woman writer in the high Middle Ages is more sharply defined by her status as a religious celibate or a secular wife and mother. In the high Middle Ages, literacy ceases to be the prerogative of the noble elite, and letters from women of the merchants' class survive along with those by women in the monasteries, in Beguinages, and at court. The proliferation of social contexts of these letters goes hand in hand with women's creative transformations of the epistolary genre. Paradoxically, this astounding literary diversification is paralleled by an increasing polarization of gender roles and expectations, which also explains the sharpening of boundaries between religious and secular lifestyles for women. Yet the gradual enclosure of religious women and their ensuing isolation and powerlessness is only a prelude to that experienced by secular women who were increasingly confined to the home—a process that came to a head in the Reformation era. As many of the letters of humanist women testify, the struggle between public and private roles for women was largely fought over the issue of women's education and literacy.[23] The problematic nature of gender polarization and the vicissitudes of negotiating a balance between the private and the public among women writers in our volume is perhaps most evident in Héloïse's correspondence with Abélard. Glenda McLeod illustrates how Héloïse examines with brutal honesty her competing claims as wife and lover versus nun and abbess.[24]

Although some women writers participated successfully in the male-dominated world of the *ars dictaminis*, the majority of medieval women produced their letters outside it. Because dictamen functioned in part as a complicated game of establishing and consolidating hierarchies among men, women were excluded from the game. In general, women's absence from this rhetorical discourse is a result of their restricted access to education and public roles, but it also coincides with two distinctly medieval phenomena: one, the discovery of the vernacular as a written means of communication, which moved the epistolary discourse away from the centers of learning, and two, the emerging role of women visionaries as legitimate figures of authority for the laity. The use of both the vernacular and the visionary mode brought into being new ways of writing and using letters. Barred from public performances as teachers, theologians, and pastoral counsellors, visionary women could sublimate these roles in part by writing letters.

In his survey of the genre, Constable argues that after "the Golden Age of medieval epistolography" in the eleventh and twelfth centuries, "epistolary style and content became degraded and mechanical." Constable links this falling off with "the decline of Latin and the spread of vernacular languages."[25] His perspective emphasizes the negative and defines cultural achievement exclusively from a masculine point of view. Constable uses as standard the economic and educational resources open only to medieval men. When one takes into consideration the correspondence of medieval women—and except in passing, Constable does not—we are faced not simply with a decline of Latinity but also with a simultaneous creative expansion of the genre in the *vernacular*. In Anglo-Norman alone, letters survived by secular authors such as Blanche, Duchess of Bretagne; Alice la Desperance; Maud Pantouff; and Alice of Winchester. In German-speaking countries, letters testify to the creativity of religious women writers such as Mechthild of Hackeborn, Christine of Stommeln, and Hadewijch.[26]

This explosion of epistolary possibilities, no matter how unappreciated and unnoticed it may have been during the Middle Ages, clearly shows the contribution of women to vernacular literature. The structures and patterns developed in these letters never effected the dominant epistolary paradigm, but their sheer existence poses a challenge for our own attempts at categorization. The Beguine Hadewijch is a case in point. Hadewijch's prose and poetic texts rank among the earliest "master"pieces of Dutch literature, and yet her *corpus* shows the challenges inherent in classifying medieval letters: Hadewijch left a collection of 31 prose letters, six rhymed letters, and eight rhymed treatises, four of which use the formulae of personal letters.[27] Her letters absorb topics that male writers treat in separate types of discourse such as theology, pedagogy, the praise of friendship, mystical teachings, and poetry.

Cloistered women such as Hildegard of Bingen or Elisabeth of

Schönau used the genre to merge spiritual direction or doctrinal instruction with personal data in highly complex ways. Women lay religious like Catherine of Siena and Maria de Hout continued to relate personal and doctrinal issues in their letters in the late Middle Ages, this time, however, in the vernacular. These letters are often touching, as when a weary Catherine asks for the prayers and support of her friends or a distraught Maria laments that her body is not made of iron.[28] As in the case of Caritas Pirckheimer and the much admired women of the Italian Renaissance such as Laura Cereta or Isabella d'Este, who left fascinating correspondence with artists such as Leonardo da Vinci or Pietro Perugino, women participated again visibly in intellectual and cultural life.[29] Simultaneously, less educated secular women writers were helping to create what Constable calls "intimate vernacular private letters."[30] It is in the letters of the Paston family that we glimpse the concerns of secular women, sometimes in a hastily dictated message, and sometimes in carefully constructed letters that one can well claim as literature.

The Problem of Gendered Writing

As this collection of essays demonstrates, women throughout the Middle Ages wrote on an astonishing array of topics and in a great variety of styles. This observation raises not only historical questions regarding the development of medieval letter writing, but also feminist issues familiar to anybody interested in the dynamics of gender stereotypes. Of the famous three elements with which women polemically have been aligned—children, the kitchen, and the church—it is only the church that appears with some frequency in medieval women's epistolary writings, and that not always uncritically. See, for example, the works of Hildegard of Bingen or Catherine of Siena.

In the attempt to delineate gendered boundaries in our primary sources, we were faced not only with a generally uncharted territory in terms of types of letters, but also with a problem caused by medieval "editors." Many letters by religious women, who produced the lion's share of medieval women's correspondence, were stripped of their beginning and ending formulae and inserted in the overall oeuvre of their authors. The letters by the thirteenth-century mystics Mechthild of Magdeburg and Mechthild of Hackeborn are a case in point. Obviously, the medieval compilers valued certain letters more for their spiritual content than for their testimony to the author's social status and impact as expressed in epistolary opening and closing lines, which often were simply chopped off. Scholars need to establish when and why compilers made such editorial decisions, and what these changes tell us about the status of women and their correspondence in a particular region and time.

If the female author's social standing could be denied, it could also be exploited. At times, the reputation of a holy woman was used to circulate false letters in her name, as in the case of the immensely popular Elisabeth of Schönau. This caused considerable distress to Elisabeth and endangered her existence in a way unimaginable in regard to male authors. For example, St. Bernard of Clairvaux experienced similar fraud, yet with no harmful results. For Elisabeth the ensuing dangers were two-fold. First, she was moved dangerously close to heretical groups, who nearly always supported women in leadership roles, be it as teachers or priests.[31] Second, the fraudulent letters pushed her over boundaries carefully defined by the Church: those other than priests were allowed to preach (if permission to preach was granted) only about moral issues, not dogmatic or theological questions.

To complicate our search further, a religious woman herself could use the genre to gain authority in a more dubious way. The nun Magdalena Beutler, herself daughter of the well-respected mystic Margareta of Kenzingen, composed and dramatically delivered a letter written in her own blood in order to find a hearing in her community. Probably hidden from view in the choir pews, she threw this "heavenly letter" (*Himmelsbrief*) among her fellow nuns during a church service and then mysteriously disappeared for three days. Upon her return, she refused to speak. This unusual staging of mail delivery brought forth the desired effects for Magdalena. For us, it raises interesting questions about the perceived efficacy and function of letters by visionary women.[32]

The freedom to speak in their own voice and have this voice preserved is one of the main issues regarding religious "women of letters." For secular women writers, the problem is our ignorance of women's (changing) roles in medieval economy, family settings, and politics. As Diane Watt's analysis of Margaret Paston's letters and Karen Cherewatuk's reading of Radegund point out, secular women writers always appear to have had access to informal routes of power through emotional or familial ties, even if the direct exercise of political power was barred. The question that is raised then is how to realign the boundaries between a medieval woman's private life and her public influence. Margaret Paston's "household rhetoric," a term chosen aptly by Diane Watt, includes more than just chatting about her need for a new necklace; it embraces the whole gamut of a life that begins in Margaret's backyard and extends to the royal court. Thus Diane Watt can characterize Margaret Paston as a "matriarchal figure dominating the household."[33]

In view of the wealth of our primary sources, this collection of essays merely touches the surface. In sum, the following themes emerged as pivotal in our discussions of the source material: the relationship between traditional models of the *ars dictaminis* and the actual letters composed by learned women; a reconsideration of the relation between public and private spheres evidenced in all of medieval women's letters; implications of the ways in which letters and letter collections were prepared and passed on; the locus of women's letters in their community (their *Sitz im Leben*); the question of a specifically "female discourse" in the Middle Ages; and, finally, women's letters as an important and unique source of medieval women's lives in all their aspects. These are not themes about which we, as editors, can make easy generalizations. We refer readers to the perceptive comments of our contributors.

In her book *Writing a Woman's Life* Carolyn G. Heilbrun asserts that "reading women's lives needs to be considered in the absence of 'a structure of critical' or biographical commonplaces. . . . It all needs to be invented, or discovered, or resaid."[34] A researcher willing to test this thesis in regard to the medieval epistle will find Heilbrun's statement confirmed. Seen as a group, medieval women do not fit snugly any kind of pattern established for the development of the epistolary genre in the Middle Ages. These models have been extracted exclusively from the correspondences of men and follow the ebb and flow of medieval men's use of the genre. Neither the twelfth nor the late fourteenth and fifteenth centuries, both representing peak periods in the production of epistolary "master"pieces in the *ars dictaminis* from the pens of male writers, brought forth more than a handful of accomplished women letter writers. Yet the centuries of epistolographical "decline," which witnessed also the rise of the vernacular in literature, meant an exciting new opening for women's epistolary productivity. Women's achievements in epistolography have generally been left unexamined. Preceding the much-needed efforts by Albrecht Classen,[35] one rare exception is Eleanor Duckett's essay on "Women and their Letters in the Early Middle Ages."[36] Duckett poignantly addresses the seemingly timeless problem of locating female writing in a male world. She recounts the response of one of her male colleagues to her submission of her first book. The scholar asked upon receipt: "Do you want me to judge it on its own merits or as the work of a woman?"[37] The book's "own merits," of course, like the criteria for "the work of a woman," were to be established on the basis of categories created by the larger male culture.

The essays in this volume demonstrate how medieval women transcended and refashioned male categories of the letter to suit their specifically female intentions. Karen Cherewatuk, Earl Jeffrey Richards, and Karen Scott show that the women who wrote within the parameters of verse epistles or *ars dictaminis* demonstrated consummate skills in applying epistographical rule; in each case, the writer created a mode of discourse to suit her individual needs. By creating as individuals, these authors also gave birth to "structure[s] and biographical commonplaces" (Heilbrun's phrase) as models for other women's experiences.[38] As Karen Cherewatuk points out, Radegund merged already existing literary patterns from both the classical and the Germanic tradition to forge a lexicon for her own experiences. Through her correspondence, as Glenda McLeod illustrates, Héloïse explored the roles she had been forced to play. As Diane Watt argues, letters give the contemporary reader a glimpse of medieval women exerting power and even dominating the Paston household. We can only speculate how many similar efforts have been destroyed by time and circumstance that could testify to at least the beginnings of a lineage of female creators of a feminine discourse in the West.

Hildegard of Bingen, Héloïse, and Christine de Pizan are among the women writers who excelled at flexing, molding, and transforming the rules of the *ars dictaminis* to suit their needs as female authors. To a contemporary reader, their epistolary creativity destroyed the self-depreciating persona that many women, especially religious women, seemed to have chosen in order to claim public authority in a man's world. Nonetheless, we can also learn from the letters how the ecclesiastical hierarchies that are made so explicit in the epistolary genre ultimately served to annihilate women as writers. As Ulrike Wiethaus demonstrates, Patricia Spacks's observations in regard to eighteenth-century women's autobiography hold true for the Beguine Maria de Hout as well: "The nature of public and private selves . . . is for women, in some ways, the reverse of what it is for men. The face a man turns to the world . . . typically embodies his strength, while the only acceptable models for women involve self-deception and yielding."[39]

Yet despite these deformities caused by asymmetrical power relations, women's religious letters also constitute a remarkable source for yet another little studied phenomenon of medieval women's spirituality: cross-sex friendships between a confessor or male spiritual protégé and a religious woman. These friendships deepen and may even revise our understanding of the relationships between medieval men and women; their oftentimes equal exchange of affection and support challenge assumptions about an all-pervasive misogynist attitude among medieval men. The exemplary relationships between Hildegard of Bingen and Guibert of Gembloux and between Maria de Hout and Gerhard Kalckbrenner are discussed in this volume.

The second distinctly medieval phenomenon that needs to be considered as a criterion for establishing gender boundaries is the high regard and need that medieval people had for visionaries and the visionary mode. Since it was predominantly women who cultivated this mode of perception, it influenced their use of letter-writing dramatically. The evidence presented in this volume suggests that religious women generally struggled to establish their own credentials in the letters more than they took recourse to already existing epistolary conventions. The novelty of visionary spirituality and women's ensuing entry into public religious discourse that began in the twelfth century thus propelled the women writers not just to explore certain altered states of consciousness, but also to utilize the epistolary genre in new ways. The use of letters as a woman's continuing reflection on her spiritual experiences and the subsequent struggle to integrate these experiences into a larger theoretical framework may well qualify as a distinct category in medieval religious women's letters. Maria de Hout's letters as a testimony of the "making of a saintly woman" are discussed in this volume. The gender dynamics involved in this process are well worth further study.

Another theme of women's visionary epistles is represented by a letter from Christina of Stommeln to the Dominican Petrus Dacus, in which she ostentatiously confides to him intimate details of hair-raising and bloody encounters with a devil. We might call this the "affliction topos."[40] Here, a religious woman establishes herself with the means of extravagant and almost intolerable suffering. What at first glance reads as a personal confession, a pouring out of intimate experiences, reveals a public dimension and curious gender dynamics. Within the safe boundaries of celibacy, the male readers—in Christina's case Petrus Dacus and a priest named Johannes—turn into voyeurs as the female author reveals her mistreated bleeding and beaten body in all its physicality.

Three women writers who claimed the visionary mode as a means to exert public authority are discussed in depth in this collection: Hildegard of Bingen, Catherine of Siena, and Maria de Hout. Gillian T. W. Ahlgren demonstrates how Hildegard's use of the greeting formula varied with each audience. The higher the social status of her addressee(s), the more Hildegard referred to the source of her visions as legitimizing her authority. Karen Scott illustrates the different ways in which Catherine of Siena, an illiterate member of the artisan class, and her confessor/disciple Raymond of Capua, a highly educated cleric, perceive her literary accomplishments. Raymond tries to reconcile his own academic standards with Catherine's astounding success and articulateness by stressing Catherine's miraculous instruction by the Holy Spirit. Catherine, on the other hand, presents herself in a surprisingly unpretentious manner. As Scott notes, "the tone of most of her letters is so ordinary and mundane that they hardly qualify as 'mystical' or 'literary' texts."[41] Somewhat similar to the case of Hildegard of Bingen, Catherine's authority as derived from visions is stressed more in regard to the well-established male ecclesiastical hierarchies than vis-à-vis common people or people closer in social standing.

Conclusion

In studying medieval texts one must always be conscious of working with an incomplete puzzle: we simply do not know the number of missing pieces. In analyzing the texts of medieval women writers, we assume that the corpus of surviving letters represent a fraction of what women originally wrote. Despite this problem of unknown loss, the epistle remains the only medium common to both religious and secular women writers throughout the Middle Ages. What emerges more clearly and consistently from letters than from any other genre employed by medieval women is the writer's sense and use of her own authority. This appropriation of authority lies not only in the status of written communication but also in the form of the letter itself. Whatever the writer's social position, whatever her role, whatever her immediate goal in writing, the letter functions as the primary vehicle for her own voice.

In her first letter Hadewijch addresses her "Dear Sister." The address "sister" is, of course, common among members of a Beguinage. We metaphorically adapt this title to refer not to the recipient of the epistles, but to their authors. This volume attempts to bring into prominence the medieval women who bridged spiritual, psychological, or physical distance and who created communities of readers through the epistle. Like Hadewijch, the religious authors Hildegard of Bingen, Catherine of Siena, and Maria de Hout employed letters for spiritual direction. Catherine shares with Radegund, a woman half a millennium her predecessor, an interest in shaping politics through the epistle. Like Radegund, Héloïse and Christine de Pizan used the epistle for literary exploration and to create a distinctly female mode of discourse. In contrast, the Paston women wrote for a particular purpose, yet their correspondence displays their power within their community. The correspondents represented in this volume are but a handful of the women who explored the epistolary genre throughout the Middle Ages. We could multiply the connections among these writers without end. We leave that task to our readers, with the hope that others will reap the field of letters planted by the dear sisters of our medieval past.

Notes

1. "Introduction," *Writing the Female Voice: Essays on Epistolary Literature,* ed. Elizabeth C. Goldsmith (Boston: Northeastern University Press, 1989), p. vii.

2. See in this volume Karen Scott, "'*To Catarina*": Ecclesiastical Politics and Oral Culture in the Letters of Catherine of Siena," p. 89 and Earl Jeffrey Richards, "'*Seulette a part*'—The 'Little Woman on the Sidelines' Takes Up Her Pen': The Letters of Christine de Pizan," pp. 162.

3. See in this volume Glenda McLeod, "'Wholly Guilty, Wholly Innocent": Self-Definition in Héloïse's Letters to Abélard," p. 82. For an in-depth exploration of scholars' responses to questions of authorship regarding the letters, see Barbara Newman, "Authority, Authenticity, and the Repression of Héloïse," *Journal of Medieval and Renaissance Studies* 22, 2 (Spring 1992): 121–57.

4. Scott, p. 96.

5. Giles Constable, *Letters and Letter Collections,* Typologie des sources du Moyen Âge occidental, fasc. 17 (Turnhout: Brepols, 1976), p. 12.

6. See in this volume Diane Watt, "'No Writing For Writing's Sake': The Language of Service and Household Rhetoric in the Letters of the Paston Women," p. 123.

7. Janet Gurkin Altman, *Epistolarity: Approaches to a Form* (Columbus: Ohio State University Press, 1982).

8. See in this volume Ulrike Wiethaus, "'If I Had an Iron Body': Femininity and Religion in the Letters of Maria de Hout."

9. Altman, *Epistolarity*, p. 200.

10. Patrocinio Schweickart, "Reading Ourselves: Toward a Feminist Theory of Reading" in *Gender and Reading*, ed. Elizabeth Flynn and Patrocinio Schweickart (Baltimore: Johns Hopkins University Press, 1986), pp. 31–57.

11. E. J. Polak, "Dictamen," in *Dictionary of the Middle Ages,* ed. Joseph R. Strayer, vol. 4 (New York: Charles Scribner's Sons, 1984), p. 173.

12. *Alberici Cassinensis rationes dictandi,* in *Briefsteller und Formelbuecher des elften bis vierzehnten Jahrhunderts,* ed. Ludwig Rockinger, vol. 1 (Munich: 1863, rpt. New York: Franklin, 1961), p. 10.

13. See in this volume Richards, pp. 162–63.

14. On women and humanist education in general see Margaret L. King, *Women of the Renaissance* (Chicago and London: University of Chicago Press, 1991), chap. three.

15 Norman Davis, "The 'Litera Troili' and English Letters," *Review of English Studies* 16 (1965): 233–44.

16. Patricia Wilson-Kastner, "Egeria," in *A Lost Tradition: Women Writers of the Early Church,* ed. Patricia Wilson-Kastner, Ann Millin, Rosemary Rader, and Jeremiah Reedy (Lanham, MD: University Press of America, 1981). *Egeria: Diary of a Pilgrimage,* ed. and trans. George E. Gingras, Ancient Christian Writers 38 (New York: Newman Press, 1970).

17. Leo Spitzer, "The Epic Style of the Pilgrim Aetheria," *Comparative Literature* 1 (1949): 225–48, quote p. 228.

18. *Dhuoda: Manuel pour mon fils,* ed. Pierre Riché, Sources Chrétiennes 225 (Paris: Éditions du Cerf, 1975); "epigramma," p. 15.

19. See *Die Briefe des Heiligen Bonifatius und Lullus,* ed. Michael Tangl, *Monumenta Germaniae Historica, Epistolae Selectae,* vol. 1 (Berlin: Weidmann, 1955), 2nd. unchanged edition, nrs. 13, 14, 15, 26, 29, and 97; see also Christine Fell, "Some Implications of the Boniface Correspondence," in *New Readings on Women in Old English Literature,* ed. Helen Damico and Alexandra Hennessey Olsen (Bloomington: Indiana University Press, 1990), pp. 29–43 and Albrecht Classen, "Female Epistolary Literature from Antiquity to the Present: An Introduction," *Studia Neophilologia* 60 (1988): 3–13, quote p. 4.

20. See in this volume Karen Cherewatuk, "Radegund and the Epistolary Tradition."

21. Amalasuntha's letters appear in Cassiodorus's *Variae X* in *Monumenta Germaniae Historica, Auctorum Antiquissimorum,* vol. XII (Berlin: Wiedmann, 1894), pp. 296–304. They are translated by Marcelle Thiebaux in *Writings of Medieval Women* (New York: Garland, 1987), pp. 18–23. Brunhilda's letter to Anastasia is discussed by Peter Dronke in *Women Writers of the Middle Ages: A Critical Study of Texts from Perpetua (†203) to Marguerite Porete (†1310),* (Cambridge: Cambridge University Press, 1984), pp. 26–27; Herchenafreda's letters to Desiderius, pp. 29–30; Berhtgyth's letters to Balthard, pp. 32–33 and in Fell, "Some Implications," pp. 37–41. The letters of Gisela and Rotrud are published in *Monumenta Germaniae Historica, Epistolarum IV, Karolini Aevi II* (Berlin: Weidmann, 1895), nr. 196, p. 232 ff. See also Classen, "Female Epistolary Literature," p. 4.

22. For a discussion of gender dichotomy in the high Middle Ages, see Susan Stuard, "The Dominion of Gender: Women's Fortunes in the High Middle Ages" in *Becoming Visible: Women in European History,* ed. Renate Bridenthal, Claudia Koonz, and Susan Stuard (Boston: Houghton Mifflin, 1987), pp. 153–75.

23. Many women writers of this era are represented in Katharina M. Wilson,

ed., *Women Writers of the Renaissance and Reformation* (Athens and London: University of Georgia Press, 1987). The following women humanists can be regarded as representative. Caritas Pirckheimer appears in *Der Briefwechsel des Conrad Celtis*, ed. Hans Rupprich (Munich: C. H. Beck'sche Verlagsbuchhandlung, 1934), nrs. 272–293. Isabella d'Este, who widely corresponded with artists, is discussed by David Wilkins in his essay "Woman as Artist and Patron in the Middle Ages and the Renaissance" in *The Roles and Images of Women in the Middle Ages and the Renaissance*, ed. Douglas Radcliff-Umstead (Pittsburgh: University of Pittsburgh Publications on the Middle Ages and the Renaissance, 1975), III, pp. 107–31. Laura Cereta is presented by Albert Rabil, Jr., in *Laura Cereta: Quattrocento Humanist*, Medieval and Renaissance Texts and Studies 3 (Binghamton, NY: Center for Medieval and Early Renaissance Studies, 1981).

24. See in this volume Glenda McLeod, "'Wholly Guilty, Wholly Innocent': Self-Definition in Héloïse's Letters to Abélard."

25. Constable, *Letters and Letter Collections* (note 5), pp. 31, 37.

26. For the women authors writing in Anglo-French see F. J. Tanquerey, ed., *Recueil de lettres Anglo-Françaises (1265–1399)* (Paris: Champion, 1916); for Mechthild of Hackeborn and Christine of Stommeln, see Wilhelm Oehl, ed., *Deutsche Mystikerbriefe des Mittelalters 1100–1500* (Munich-Vienna: Langen-Müller, 1931; rpt. Dornstadt: Wissenschaftliche Buchgesellschaft, 1972); for Hadewijch, see Mother Columba Hart, *Hadewijch, the Complete Works* (New York: Paulist Press, 1980).

27. Hart, p. 32.

28. See in this volume Scott, p 102, and Wiethaus, p. 187.

29. See note 22. For a collection of primary sources especially on Italian women humanists, including letters, see Margaret L. King and Albert Rabil, Jr., eds., *Her Immaculate Hand: Selected Works By and About the Women Humanists of Quattrocento Italy*, Medieval and Renaissance Texts and Studies 20 (Binghamton, NY: Center for Medieval and Renaissance Studies, 1983).

30. Constable, *Letters and Letter Collections*, p. 40.

31. On Elisabeth of Schönau, see Anne L. Clark, *Elisabeth of Schönau: A Twelfth-Century Visionary* (Philadelphia: University of Pennsylvania Press, 1992). Unfortunately, no comprehensive work on the important roles of women in medieval dissent has yet been written; see Malcolm Lambert for references in passim, *Medieval Heresy: Popular Movements from Bogomil to Hus* (London: Edward Arnold Publishers, 1977).

32. For material on Magdalena Beutler, see Oehl, ed., *Deutsche Mystikerbriefe des Mittelalters* (note 26); Kate Greenspan, *Magdalena of Freiburg: Selections* (Brookline, Village, MA: Focus Library of Medieval Women, forthcoming).

33. See in this volume, Watt, p. 132.

34. Carolyn G. Heilbrun, *Writing a Woman's Life* (New York: Ballantine Books, 1988), pp. 18, 19.

35. Albrecht Classen, "Female Epistolary Literature"; Classen, "From *Nonnenbuch* to Epistolarity: Elsbeth Stagel as a Late Medieval Woman Writer," in *Medieval German Literature. Proceedings from the 23rd International Congress on Medieval Studies Kalamazoo, Michigan, May 5–8, 1988*, ed. Albrecht Classen, GAG 507 (Göppingen: Kümmerle Verlag, 1989), pp. 147–70.

36. Eleanor Duckett, *Women and Their Letters in the Early Middle Ages* (published by Smith College, Baltimore: Barton-Gillet Company, 1965).

37. Duckett, *Women and Their Letters*, p. 3.

38. Heilbrun, *Writing a Woman's Life*, p. 19.

39. Patricia Spacks, *Imagining a Self* (Cambridge, MA: Harvard University Press, 1976); quoted in Heilbrun, *Writing a Woman's Life*, p. 22.

40. The term "affliction topos" is coined by Ulrike Wiethaus; the following analysis of Christine's possession is part of a larger project on violence and sexuality in the writings of medieval women mystics. The letter is printed in Friedrich-W. and Erika Wentzlaff-Eggebert, *Deutsche Literatur im späten Mittelalter 1250–1450* (Hamburg: Rowohlt Verlag, 1971), II, pp. 214–17.

41. Scott, p. 96.

Karen Cherewatuk

Radegund and Epistolary Tradition

Three extant verse epistles in Latin are ascribed to the sixth-century saint Radegund (c. 520–87).[1] In keeping with her practice of corresponding with the most powerful ecclesiastical and political figures of her day, the second poem is addressed to the Emperor Justin II and the Empress Sophia of Byzantium.[2] The first and third verse epistles Radegund addresses to members of her family, her cousin Hamalafred and her nephew Artachis. These men living in the east constituted the scattered remnants of the royal house of Thuringia, which had fallen to the Franks in 531.

Radegund was well versed in both classical and Germanic poetry. In her epistles she blends these two traditions through the female voice. Given the nature of her audience—Hamalafred and Artachis were Germanic exiles living in Constantinople, the seat of classical learning—Radegund's merging of the two traditions is especially apt. Perhaps because of her technical mastery, however, it is hard to distinguish the poet's personal voice in the letters. She assumes so many literary masks from both Latin poetry and Germanic tradition that it is difficult to penetrate them. Here I will examine how Radegund explores available female personae to project her concern and analyze the presentation of self Radegund constructs from classical and Germanic traditions in the letters to Hamalafred and Artachis.

Hagiographers, Poets, and Royal Politics

The problem of interpreting Radegund's letters is oddly compounded by the extensive documentation of her life. Gregory of Tours treats her in his *Historia Francorum* and in his *Liber in confessorum gloria*, which is the eighth chapter of his book of miracles, the *Libri octo miraculorum*. Two other *vitae* survive: the first by Venantius Fortunatus, the Italian poet who later became Bishop of Poitiers; and the second by Baudonivia, a nun of Rade-

gund's religious community who wrote twenty years after Radegund's
death. All three of Radegund's biographers personally knew her. Gregory
performed her funeral rites (*In gloria* 104.815); Fortunatus acted as her close
advisor, and some critics argue that the verse epistles represent their collab-
orative effort;[3] Baudonivia was raised by Radegund in her household at the
monastery of Holy Cross (Baudonivia, *prologus* 377). A summary of her life,
borrowing from these three biographers, shows Radegund to be, in Jane
Tibbetts Schulenberg's phrase, a "queen saint," that is, a female saint of the
early church who because of her political and economic power receives
praise and ultimately canonization for both her private sacrifices and her
public works.[4] As we will see, the strong character who emerges from
Gregory's *Historia* and Fortunatus's and Baudonivia's *vitae* sharply contrasts with the weak and vulnerable persona Radegund creates for herself in
the two verse epistles.

Radegund's personal history is intimately linked with that of her
nation. The kingdom of Thuringia (now a part of Germany bordering on
Czechoslovakia) was brutally sacked by the Franks under the command of
Clovis's two sons Theoderic and Lothar in 531. Gregory of Tours writes,
"There was made such slaughter of them [the Thuringians] that the bed of
the stream was choked with their dead bodies, and the Franks used them as
a bridge on which to cross to the other side" ("Ibique tanta caedes ex
Thoringia facta est, ut alveus fluminis a cadaverum congerie repleretur,
et Franci tamquam per pontem aliquod super eos in litus ulterius tran-
sirent").[5] The young princess Radegund and her brother became royal
booty to Lothar. Gregory succinctly summarizes the main points of Radegund's life from her captivity:

> Lothar, returning home, took with him as his captive Radegund,
> daughter of King Berthar; her he wedded, though afterwards he
> caused her brother to be slain by evil men. This queen turned to God
> and, changing her habit, built for herself a monastery in Poitiers.
> (Dalton, p. 91)

> Clothacharius vero rediens, Radegundem, filiam Bertecharii regis,
> secum captivam abduxit sibique eam in matrimonio sociavit; cuius
> fratrem postea iniuste per homines iniquos occidit. Illa quoque ad
> Deum conversa, mutata veste, monastirium sibi intra Pectavensem
> urbem construxit. (*Hist. Fr.* III.7.115)

Radegund's hagiographers supply more explicit detail than Gregory. Fortunatus relates that Lothar won from his brother Theoderic the "regalis puella" and consequently the claim to Thuringia through a judicial contest ("transacto certamine," II.4.38). Lothar placed Radegund in his royal villa, Athiers, where she was converted and then educated until she was of marriageable age. Following hagiographic convention, Fortunatus writes that even as a child Radegund performed extraordinary works of mercy: gathering to herself poor children, she would wash their hair and feet and clothe and feed them (II.6.39). Radegund's ascetic practices continued after her marriage. While living in Lothar's palace, the queen would attend the poor and sick (IV.12.39). She wore a hairshirt and at night exposed her flesh to the cold in hopes of thwarting Lothar's sexual advances (V.14.40). Fortunatus summarizes that "Because of these practices, the king was said to have married a nun, not a queen" ("De qua regi dicebatur habere se potius iugalem monacham quam reginam," V.15.40).

Despite the polygamous king's unhappiness with his ascetic bride, Radegund remained at the palace until Lothar had her brother murdered (Fortunatus XII.26.41). She then sought permanent shelter away from the court. She fled to Noyon and, laying her royal jewels on the altar, asked Bishop Medard to consecrate her as deaconess. Fearing royal retribution, the bishop hesitated, for the king's officials had dragged him from the altar. Fortunatus relates, however, that Radegund convinced Medard with these words: "If you refuse to consecrate me and fear a man more than God, from your hand, shepherd, will be demanded the soul of your sheep" ("Si me consecrare distuleris et plus hominem quam deum timueris, de manu tua, pastor, ovis anima requiratur," XII.28.41). This argument forcefully exemplifies Radegund's strength of commitment and of will. Baudonivia, who fashioned her work to supplement Fortunatus's *vita*,[6] provides an earlier example of Radegund's forceful will. While traveling with a small royal escort, Radegund passed a pagan temple and ordered it destroyed. Despite the loud protest of the local people, who came armed with swords and clubs, "unshaken, the holy queen persevered . . . the horse on which she sat did not move at all . . . for which all admired her strength and self possession" ("sancta vero regina inmobilis perseverans . . . equum quem sedebat in antea non movit . . . Quo facto, virtutem et constantiam reginae omnes admirantes," 2.380).

After Radegund's desertion, Lothar made several attempts to regain her. According to Baudonivia, Radegund "would choose to end her life rather than be wed to the earthly king again" ("optaret vitam finire, quam regi terreno iterum iungi," 4.381). Radegund appealed for aid to Bishop

Germanus of Paris, who convinced Lothar not only to release her from marriage but also to provide her with wealth and land at Poitiers (7.382). There Radegund established a monastery for women, eventually named Holy Cross, and appointed Agnes abbess (5.381). Radegund's presence in his diocese must have proven threatening to the local bishop, Maroveus, for he refused to offer direction to the new foundation. Maroveus continued this unsupportive, if not hostile, behavior toward Radegund throughout her life.[7] As Gregory relates, Radegund, not to be daunted, sought direction for her community outside the bishop's diocese. She obtained a copy of the rule of St. Caesarius, the first rule written for women, from the Abbess Caesaria the Younger of Arles (*Hist. Fr.* IX.40.397). Radegund modeled her community on this rule, which provides for strict enclosure and literacy for nuns. The rule prescribes that the sisters spend at least two hours a day in reading and lessons (Caesarius 19.105).[8] The Abbess Caesaria writes to Radegund in a letter of 567, "Let there be no sister entering who does not know letters" ("Nulla sit de intrantibus, quae non litteras discat"). Hearing of Radegund's fiercely ascetic habits, practises which both hagiographers stress,[9] Caesaria also cautions, "I have learned that you are fasting to excess. Act reasonably in all things" ("Pervenit ad me, quod nimis abstineas. Totum rationabiliter fac").[10] In contrast, a gentle Radegund emerges in this story of the daily lesson related by Baudonivia:

> When the lesson was read, she [Radegund], administering to our souls with pious concern, would say: "If you do not understand what is read, why is that? Is it because you do not seek diligently a mirror for your soul?" Even when the least [of the community] respectfully undertook to question her, she with pious concern and motherly affection did not cease preaching about what the lesson contained for the health of our souls.

> Cum lectio legebatur, illa sollicitudine pia animarum nostrarum curam gerens, dicebat: 'Si non intellegitis quod legitur, quid est, quod non sollicite requiritis speculum animarum vestrarum?' Quod etsi minus pro reverentia interrogare praesumebatur, illa pia sollicitudine maternoque affectu, quod lectio continebat ad animae salutem praedicare non cessabat. (9.384)

Here Radegund acts as the maternal shepherd of her flock, gently exhorting, leading, and teaching them.

Despite her retreat from the world and the political turmoil resulting from Lothar's death, Radegund retained ties with the Merovingian court. Suzanne Wemple argues that Radegund, recognizing rather than repudiating familial obligations, attempted "to set up the convent as an intermediary between royalty and divinity."[11] Baudonivia's *vita* convincingly supports Wemple's claim:

> Always concerned about peace, worried about the country, [Radegund perceived that] relations among them [the kings] were shaken. Since she cared for each of the kings, she prayed for their lives and instructed us to pray without ceasing for their stability. Whenever she heard that they had stirred up strife against each other, she was very upset and sent letters to the one and the other, so that they would not wage war and arms against each other, but would fashion a peace so that the country would not perish . . . She imposed continuous vigils on the congregation and through tears taught us to pray for the kings without interruption.

> Semper de pace sollicita, de salute patriae curiosa, quandoquidem inter se regna movebantur, quia totos diligebat pro omnium vita orabat et nos sine intermissione pro eorum stabilitate orare docebat. Ubi eos inter se amaritudinem moveri audisset, tota tremebat, et quales litteras uni, tales alteri dirigebat, ut inter se non bella nec arma tractarent, sed pacem firmarent, et patria ne periret . . . Congregationi suae assiduas vigilias inponebat et, ut sine intermissione pro eis orarent, cum lacrimis docebat. (10.384)

Radegund's concern for political stability may underlie her campaign for collecting relics. First she acquired a relic of St. Andrew, then of the holy man Mammes, and ultimately of the true cross (Baudonivia 13.386, 14.386–87, 16.387–89). Despite the hostility of Bishop Maroveus, in 573 Radegund had the fragment of the cross installed in the convent church, for which occasion Fortunatus composed the famous hymn, "Vexilla regis prodeunt." Baudonivia claims that Radegund, acting as a second St. Helen, sought the relic of the cross "for the health of the entire country and the stability of the kingdom" ("pro totius patriae salute et eius regni stabilitate" 16.388).

Radegund died in 587, and although she refused to serve her sisters as abbess, she had met their needs for security and independence. According to Gregory's account, a community of 200 (educated) women mourned at her funeral (*In gloria* 104.815). Jo Ann McNamara shrewdly notes that the queen left the community with relics that would ensure pilgrims to Holy Cross and hence financial prosperity for years to come.[12] Radegund thus retired to the cloister but had hardly left behind secular concerns. She maintained an influence in royal politics while strongly administering her community.

It is notoriously difficult to sort out fable from fact in hagiography. In attempting to do so, I have omitted the most graphic details narrated by Radegund's three biographers: scenes of her cleaning lepers and embracing them, of her scouring the streets, of her quelling a storm, of her healing the sick, of her raising the dead.[13] Other sources temper the formidable view of the saint, among them Fortunatus's poem "Ad Radegundem." Concerning their exchange of verses, he writes,

> You gave me great poems on short tablets,
> honeyed poems which you are able to return in wax . . .
> You send perfected little verses with gentle speech,
> in whose words you bind our hearts.

> In breuibus tabulis mihi carmina magna dedisti,
>   Quae vacuis ceris reddere mella potes . . .
> versiculot mittis placido sermone refectos,
>   In quorum dictis pectora nostra ligas.[14]

Fortunatus paints the saint as a tenderhearted and thoughtful woman of letters.

Despite sometimes contradictory views of Radegund, several traits clearly emerge. The saint displayed an extraordinary assertiveness in achieving her goals and enforcing her will, a quality perhaps most evident in her escape from Lothar and foundation of the monastery. Her conviction and her courage thread throughout her history. Gregory recounts, for example, that Radegund thwarted King Chilperic's plan to remove his daughter from the monastery for a political marriage by insisting, "It is unseemly that a maid dedicated to Christ should return to the pleasures of the world" ("Non est enim dignum, ut puella Christo dedicata iterum in saeculi voluptatibus revertatur," *Hist. Fr.* VI.34.274). Although she gave all her wealth to the convent and would willingly perform menial labors, Radegund never yielded her queenly status. Baudonivia reports that after Radegund's death her serving girl Vinoperga dared to sit on her throne; she was tortured with smoke and a burning sensation for three days and nights until the assembled community invoked the deceased queen for mercy (12.385–86). In a less fabulous way Radegund's regal position is evident in her sustained relationships with the Merovingian court and ecclesiastical authority. In the intimate circle of her sisters, she displays maternal concern; in her friendship with Fortunatus, affection and wit. Ultimately, Radegund emerges as a shrewd and learned woman, capable of influencing royal politics and of crafting "carmina magna."

Rhetoric and the Roman Woman

The image of the resourceful woman who emerges in the biographical sources diametrically opposes the personae Radegund creates for herself in her verse epistle to her cousin Hamalafred, entitled "De excidio Thoringiae" ("The Fall of Thuringia"), and the epistle to her nephew Artachis, "Ad Artachin" ("To Artachis"). In these poems Radegund is primarily concerned to depict her own personal grief through female suffering. She does so by incorporating motifs from a number of genres and from two traditions, classical Latin and Germanic poetry. Hence Radegund weaves into the tapestry of her epistles various threads: allusions to classical epic; details from the Latin lament for the dead, the *epicedium*; the exaggerated rhetoric of Ovid's fictive epistles, the *Heroides*; and the plaintive tone of Germanic lament. In these letters Radegund ostensibly seeks communication from her nearest living relatives. The sophisticated mingling of various female masks, however, suggests Radegund's calculated attempt to elicit her relatives' sympathy.

Radegund's "De excidio Thoringiae" opens with the strains of the classical epic: "The condition of harsh war, the jealous fate of things! / How suddenly the proud kingdoms tumble down!" ("Condicio belli tristis, sors invida rerum! / quam subito lapsu regna superba cadunt!" 1–2). Radegund explicitly recalls the epic by comparing the fall of Thuringia with that of Troy.

> Troy can no longer lament her ruin alone:
> The land of Thuringia endured to the end an equal slaughter.

From here the wife, bound, was dragged away by her mangled hair,
She could not bid a tearful farewell to her household gods.
The prisoner was not permitted to fix kisses on her doorpost
or to turn her gaze on familiar places.
The wife's naked foot trod through her spouse's blood
and the charming sister stepped over her fallen brother.
The child, torn from his mother's embrace, lingered on her lips.

non iam sola suas lamentet Troia ruinas:
   pertulit et caedes terra Thoringa pares.
hinc rapitur laceris matrona revincta capillis,
   nec laribus potuit dicere triste vale.
oscula non licuit captivo infigere posti
   nec sibi visuris ora referre locis.
nuda maritalem calcavit planta cruorem
   blandaque transibat fratre iacente soror.
raptus ab amplexu matris puer ore pependit. (19–27)

Radegund depicts the pain women suffer in war through a catalogue of heart-wrenching images. She drew inspiration for these images from the most famous description of the fall of Troy, book two of Virgil's *Aeneid,* yet heightening the pathos of each Virgilian image. In the *Aeneid* the virgin Cassandra "was dragged by her streaming hair" ("trahebatur passis . . . crinibus" II.403–4). Radegund increases the outrageousness of abduction by making her victim not a "virgo," a maiden, but a "matrona," a wife. In describing the brutal devastation of Priam's home, Virgil focuses on the women who "roam, clinging fast to the doors and imprinting kisses on them" ("errant, / amplexaeque tenent postis atque oscula figunt" II.489–90). Radegund describes the sack of Thuringia as happening so suddenly that the woman, already captive, is not able to kiss the doorpost. In the *Aeneid* it is Priam who slips "in his son's streaming blood" ("in multo . . . sanguine nati" II.551). Radegund doubles this image of suffering and makes it explicitly female: the wife walks through her husband's blood, the sister passes over her brother's body. Virgil gives Creusa, Aeneas's wife, a moment to cling to her little boy Iulus (II.673), while Radegund laments with the woman whose son is ripped from her arms. Through indirect comparison with the *Aeneid* Radegund shows the suffering of the Thuringian women surpassing that of the Trojan women.

The emotional pitch of this verse epistle remains high as Radegund comes to her own role in that fallen community:

> I, a foreign woman, cannot cry enough tears
> were I able to swim in a lake full of my tears.
> Each has tears, but I alone weep for all:
> For me the private grief is public.

> non aequare queo vel barbara femina fletum
>   cunctaque guttarum maesta natare lacu.
> quisque suos habuit fletus, ego sola sed omnes:
>   est mihi privatus publicus ille dolor. (31–34)

Radegund's plight is to be both family member—daughter, sister (and as she here casts herself, wife, mother) and queen to this fallen people. She thus simultaneously defines her loss in personal and political terms. "De excidio Thoringiae" is a lament for the dead that embraces both loss of family and of nation. It is a lament that only could be sung by a grieving queen, and this is the persona Radegund powerfully depicts in the opening section of the poem.

While these images of past losses at Thuringia are gripping, equally poignant is Radegund's description of the death of her brother, killed at Lothar's command. About her recent loss, Radegund questions Hamalfred,

> Why are you silent about the murder of my brother, the deep pain
> how innocent he fell by a treacherous ambush? . . .
> A gentle boy with a downy beard, he was pierced through,
> Absent, I, his sister, did not see his cruel death.
> Not only did I lose him, but I did not close his pious eyes
> nor did I throw myself on him and speak a final message to him.
> I did not warm his cold heart with my hot tears,
> nor did I receive kisses from my dying beloved.
> I did not, crying, grasp his neck in a miserable embrace
> or, panting, clutch his ill-omened body to my breast.
> Life was denied him: Why couldn't his passing breath
> be preserved in the brother's mouth for his sister?

de nece germani cur, dolor alte, taces,
qualiter insidiis insons cecidisset iniquis . . .
percutitur iuvenis tenera lanugine barbae,
    absens nec vidi funera dira soror.
non solum amisi, sed nec pia lumina clausi
    nec superincumbens ultima verba dedi.
frigida non calido tepefeci viscera fletu,
    oscula nec caro de moriente tuli,
amplexu in misero neque collo flebilis haesi
    aut fovi infausto corpus anhela sinu.
vita negabatur: quin iam de fratre sorori
    debuit egrediens halitus ore rapi? (124–26, 133–42)

Just as Radegund turned to the classical epic to describe her pain at the devastation of Thuringia, here she relies on the Latin lament for the dead, the *epicedium*, to depict her personal grief. Traditional *epicedia* break down into the constituent elements of eulogy, lamentation, and solace for the bereaved survivors.[15] In praising the deceased Radegund defines her brother's goodness in terms of her own needs, a rhetorical strategy typical in *epicedia* spoken in first person: "Because he avoided giving hardship to me, he pierced himself with wounds, / Since he feared to hurt me, he became the cause of my pain" ("dum dare dura mihi refugit, sibi vulnera fixit: / laedere quod timuit, causa dolores adest" 131–32).[16] In describing her brother as "a gentle boy with downy beard" ("iuvenis tenera lanugine barbe" 133), Radegund echoes the traditional lament for lost youth heard in the *epicedia* of Virgil (*Aeneid* VI.860–85), Propertius (III.18.15–16), and Ausonius (*Parentalia* VII.10, 11, 14, 17, 20, and 23).

But while Radegund incorporates these motifs of praise for the deceased and the lament for youth, she inverts a third expectation of the genre. *Epicedia* often describe the consolation the survivor feels in sharing the last moments of a loved one's life. Statius describes Claudius Etruscus reverently helping his aged father meet death:

    . . . Lo! Gently in his arms he holds the aged face and lets his tears bedew the sacred white hairs of his sire, and lovingly he gathers the last cold breath.

> . . . tenet ecce seniles
> leniter implicitos vultus sanctamque parentis
> canitiem spargit lacrimis animaque supremum
> frigus amat. (*Silvae* III.3.17–20)

The consolation Claudius enjoys is denied Radegund, who is not present to receive her brother's final breath (141–42). In an unusual variation of the genre, Propertius has a wife speak from the grave to her husband: "You . . . are my comfort even in death; in your bosom were my eyelids closed" ("tu . . . meum post fata levamen; / condita sunt vestro lumina nostra sinu" IV.11.63–65). The *epicedia* frequently reserve for women the act of closing the eyes of the loved one and weeping over him (cf. Ovid, *Amores* III.9.49–54). In describing her brother's death, Radegund relies entirely on a series of negative statements: "I did not close his eyes," "did not . . . speak a final message," "did not receive kisses," "crying, did not grasp his neck," "did not clutch his body" ("nec . . . lumina clausi / nec . . . ultima verba dedi / . . . oscula nec . . . tuli / . . . neque collo . . . haesi / aut fovi . . . corpus" 135–40). These negative statements cumulatively present the image of a woman who enjoys no comfort, who is denied even the right to weep over the corpse. Radegund thus incorporates the elements of eulogy and lamentation traditional in *epicedia* while she inverts the genre's message of consolation. Radegund speaks here as the inconsolable mourner.

Radegund's familiarity with classical poetry is most evident in the exaggerated rhetoric she employs to describe the pain she feels in being separated from her cousin. Addressing Hamalafred in Constantinople, she writes,

> I used to be troubled, anxious, if one house did not cover us.
> Now the east hides you in shadows and the west me,
> the tide of the ocean detains me, and the tide of the red sea you.
> The whole orb separates us lovers.

> anxia vexabar, si non domus una tegebat,
>   egrediente foris rebar abisse procul.
> vos quoque nunc Oriens et nos Occasus odumbrat,
>   me maris Oceani, te tenet unda rubri,
> inter amatores totusque interiacet orbis. (63–67)

As Peter Dronke remarks, however innocent Radegund's emotions for her cousin, the language she uses to express her longing is the passionately charged language of Ovid's *Epistulae Heroidum*,[17] his fictive collection of poetic epistles written in the voice of the abandoned lovers and wives of famous heroes. In the *Heroides* Ovid employs the form of the verse epistle to give voice to a distinctly female point of view as imagined by this male poet. Ovid's *Heriodes* thus stands, in the words of Joan DeJean, as a model "for epistolarity and for women's writing."[18]

In composing her poetic epistles, Radegund quite naturally turns to the form and rhetoric of the *Heroides*. Like nine of Ovid's fifteen heroines, Radegund is separated by the sea from her beloved.[19] And like all of Ovid's heroines, Radegund writes not only to express her loneliness or sense of desertion, but also to induce guilt:

> If the fortress of the holy monastery did not hold me,
> I would travel immediately to you in whatever quarter you dwelled.
> Boldly in a ship I would cross waves chilled by violent storms,
> Happily I would be rushed over the water by the wintry breeze.
> Uncertain but strong I would press the driven waves,
> And what the sailor fears would not panic her who loves you.
> If a wave driven by hostile rains smashed my hull,
> I would seek you, carried on the sea by an oarsman on a plank.
> If by chance I couldn't grasp the wood,
> I would come to you swimming with exhausted hands.
> When I beheld you, I would deny the dangers of the journey;
> You, sweet one, would relieve the burden of shipwreck;
> Or if fate ultimately should take my complaint-filled life,
> at least the sand with your hands would form a grave for me.
> Before your eyes I, a corpse, would pass without light,
> so that you would be stirred to perform my funeral rites.
> You who now scorn the tears of the living, you then tearful
> would give lament, you who now refuse even words.

> sacra monasterii si me non claustra tenerent,
>   inprovisa aderman qua regione sedes.
> prompta per undifragas transissem puppe procellas,
>   flatibus hibernis laeta moverer aquis.

fortior eductos pressissem pendula fluctus,
    et quod nauta timet non pavitasset amans.
imbribus infestis si solveret unda carinam,
    te peterem tabula remige vecta mari.
sorte sub infausta si prendere ligna vetarer,
    ad te venissem lassa natante manu.
cum te respicerem, peregrina pericula negassem,
    naufragii dulcis mox relevasses onus;
aut mihi si querulam raperet sors ultima vitam,
    vel tumulum manibus ferret harena tuis.
ante pios oculos issem sine luce cadaver,
    ut vel ad exequias commoverere meas.
qui spernis vitae fletus, lacrimatus humares
    atque dares planctus qui modo verba negas. (105–22)

Radegund's claim that she would brave the sea to be buried by the hands of her heartless cousin recalls that of Ariadne: "These hands, wearied with beating of my sorrowful breast, unhappy I stretch toward you over the wide seas . . . If I have died before you come, 'twill be you who bear away my bones!" ("Has tibi plangendo lugubria pectora lassas / infelix tendo trans freta lata manus / . . . si prius occidero, tu tamen ossa feres!" *Her.* X.145–46, 152). Radegund specifically echoes Ariadne in her use of the phrase "exhausted hands" ("lassa . . . manu" *De excidio* 114; "lassas . . . manus" *Her.* X.145–46) and generally in her view of consolation in death. Perhaps implicit in Radegund's description of her voyage is a suicide threat like that of Phyllis:

> To throw myself hence into the waves beneath has been my mind; and, since you still pursue your faithless course, so shall it be. Let the waves bear me away, and cast me upon your shores, and let me meet your eyes untombed!

> hinc mihi suppositas inmittere corpus in undas
>   mens fuit; et, quoniam fallere pergis, erit.
> ad tua me fluctus proiectam litora protent,
>   occurramque oculis intumulata tuis! (*Her.* II.133–36)

Radegund less directly employs guilt than does Ovid's heroine. In a back-handed compliment, she claims that even the sight of Hamalafred would ease the burden of shipwreck she would have to endure to reach him (115–16). Yet Radegund threatens to place her cousin in the same position as Phyllis would Demophoon: the man who shunned communication with the woman must face her silent corpse.[20]

The exaggerated claims of Ovid's heroines sound throughout the "De excidio Thoringiae." Asserting that her lover fulfills all familial roles for her, Briseis writes to Achilles, "For so many lost to me I still had only you in recompense; you were my master, you my husband, you my brother" ("tot tamen amissis te conpensavimus unum; / tu dominus, tu vir, tu mihi frater eras" *Her.* III.51–52). Radegund offers Hamalafred a parallel compliment: "What my slaughtered father could be, what my mother / What my sister or my brother—you alone were to me" ("quod pater extinctus poterat, quod mater haberi, / quod soror aut frater tu mihi solus eras" 51–52). Perhaps alluding to her abduction by Lothar, Radegund calls herself "twice captive" ("bis capta" 147) as does Ovid's Briseis ("iterum . . . visa capi" *Her.* III.16) and Helen ("bis . . . rapi" *Her.* XVII. 22). Perhaps alluding to her position in the Frankish kingdom, Radegund refers to herself as "barbara" (31), a foreign woman, an outsider, as does Ovid's Medea (*Her.* XII.104). It is the persona of the *barbara* Radegund assumes in adopting Ovidian rhetoric. She depicts herself as a woman whose desperate loneliness has made her a stranger to the whole world, and like all the women who speak in the *Heroides*, Radegund claims that only one man can vanquish her pain.

The Lamenting Voice of the Germanic Tradition

As skillful as her merging of the motifs of classical epic, *epicedium*, and verse epistle may be, Latin poetry is not the only tradition Radegund draws upon. As is appropriate in a work entitled "De excidio Thoringiae," Radegund also turns to her native Germanic poetic traditions for inspiration. As Marcelle Thiebaux notes, Radegund's description of the sack of Thuringia sounds "the notes of exile and elegy heard in early Germanic poetry":[21]

> Roofs that stood happily for a long time
> lie conquered, burnt to ashes under the great scourge.

The hall which flourished earlier with kingly tending
is covered not with vaults but with gloomy ash.
The steep roofs decorated with bright red metal
pale fire crushed.
Its king is sent to a hostile realm,
its high glory in subjection.
The crowd of bright retainers who stood ready together
lie dirty, having suffered the funereal dust on the same day.

quae steterant longo felicia culmina tractu
   victa sub ingenti clade cremata iacent.
aula palatino quae floruit antea cultu,
   hanc modo pro cameris maesta favilla tegit.
ardua quae rutilo nituere ornata metallo,
   pallidus oppressit fulgida tecta cinis.
missa sub hostili domino captiva potestas,
   decidit in humili gloria celsa loco.
stans aetate pari famulorum turba nitentum
   funereo sordet pulvere functa die. (3–12)

Radegund's passage evokes a similar scene of destruction from the Anglo-Saxon elegy "The Wanderer":

The winehalls crumble, lords lie dead,
deprived of joy, all the proud followers
have fallen by the wall.

Woriað þa winsalo,   waldend licgað
dreame bidrorene,   duguþ eal gecrong,
wlonc bi wealle.[22]

Like the speaker of the "Wanderer," Radegund laments the passing of the glorious hall, its lord, and his thanes. The society her description recalls is traditionally Germanic, as is her theme of transcience and her tone of desolation. Yet it is Radegund's tone that most echoes the Germanic elegist. Like the wanderer, Radegund speaks as one "Mindful of hardships, grievous slaughter / the ruin of kinsmen" ("earfeþa gemyndig, / wraþra wæl-sleahta, winemæga hryre" 6–7). The wanderer complains,

Time and again at the day's dawning
I must mourn all my afflictions alone.
There is no one still living to whom I dare open
the doors of my heart.

Oft ic sceolde ana   uhtna gehwylce
mine ceare cwiþan.   Nis nu cwicra nan
þe ic him modsefan   minne durre
sweotule asecgan. (8–11)

Radegund reports the same sense of alienation:

Often pressing my eyes shut on my damp face,
my complaints lie hidden, enclosed, but my cares are not silent.
Gladly I would look to see whether the wind reports a greeting,
and yet no shade of my relatives approaches.

saepe sub umecto conlidens lumina vultu;
    murmura clausa latent nec mea cura tacet.
specto libens, aliquam si nuntiet aura salutem,
    nullaque de cunctis umbra parentis adest. (39–42)

Radegund's image of the shades of her kin recalls the detail from the Anglo-Saxon elegy in which the wanderer imagines he greets his relatives, but "they drift away again" ("swimmað eft on weg" 53). In tone and imagery, then, "De excidio Thoringiae" bears a striking resemblance to the most poignant of the early Germanic elegies.

And just as she assumed the classical female persona familiar from Ovid's *Heroides*, so too does Radegund employ the female voice of the Germanic tradition, the lamenting woman lover of the *winileod* or love song (literally, "song for a friend"). The *winileod* is an elegy, narrated by a woman, which gives voice to her feelings.[23] Radegund's strongly expressed female emotion, her evocation of love and tears, and even the separation of the man and the woman by the sea has precise parallels in the two earliest surviving examples of this genre, the Anglo-Saxon "Wife's Lament" and "Wulf and Eadwacer." A comparison of these Anglo-Saxon poems with the Latin poetry above suggests that the Germanic tradition is distinct from and most likely uninfluenced by Virgil or Ovid. Whereas the Roman poets achieve emotional appeal through poignant images of women suffering and exaggerated rhetoric, particularly in the *Heroides*, the Anglo-Saxon poets rely on typically Germanic techniques—riddles, understatement, aphorism—and themes—desolation, transience, and fate.[24]

The female speaker of the "Wife's Lament" begins her song of lament as a riddle:

> I draw these words from my deep sadness,
> my sorrowful lot. I can say that,
> since I grew up, I have not suffered
> such hardship as now, old or new.
> I am tortured by the anguish of exile.

> Ic þis giedd wrece   bi me ful geomorre,
> minre sylfre sið.   Ic þæt secgan mæg,
> hwæt ic yrmþa gebad,   siþþan ic up weox,
> niwes oþþe ealdes,   no ma þonne nu.
> A ic wite wonn   minra wræcsiþa. (1–5)

While Radegund is more direct about her identity than is the speaker of the "Wife's Lament," they nonetheless share the theme of old and new hardships, the pain of living among a hostile people, and most important, a sense of desertion. The wife bemoans her desertion with understatement typical of the Anglo-Saxon elegy:

> . . . How often
> we swore that nothing but death should ever
> divide us; that is all changed now;
> our friendship is as if it had never been.

> . . . ful oft wit beotedan
> þæt unc ne gedælde   nemne deað ana
> owiht elles;   eft is þæt onhworfen,
> is nu * * * swa hit no wære
> freondscipe uncer. (21–25)

Like the wife, Radegund is careful not to place blame but to describe the severed relationship: "Hostile fate loosened me from the embrace / of him who used to love me with a tender glance" ("cuius in aspectu tenero solabar amore / solvit ab amplexu sors inimica meo" 43–44). Voicing similar grief, the female speaker of "Wulf" laments,

> Wulf, my Wulf, my yearning for you
> and your seldom coming have caused my sickness,
> my mourning heart, not mere starvation.

> Wulf, min Wulf,   wena me þine
> seoce gedydon,   þine seldcymas
> murnende mod,   nales meteliste. (13–15)

Radegund too employs direct address to vent her pain: "at least be mindful how from your earliest years, Hamalafred, I was your Radegund" ("vel memor esto, tuis primaevis qualis ab annis, / Hamalafrede, tibi tunc Radegundis eram" 47–48). The speaker of the "Wife's Lament" concludes her song by aphoristically noting, "Grief goes side by side with those / who suffer longing for a loved one" ("Wa bið þam þe sceal / of langoþe leofes abidan" 52–53). Radegund likewise expresses her longing for Hamalafred in fatalistic aphorism: "fate was an indication that suddenly I would be separated from you, dear one: / Stormy love does not know how to endure a long time" ("sors erat indicium, quia te cito, care, carerem: / inportunus amor nescit habere diu" 62–63). Although women are sometimes treated with great sympathy in Anglo Saxon poetry (for example, in the "Song of Finnesburg" of *Beowulf*), it is only in these two *winileodas* that a female narrator speaks directly in her own voice. Radegund thus shares with the lamenting women of the "Wife's Lament" and "Wulf" the poetic techniques of understatement and direct address as well as the desolate tone she strikes in the "De excidio Thoringiae."

Although these Anglo-Saxon poems post-date Radegund's compositions, the earliest surviving poems in vernacular languages—Anglo-Saxon, Old and Middle Irish, and early Welsh—all share a poetic tradition of lament as narrated by a female voice.[25] In the later Middle Ages, the voice of the lamenting woman is fully explored in Germanic poetry, in Middle High German *Minnesang* and in the Icelandic *Poetic Edda*. The *Minnesang* clearly testify to the influence of Provençal and French lyric. However, the laments of the *Poetic Edda* which are spoken by women—the first and second lays of Gudrun, "Guðrunarqviða in fyrsta" and "Guðrunarqviða ǫnnor"; Odrun's lament, "Oddrúnargrátr"; and Gudrun's final lay, "Guðrunarhvǫt"—hark back to traditional Germanic material. Arguing backwards from Anglo-Saxon and Icelandic poems, Joseph Harris argues for a common Germanic elegy that developed during "the Continental period before the Anglo-Saxon invasions."[26] This "common" elegy was probably a dramatic monologue spoken in the first person, often by a woman, which focused on the contrast between past joy and present grief. Radegund's "De excidio" exemplifies each of these features. One can only speculate about the poems which have not survived but which Radegund heard as the royal daughter of a Germanic court. Given the poverty of poetic texts surviving from the early Middle Ages, the distinctly Germanic tone of Radegund's epistle suggests an ancient oral tradition of female lamentation. The pose of the lamenting woman, familiar to us in early Germanic elegy and *wineleod*, is a powerful tool in Radegund's hands, calculated to evoke Hamalafred's sympathy and guilt.

Female Personae in the Letters

Radegund's "Ad Artachin" is one-fifth the length of the first epistle. Corresponding to its length, the poem displays less emotion than the "De excidio Thoringiae." Here Radegund addresses a man to whom she is less directly related, a nephew rather than the cousin with whom she was raised. Her verse epistle to Artachis reads like a story told to one who did not witness the devastation:

> After my homeland was burnt to ashes, and the high roofs of my
>   relatives fell,
> a devastation which the land of Thuringa endured through the
>   enemy's blade,
> how could I speak, I a woman harassed by war's unfortunate
>   struggle?
> What should I, a captive in tears, tell of first?
> What did I have time to mourn? This nation crushed by death
> or my sweet people cast down by various fates?

> Post patriae cineres et culmina lapsa parentum,
>   quod hostili acie terra Thoringa tulit,
> si loquar infausto certamine bella peracta,
>   quas prius ad lacrimas femina rapta trahar?

quid mihi flere vacet? pressam hanc funere gentem
an variis vicibus dulce ruisse genus? (1–6)

While Radegund perhaps summarizes action more than in the first verse
epistle, the personae she adopts are familiar. Borrowing Roman poetic
diction, she becomes the queen grieving for her "nation" and "people,"
the woman mourning her "relatives," and the captive or *barbara* missing
her "homeland." At the same time, Radegund emerges as the lamenting
woman of Germanic elegy who tells her story directly to us and comments
on her inexorable fate. Later in the letter, Radegund notes the impetus of
her writing, the death of Hamalafred:

Dear foster-son Artachis, why do I recall these things for you
To add even your tears to my weeping?
Rather I should have offered you the solace of family,
but grief for the dead compels me to speak bitterly.

cur tamen haec memorem tibi, care Artachis alumne
    fletibus atque meis addere flenda tuis?
debueram potius solamina ferre parenti,
    sed dolor extincti cogit amara loqui. (27–30)

As even this short passage indicates, Radegund's letter is not so much a
message of solace, an *epicedium* addressed to Artachis, but a reminder of his
relationship to her. Radegund here shows great subtlety. She does not play
on Artachis's guilt or even mention his familial obligations. Instead she
retains the position of the forelorn woman seeking a response from family.
She gently beseeches, "you, dear nephew Artachis, return to me the kind-
ness of that kinsman / and be mine in love as he first was" ("vel tu, care
nepos, placidum mihi redde propinquum / et sis amore meus quod fuit ille
prius" 35–36).

At first glance it is not easy to reconcile the strong woman who
emerges from Radegund's biographies with the desperately needy woman
she depicts in these two verse epistles. One wonders what prompted Radegund to write them. The letters are not dated and interior historical references are scarce. We know only that she composed the "De excidio Thoringiae" after her brother's death and her retreat to the monastery and
the "Ad Artachin" after Hamalafred's death. Interpreted from a psycho-

biographical perspective, the poems might have been composed shortly after Radegund fled Lothar, when she was feeling most vulnerable to her husband's power and most in need of her family's protection. Perhaps the expressive outlet provided by the verse epistles allowed Radegund to stand strong in the public arena.

Given Radegund's political astuteness, it seems just as likely that the personae she assumes in the letters represent an alternate strategy for survival. Sandwiched between the letter to Hamalafred and that to Artachis is another verse epistle addressed to Justin II and Sophia, "Ad Iustinum et Sophiam Augustos," in which Radegund thanks them for the relic of the true cross. Perhaps Radegund had earlier sent the two letters to her kin, who were living in Constantinople, in hopes that they would support her request to the emperor and empress. These two theories remain a matter of speculation.

It is nonetheless evident from the poems to Hamalafred and Artachis that, even while in the convent, Radegund attempted to maintain her ties not only with the ruling Merovingian crown but also with the Thuringian crown to which she was legitimate heir. Radegund's verse epistles thus stand not merely as a brilliant marriage of classical and Germanic poetic tradition, but the strategic act of an erudite queen who never yielded the voice of authority derived from her noble status.

I am grateful to Richard J. DuRocher, James M. May, Jo Ann McNamara, Karen Swenson, and Ulrike Wiethaus for their help on this essay.

Notes

1. Radegund's poems appear in *Monumenta Germaniae Historica, Auctores Antiquissimi,* ed. F. Leo, vol. 4, part I, pp. 271–79. All quotations from the poems are cited from this edition. All other Latin sources are from the *Monumenta Germaniae Historica,* the *Patrologia Latina* or the Loeb Classical Library from which I have cited both texts and translations. Beyond the Loeb volumes, I have used standard translations of sources when they exist and parenthetically indicated the translator's name. All other translations into English are my own. Poems are cited by line numbers.

2. The evidence for this correspondence is preserved in Gregory of Tours' *Historia Francorum,* ed. W. Arndt, *MGH: Scriptores rerum Merovingicarum* I.i (Hanover: 1885) and the nun Baudonivia's *vita* of Radegund, ed. B. Krusch, *MGH: Scriptores rerum Merovingicarum* II (Hanover: 1888). Gregory quotes in full a lengthy prose letter composed by Radegund before her death which is addressed to several unnamed bishops (*Hist. Fr.* IX.42.401–5). It is likely that these bishops are Eu-

fronius of Tours, Praetextatus of Rouen, Germanus of Paris, Felix of Nantes, Domitianus of Angers, Victorius of Rennes, and Domnolus of Le Mans, the same seven bishops who addressed a joint letter to Radegund shortly after the founding of her community (*Hist. Fr.* IX.39.394–96). In her letter Radegund seeks ecclesiastical and royal support for her foundation after her death.

Other evidence for Radegund's correspondence is indirect. Baudonivia relates that after Radegund fled her husband, she sent letters to Bishop Germanus asking him to intercede with Lothar (7.382), and that after her husband's death, Radegund attempted through letters to act as peacemaker among Lothar's warring sons (10.384). Baudonivia's *vita* further associates Radegund's acquisition of relics with her correspondence. Radegund secured King Sigibert's aid in seeking a relic of the true cross for France by writing to him; Sigibert sent petitions to the Emperor Justin II, Radegund's own among them (16.388). Justin complied with Radegund's wish in 569 by sending the relic to Poitiers in a beautiful enamel reliquary which Sophia had commissioned. The Poitiers reliquary is the earliest surviving specimen of Byzantine enamel in the west. Baudonivia also mentions letters of thanks which Radegund sent to the emperor and empress upon receiving the relic of the true cross and the reliquary (17.389). Radegund's second verse epistle, entitled "Ad Iustinum et Sophiam Augustos," praises the emperor and empress for their gifts. Perhaps this poem is one of the letters of gratitude to which Baudonivia refers. These references to Radegund's correspondence suggest that the written word was the only means by which a powerful but cloistered woman could maintain her ties with the outside world.

3. Fortunatus came to Poitiers in 567 and served as Radegund's advisor for twenty years until her death in 587. Since the late nineteenth century most critics have argued that these two metrical epistles were composed not by the saint but by her friend and advisor. See W. Lippert, "Zur Geschichte der hl. Radegunde von Thüringen," *Geschichte und Altertumkunde* 7 (1890): 16–38; E. Rey, "De l'authenticité de deux poèmes de Fortunat attribués à tort à Ste. Radegonde," *Revue de philologie* n.s. 30 (1906): 124–38; and more recently Josef Szövérffy, *Dichtungen des Lateinischen Mittelalters* (Berlin: Erich Schmidt, 1970), pp. 281–84. Noting the painfully depicted female emotion in the poems, other critics, such as Charles Nisard, "Des poésies de sainte Radegonde attribués jusqu'ici à Fortunat," *Revue historique* 37 (1888): 1–6, posited that the works must be Radegund's. Although the epistles are attributed in one MS to Fortunatus (MS Σ, cod. Paris. Nat. lat. 13,048), Szövérffy's accusation that Fortunatus composed in Radegund's name is, according to Peter Dronke, *Women Writers of the Middle Ages: A Critical Study of Texts from Perpetua (†203) to Marguerite Porete (†1310)* (Cambridge: Cambridge University Press, 1984), p. 298 n. 14, "inappropriate, since Fortunatus refers explicitly to poems of hers that Radegund had sent him." Marcelle Thiebaux, who has recently translated the two poems into English in *The Writings of Medieval Women* (New York: Garland, 1987), attributes them directly to Radegund. In my "Germanic Echoes in Latin Verse: the Voice of the Lamenting Woman in Radegund's Poetry" (forthcoming, *Allegorica*), I argue that the Germanic elements in the poems attest at the very least to the saint's partial authorship.

Perhaps the strongest evidence for attributing authorship of the letter to Radegund is internal evidence. Each of the three verse epistles uses her name as the author. In the first epistle, entitled "De excidio Thoringiae," the author writes, "Hamalafred, I was your Radegund" ("Hamalafrede, tibi tunc Radegundis eram," l. 48). In the second epistle, "Ad Iustinum et Sophiam Augustos," the author calls herself "Radegund of Thuringa" ("Radegunde Thoringa," l. 57), "the suppliant Radegund" ("supplex Radegundis," l. 87), and simply "Radegundis" (l. 96). In the third poem, "Ad Artachin," the author questions, "Should I, Radegund, ask after so long a time?" ("sic Radegundis enim post tempora longa requiror?" l. 13). In this essay I refer to the poems as Radegund's since she is the narrator of the "De excidio" and "Ad Artachis" and since recent scholarship has argued for her authorship.

4. Schulenberg, "Female Sanctity: Public and Private Roles, ca. 500–1100," in *Women and Power in the Middle Ages* (Athens: University of Georgia Press, 1988), p. 106.

5. *Hist. Fr.* III.7.15, trans. O. M. Dalton, *History of the Franks* (Oxford: Clarendon Press, 1927).

6. In the prologue to her *vita* Baudonivia writes, "Let us not repeat what the holy man Bishop Fortunatus told in his life of the blessed one, but those things which he passed over quickly" ("Non ea quae vir apostolicus Fortunatus episcopus de beatae vita conposuit iteramus, sed ea quae prolixitate praetermisit," *prologus*.387). Both Fortunatus's and Baudonivia's *vitae* were put forward as supporting material for Radegund's canonization.

7. According to Gregory of Tours, when the relics of the true cross arrived in Poitiers Radegund requested that Maroveus "deposit them in the convent with chanting of psalms and all due honour. But he disregarded her proposal, mounting his horse, and going off to a country estate" ("ut cum honore debito grandique psallentio in monastryrim locarentur. Sed ille dispiciens suggestionem eius, ascensis equis, villae se contulit" *Hist. Fr.* IX.40.397). Baudonivia attributes the same behavior to him (16.388). Maroveus also refused to preside at Radegund's funeral, and Gregory himself performed the rites (*In gloria* 104.815).

8. According to Mother Maria Caritas McCarthy S.H.C.J., *The Rule for Nuns of St. Caesarius of Arles: A Translation with a Critical Introduction* (Washington, DC: Catholic University of America Press, 1960), the *vita* of Saint Caesaria the younger indicates that the nuns at Arles also worked at copying manuscripts and that the convent likely had a scriptorium. On p. 25 McCarthy quotes the *vita*: " . . . the mother Caesaria, whose work with her community so flourished, that amidst psalmody and fasting, vigils and readings, the virgins of Christ lettered most beautifully the divine books, having the mother herself as teacher." Radegund's biographers do not state that Holy Cross had a scriptorium, yet MS Σ, the definitive collection of Fortunatus's poems, was copied there. In addition, the exchange of poems of Fortunatus, Radegund, and Agnes, Radegund's own exquisite verse epistles, and the rhetorically rich style of Baudonivia's *vita* indicate that Holy Cross was a center for humane letters.

9. Although Fortunatus emphasizes Radegund's asceticism far more than does Baudonivia, the details are present in both *vitae*. See, for example, Fortunatus XV.35.42; XVII.39.42, 40.43, 41.43; XVIII.43.43; XIX.44.43, 45.43, 46.43; XXI.50.44; XXII.52.44; XXIII.54.44; XXIV.58.45; XXV.60.45; XXVI.61.45; and Baudonivia 5.381–82 and 8.382–83.

10. Caesaria, "Epistola ad Richildam et Radegundim," *PL, Supplementum,* vol. 4, cols. 1406, 1407.

11. Wemple, *Women in Frankish Society: Marriage and the Cloister, 500–900* (Philadelphia: University of Pennsylvania Press, 1981), p. 184.

12. McNamara, "A Legacy of Miracles: Hagiography and Nunneries in Merovingian Gaul," in *Women in the Medieval World,* ed. Julius Kirshner and Suzanne Fonay Wemple (Oxford: Blackwell, 1985), p. 47.

13. My summary is not meant to level the differences in the two *vitae* found by astute critics. In *Women in Frankish Society,* p. 184, Wemple attributes the contrasting emphases in Fortunatus's and Baudonivia's *vitae* to gender difference: "In contrast to Fortunatus's portrait of Radegund as the withdrawn wife and reluctant queen whose main object was to transform her femininity and escape from her husband, Baudonivia described Radegund as an outgoing and emotional woman, who was as concerned about the affairs of the convent as about the developments in the kingdom" (184). In *The Small Sound of the Trumpet: Women in Medieval Life* (Boston: Beacon Press, 1986), p. 78, Margaret Wade Labarge comments in a similar vein: "The difference in point of view is striking, for unlike Fortunatus, Baudonivia's emphasis is not on Radegund's expected feminine virtues of piety and self-denial, but, more realistically, on her feminine attributes of maternal solicitude for her nuns, her attempts to serve as a peacemaker among her husband's kin, and her effort to develop her monastery into a centre of intercession for the French kings."

14. *MGH Auctores Antiquissimorum,* vol. IV, appendix XXXI.

15. Famous *epicedia* include Catullus 101; Virgil, *Ecologues* V.20–44 and *Aeneid* VI.860–86; Horace, *Odes* I.24; Propertius III.7, 18 and IV.11; Ovid, *Amores* III.9 and *Epistulae ex ponto* I.9; Martial *Epigrams* V.37, VI.37, VI.28 and 29, and 85; Statius, *Silvae* II.1, 6, III.3, V.1, 3, and 5; and Ausonius, *Parentalia.*

16. Ovid employs a similar strategy and self-pitying tone in his *epicedium* on Celus's death, when the poet praises the deceased for loyalty:

But no hours came to my mind more frequently than
those—would they have been the latest of my life—when
my house on a sudden collapsed in utter ruin and fell
upon its master's head. He stood by me when the
greater part abandoned me . . .

nulla tamen subeunt mihi tempora densius illis,
    quae vellem vitae summa fuisse meae,
cum domus ingenti subito mea lapsa ruina
    concidit in domini procubuitque caput.
adfuit ille mihi, cum me pars magna reliquit . . . (*Ex ponto* I.9.11–15)

17. Dronke, *Women Writers of the Middle Ages* (note 3), p. 86.

18. DeJean, *Fictions of Sappho, 1546–1937* (Chicago: University of Chicago Press, 1989), p. 60. On pp. 60–71, DeJean provides a helpful summary of recent scholar-

ship on the *Heroides*. See Howard Jacobson's *Ovid Heroides* (Princeton: NJ: Princeton University Press, 1974), a reading of the *Heroides* as a rejection of Augustan and Virgilian heroism (p. 7); Florence Verducci's *Ovid's Toyshop of the Heart: Epistulae Herodium* (Princeton, NJ: Princeton University Press, 1985), a reading of the *Heroides* as a debasement of the female characters, an Ovidian rhetorical slide from pathos "into selfish bathos" (p. 285); and Linda Kauffman's *Discourses of Desire: Gender, Genre, and Epistolary Fictions* (Ithaca, NY: Cornell University Press, 1986), a reading of the *Heroides* as a skeptical exposé of language's inability to represent "a center, a self, and hence gender" (p. 19). My purpose here is not to enter the debate on interpreting the *Heroides*, but simply to claim these poems as precursors to Radegund's verse epistles.

19. Ovid originally composed fifteen *Heroides* (numbers I–XV), all of which are narrated by women. At a later date, he wrote a series of verse epistles which probably formed a second volume of the *Heroides*. These are the paired letters (numbers XVI–XXI) in which a man addresses a woman in one letter and she responds in the next.

Of Ovid's original fifteen heroines, nine are separated from their lovers by the sea or fear they will be. See Penelope to Ulysses, *Her.* I.73–74; Phyllis to Demophoon, *Her.* II.11–12, 25–26, 45–46, etc.; Briseis to Achilles, *Her.* III.57–58, 63–66; Oenone to Paris, *Her.* V.53–57, 63–64, etc.; Hypsipyle to Jason, *Her.* VI. 1–5, 57–58, 65–68, etc.; Dido to Aeneas, *Her.* VII.7–10, 35–44, etc.; Ariadne to Theseus, *Her.* X.1–6, 25–36, etc.; Laodamia to Protesilaus, *Her.* XIII.3–11, 15–24, etc.; and Sappho to Phaon, *Her.* XV.95–96, 211–20.

20. Further evidence for Radegund's use of the *Heroides* in describing her imagined voyage to Hamalafred may be found in the letters of Hero and Leander, which appear among the second series or paired letters of the *Heroides*. Leander predicts his death in the following passage:

> I shall pray to be cast up on yonder shores, and that my
> shipwrecked limbs may come into your haven; for you will
> weep over me, and not disdain to touch my body, and you will
> say: "Of the death he met, I was the cause!"

> optabo tamen ut partis expellar in illas,
>   et teneant portus naufraga membra tuos;
> flebis enim tactuque meum dignabere corpus
>   et "mortis," dices, "huic ego causa fui!" (*Her.* XVIII.197–200)

The tone of Leander's speech and his attempt to elicit guilt is quite similar to "De excidio" 112–20. In her response to Leander, Hero questions, "Ships wrought with skill are overwhelmed by the wave; do you think your arms more powerful than oars?" ("arte laboratae merguntur ab aequore naves; ·/ tu tua plus remis bracchia posse putas?" *Her.* XIX.183–84). Perhaps this passage suggested to Radegund her exaggerated claim that, if ship or oars should fail, she would reach Hamalafred "swimming with exhausted hands" ("lassa natante manu," 114).

21. Thiebaux, *Writings of Medieval Women* (note 3), p. 29.

22. "Wanderer," *The Exeter Book*, ed. George Philip Krapp and Elliott van Kirk Dobbie, Anglo-Saxon Poetic Record, vol. 3 (New York: Columbia Univ. Press, 1936), ll. 78–80. Translations of the Anglo-Saxon are from Kevin Crossley-Holland, *The Anglo-Saxon World* (New York: Oxford University Press, 1982). The "Wanderer," "Seafarer," "Wife's Lament," and "Wulf and Eadwacer" survive in this single manuscript, the *Exeter Book*, and henceforth I will note them parenthetically by line numbers.

The poet of the "Seafarer," an elegy which critics often treat as a companion piece to the "Wanderer," describes a scene parallel to the one discussed above:

> kings and kaisers and gold-giving lords
> are no longer as they were
> when they wrought deeds of greatest glory
> and lived in the most lordly splendour;
> their host has perished . . .

> næron nu cyningas   ne caseras
> ne goldgiefan   swylce iu wæron,
> þonne hi mæst mid him   mærþa gefremedon
> ond on dryhtlicestum   dome lifdon.
> Gedroren is þeos duguð eal, . . . (82–86)

23. Dronke discusses the *winileodas* and their popularity among nuns of the Carolingean Age in *The Medieval Lyric* (Cambridge: Cambridge University Press, 1977), p. 26. He also analyzes "Wulf and Eadwacer" as an early example of this genre on pp. 91–93.

24. For a fuller discussion of the distinctive features of female lament in the Germanic tradition, see my article, "Germanic Echoes in Latin Verse."

25. Laments spoken by women in Old and Middle Irish include "Líadan's Song," "the Lament of Créide . . . for Dínertach," "Créide's Lament for Cáel," "Gráinne Speaks of Díarmait," and "Díarmait's Sleep" in Gerard Murphy, *Early Irish Lyrics* (Oxford: Clarendon Press, 1956), pp. 83–84, 86–89, 148, 160–61. In Welsh the "Eagle of Pengwern" ("Eryr Pengwern") is spoken by Heledd, sister to the warrior Cynddylan in Sir Ifor Williams, *The Burning Tree* (Dublin: Institute for Advanced Studies, 1954), pp. 30–31.

26. "Elegy in Old English and Old Norse: A Problem in Literary History," in *Old English Elegies,* ed. Martin Green (Rutherford, NJ: Fairleigh Dickinson University Press, 1983), p. 52.

Gillian T. W. Ahlgren

Visions and Rhetorical Strategy in the Letters of Hildegard of Bingen

The letters of Hildegard of Bingen (1098–1179) provide a unique opportunity to analyze the interplay of religious experience, prophetic authority, and rhetorical skill in the life of a twelfth-century visionary. Hildegard's visions and the manuscript illuminations which they inspired are now well known,[1] but the relationship between the modes of expression of visionary experience and Hildegard's status among her peers has not been studied in enough detail.[2] This essay examines the ambiguity of Hildegard's role as both visionary and spiritual adviser as reflected in her correspondence. Hildegard scholar Barbara Newman has already noted that Hildegard and her protégé Elisabeth of Schönau shared a preoccupation with the ridicule that could be or was in fact aroused by their gender, and consequently with authentication through and despite their sex. Thus many of their visions obliquely sanctioned a role reversal by presenting men as negligent or weak, women as prophetic and powerful, and aspects of God as feminine. In cases of conflict, divine authority could override that of a powerful male, such as an abbot, and thus vindicate the visionary.[3] In fact, Hildegard consciously developed concrete rhetorical strategies to express her visions in her personal correspondence, and the literary formulae which she used depended on the gender and socio-religious status of the recipient. The expression of her visionary experience in her letters involved three basic formulations: reportorial, in which Hildegard merely reports visions in her letters; instrumental, in which Hildegard describes both her vision and her own role as an unworthy vessel of this vision; and representative, in which Hildegard speaks in the first person as both the medium and the source of her visions.

One of the most interesting characteristics of Hildegard's extant correspondence is that the majority of her letters include mention of a vision she has experienced. Such prominent reference to her visionary experience indicates the complex and important role that visions played in Hildegard's communications with her contemporaries. References to the "living light" ("lux vivens"), or to what she "saw and heard" ("vidi et audivi") abound in her letters. Such references to visions go farther until at times Hildegard proclaims the will of God in the first person ("I, the living fountain . . ." "Ego fons vivus . . ."). Hildegard's visionary experiences informed and supported many of her letters, granting her a voice in an ecclesiastical conversation dominated by men.

Hildegard's Visions and the Problem of Authority

Because of her visions, Hildegard enjoyed a special status in medieval Europe as prophetess and spiritual adviser. Her visions aroused both the curiosity and respect of ecclesiastical leaders, monastic figures and lay-people, who solicited her advice on questions of spiritual and moral importance.[4] Because her visions validate her message to her contemporaries, Hildegard's explanation of how she received messages from God is important to understanding her claims to authority. The extant letters show that Hildegard began an active epistolary career right after the Council of Trier (1147–48) when Pope Eugene III read portions of her unfinished *Scivias* to the assembled cardinals and bishops. Hierarchical officials encouraged her to write down the doctrine, theological insights and counsels she received through her visions. After this critical juncture, Hildegard looked to her visions to provide her with the ecclesiastical authority she might need in her correspondence with others.[5] Rather than expressing any doubt in her visions or even in herself, she presented the content of her visions forcefully, employing specific formulae for their expression.

Interestingly, in the first extant letter addressed to Bernard of Clairvaux, Hildegard uses none of the visionary formulae which we come to expect in her correspondence. Van Acker dates this letter to 1146/7. In the letter Hildegard appears to be an anxious woman, in need of some official recognition of her visions and the ministry to which she feels called. In addition to honoring Bernard with titles like "O venerable Father" ("O venerabilis Pater") and "most dependable and gentle Father" ("certissime et mitissime Pater"), Hildegard presents herself as an unworthy instrument of the Holy Spirit, writing:

Father, I am greatly troubled from this vision, which appears to me in the spirit of mystery, which I have never seen with my external physical eyes. I, a miserable and worse than miserable woman, from my infancy have seen great marvels, which my tongue [alone] could not proclaim, except that the Spirit of God teaches me, that I may believe.

Pater, ego sum valde sollicita de hac visione, que apparuit mihi in spiritu mysterii, quam numquam vidi cum exterioribus oculis carnis. Ego misera et plus quam misera in nomine femineo, ab infantia mea vidi magna mirabilia, que lingua mea non potest proferre, nisi quod me docuit Spiritus Dei, ut credam.[6]

In this case, Hildegard is soliciting Bernard's approval of her visions (and thus his authority) and indicates her willingness to submit to his authority while at the same time vouching for the authenticity and orthodoxy of her visions. Indeed, Hildegard conducted her search for ecclesiastical authority within an orthodox framework: she carefully points out that her visionary experience was not physical, thus fitting into Augustinian standards of orthopraxy.[7]

Toward the end of her life, Hildegard gave several details about the way she experienced her visions in her first letter to Guibert of Gembloux (1124/5–1213/4), written before he became her secretary in 1177.[8] Guibert had heard of Hildegard's remarkable visionary gifts and wanted to know all the details about her experience. In her response Hildegard describes a vision in which she sees and hears things:

not with my physical ears, nor with the thoughts of my heart, nor do I perceive them with the use of my senses; but only in my soul, with my external eyes open, thus I never experience in them the defect of ecstasy, but I see these things vigilantly, day and night.

Ista autem nec corporeis auribus audio, nec cogitationibus cordis mei, nec ulla collatione sensuum meorum quinque percipio; sed tantum in anima mea, apertis exterioribus oculis, ita ut nunquam in eis defectum extasis paciar, sed vigilanter die ac nocte illa video.[9]

Hildegard is careful to transmit exactly that which she sees and hears in her visions, explaining:

And the things that I write in vision I see and hear; nor do I add words, for that which I hear and make known are not elegant Latin words, just like those which I hear in the vision: for in this vision I am not taught to write as philosophers do; and the words in that vision are not like words which resound from the human mouth, but like a sparkling flame and clouds moved through clear air.

Et ea que scribo illa invisione video et audio; nec alia verba pono, quam illa que audio et latinisque verbis non limatis ea profero, quemadmodum illa invisione audio, quoniam sicut philosophi scribunt, scribere in visione hac non doceor. Atque verba que in visione ista video et audio non sunt sicut verba que ab ore hominis sonant, sed sicut flamma choruscans, et ut nubes in aere puro mota.[10]

There is an implicit criticism here of philosophical rhetoric and the evolving course of medieval education from which Hildegard was excluded.[11] Although Hildegard excuses her "rustic" style, some scholars believe that her words have the advantage of being both accessible and more poignant than those of contemporary theologians.[12] We should certainly be careful not to read Hildegard's protestations of ignorance too literally here. Hildegard's portrayal of herself as merely a transmitter of the divine message masks her creativity in the formulation and presentation of her visions. In her correspondence Hildegard describes her visions with adroitness, matching rhetorical force to both the function and the recipient of her letters.

Hildegard's Correspondence

This study analyzes Hildegard's letters now available in the new critical edition prepared by L. Van Acker for *Corpus Christianorum*.[13] Van Acker's study provides new information on the difficult question of Hildegard's initiative as a correspondent. The primary source for Hildegard's letters is the Wiesbaden Riesenkodex, produced between 1180 and 1190 in Rupertsberg by her nephew Wezelin.[14] This manuscript presents pairs of letters in a pattern of solicitation/response which portrays Hildegard as more passive than she was. Earlier editions of Hildegard's letters followed this interpretation, thus skewing our perception of her interaction with her contemporaries. Indeed, in the first volume of Van Acker's critical edition letters which Hildegard wrote on her own initiative appear in nearly equal numbers as those in which she responds to a specific request or concern.

An overview of the collection gives the reader some idea of the kind of audience Hildegard had, the reasons people wrote to her, and the way she expressed her beliefs and experiences. Hildegard's correspondence reflects her widespread reputation as a visionary with special access to God. The letters she received came from such places as Saxony, Flanders, Thuringia, Bohemia, Champagne, and Bavaria; she wrote to popes, bishops and *magistri* in Paris. Hildegard's influence as a visionary is reflected in the number of people who sought her theological insight and spiritual counsel. Many of the letters she received incorporate implicit references to Hildegard's reputation, either in their greeting or in the body of the letter. Although these salutations usually follow a standard form, the accolades or titles ascribed to Hildegard can be remarkable. Often, as in the request for prayers from Arnold, Archbishop of Mainz, writers will explicitly offer Hildegard the title of "teacher" ("magistra").[15] Other letters call her a "burning lamp in the house of the Lord" ("Lucerne ardenti in domo Domini")[16] or a woman "miraculously infused by the divine breath" ("divino spiramine mirabiliter infusae").[17]

Formulae for the Expression of Hildegard's Visions

The majority of Hildegard's 284 letters (191 letters, or 67% of the total sample) include mention of Hildegard's visionary experience. They use one of three different levels of literary formulae which represent increasingly forceful expressions of authority. The delineation of three levels of literary formulae which Hildegard employs to express her visionary experience permits us to assess the intensity of her need to claim authority. Briefly stated, at the first level, in what I call a *reportorial* depiction of her visions, Hildegard writes that she "saw and heard in a true vision . . ." ("vidi et audivi in vera visione . . ."), whatever her message was. At the second, *instrumental* level of intensity, she describes a vision but separates herself from the message, underscoring her participation solely as a vessel of divine testimony. At the third, *representative* level, Hildegard omits reference to her intermediary position altogether, writing the divine message in the first or third person. After defining more clearly these three classes of literary formulae, I will analyze their prevalence in the epistolary *corpus* and discuss the relationship of the formulae and the recipients of Hildegard's letters.[18]

Hildegard's most commonly used formula, the reportorial level of visionary expression, is represented by the words "I saw and heard" ("vidi et audivi") or "In a true [or mystical or spiritual] vision I saw and heard these words . . ." ("In vera [mystica/spirituali] visione haec verba vidi et audivi . . .").[19] A corollary to this formula is the more personal "I heard a voice saying to you . . ." ("Audivi vocem ad te dicentem . . ."). I call this level of visionary expression "reportorial" because Hildegard announces that she is merely repeating what she saw and heard. While Hildegard is clearly making recourse to a source of authority greater than herself, reportorial expressions are the least forceful of the three groups. They represent a claim to visionary experience which Hildegard implies that she had in response to, or coincidental with, a particular request for help that she received. The implication, of course, is not only that Hildegard had a vision, but that she received the vision more or less on request, since she was commissioned to act as the medium between the letter-writer and the source of her visions. The personal and episodic nature of the reportorial formula is further emphasized by its corollaries, in which Hildegard directs the vision to the writer by modifying the formula. Hildegard invokes the reportorial formula for the expression of her visions in approximately 42% of the letters which incorporate some sort of visionary formula. The reportorial formula establishes Hildegard's visionary credentials as an adviser to others. Hildegard commonly uses this expression to people of approximately the same religious status as herself in order to add force to her advice, instruction, or predictions. However, the authority claimed through this formulation appears not to have been sufficient for Hildegard to make significant criticisms of others.

The second level of claim for divine authority includes the same formula as above, but with the addition of a protestation of either Hildegard's own weakness or her lack of education. The instrumental formulation concurrently asserts humility and authority, combining some reference to Hildegard's status as "poor woman" ("paupercula femina") with authoritative vision which enables her to speak. One example of this formula is found in her letter to Pope Eugene III, which begins:

I, a poor woman, write this to you in a true vision, in the mystical breath, just as God wanted me to teach.

Ego paupercula forma scripsi tibi hec in vera visione in mystico spiramine, sicut Deus voluit me docere.[20]

In this instrumental mode Hildegard stresses her role as transmitter even though she claims to be unworthy of this responsibility. By using this formula in her letters, Hildegard replicates in microcosm the prefaces of many of her theological works, in which her self-effacement reinforces the divine nature of her message and her duty as a prophet to promulgate it.[21] This second formula for the expression of a vision underscores the divine source of Hildegard's visions by differentiating between Hildegard as a poor creature and the divinity whom she represents. The instrumental formula reveals the precarious nature of Hildegard's authority; significantly, Hildegard employs it mostly in her letters to men. These instrumental formulae constitute 10% of the formulae used in Hildegard's letters or 7% of the overall sample of Hildegard's letters. These figures are low because Hildegard typically used this formula in special cases.

When Hildegard is unsure of her religious status or authority in the mind of the recipient of her letter, she tends to fall back on an instrumental formulation, as in the case of her letter to Bernard of Clairvaux.[22] Hildegard commonly incorporates an instrumental formula when she writes to a man of high ecclesiastical rank for the first time.[23] By using this formulation Hildegard assigns herself an inferior status: she is only a "poor woman" ("paupercula femina"). This formulation serves two purposes. Hildegard's own weakness makes her message all the more clearly inspired: how could an unlettered woman speak with such a powerful voice? Second, Hildegard reassures her religious superiors of her allegiance to the hierarchical church and her willingness to be obedient.

Finally, the representative formula for the expression of Hildegard's visions makes the boldest claim to divine authority. Here, Hildegard invokes the voice of "Wisdom" ("Sapientia"), the Living Light ("Lux vivens"), or simply "the One who . . ." ("Qui est") directly, as in the formulae "The living light says . . ." ("Lux vivens dicit . . .") and "The living fountain says . . ." ("Fons vivus dicit . . .")[24] These expressions of the will of God in the third or first person are "representative," since Hildegard has actually blended her identity with that of the source of her visions. This representative formulation of her visions bypasses Hildegard's role as the instrument of divine wisdom or the seer, thus making the appeal to the recipient of the letter more direct: the recipient is addressed by the source of Hildegard's vision. Formulae of this category are found in 92 letters (48% of the formulae and 32% of the entire correspondence).

In the representative formulation of her visions, Hildegard incorporates a variety of sources of authority. Although I cannot discern a significant pattern in Hildegard's use of voices like the "living light" ("lux vivens"), the "mysteries of God" ("mystica dei"), or "the one who is" ("qui est"), these differences clearly involve distinct appeals to divine authority. Much of this authority is implicitly scriptural; Hildegard uses phrases which remind the recipients of her letters of important encounters between biblical figures and God. For example, in a letter to Pope Anastasius Hildegard begins with the words: "Listen, o man" ("Audi o homo").[25] This exhortation to listen recalls that of the Old Testament prophets who preface their divine message with the words, "Hear the word of Yahweh."[26]

Even stronger are Hildegard's references to God, as in the case of "The one who is says . . ." ("Qui est dicit . . .")[27] These words clearly echo Moses' encounter with God in Exodus 3:1–22.[28] In another case Hildegard writes, "The one who gives life to the living says . . ." ("Qui vitam dat viventibus dicit . . .")[29] Hildegard often refers to the "living light" ("lux vivens") as the source of her prophetic gift.[30] Here Hildegard connotes the creative power of God as expressed in the first chapter of John.[31] Finally, Hildegard uses the voice of the "the one who is, who was and who is to come," establishing a prophetic authority parallel to that of John of Patmos.[32]

In another strategy, Hildegard describes the source of her vision as a virtue, functioning as attributes of God, such as "Wisdom" ("Sapientia") or "Charity" ("Charitas").[33] Hildegard invokes these virtues in thirteen different letters.[34] Her rhetorical intention in the use of the virtues appears to be two-fold. First, Hildegard's reform agenda on the practical, moral level as expressed through her correspondence is a microcosm of her vision of the ordered virtues, an attempt to instill through her correspondence her perception of heavenly order. Second, by invoking traditional figures of authority which are female, Hildegard legitimizes her role as a female teacher in the church. Her use of the virtues reads as a reinforcement of Hildegard's general position that in "feminine times" women must take responsibility for reforming the church, since the men who were given this charge have not proven capable trustees.[35] Interestingly enough, none of the recipients of letters in which Hildegard refers to visions given to her by the virtues is female. The implication here is clear: the voice of an authoritative female figure is needed to establish order among male church leaders. Indeed, Hildegard commonly uses the more forceful representative formula when her letters are critical of the recipient; this mode of expression often conveys the image of a judging God. In her letter to Henry, Bishop of Liège, Hildegard reminds him of his pastoral responsibility, combining the voice of the "living light" ("lux vivens") with a reference to the parable of the talents and thus the Last Judgment.[36] Hildegard uses this type of formula in exhortations to reform, to humility, and to perseverance in good works.[37]

The added force of this representative formula in terms of the authority it represents is apparent. Its corollary, in which the recipient is addressed by the source in the first person, is clearly the most forceful and may strike us as a bold or presumptuous move on Hildegard's part. Gone are the dismissals of her own "paupercula forma"; instead, the speaker is addressed by an often nameless, though clearly supra-human figure. Although not concerned with the typology of formulae for visions which I develop here, Peter Dronke notes "a frightening hint of megalomania here," when he examines Hildegard's conflation of the third and the first person, explaining that Hildegard is "never less than certain that she knows the will of God; doing God's will and doing her will are seen as identical."[38] A study of the correlation between audience and the representative formulation of visionary expression shows, however, that Hildegard's claims of authority are not willful and distorted but rather a sophisticated rhetorical strategy.

Indeed, Hildegard's use of visionary formulae enabled her to influence ecclesiastical reforms on many levels, although her program is far from radical. In her letters Hildegard criticizes the clergy's negligence in their pastoral duties to the laity.[39] For example, in her letter to cardinals Bernard of St. Clement and Gregory of St. Angelus, both legates of Pope Eugene, Hildegard asks them to be more vigilant of their prelates, writing that they have abandoned the responsibilities of pastoral care.[40] Many of Hildegard's letters to hierarchical figures exhort them to justice and its promotion.[41] Without challenging their authority, Hildegard emphasizes their roles as servants and charges that many of them display too much pride. In the case of Henry, archbishop of Mainz, Hildegard uses the example of Nebuchadnezzar losing his kingdom because of his arrogance and sinful ways.[42]

Hildegard frequently saw visions that were defined by questions or concerns addressed to her in letters. People would write to her, asking her advice on such matters as vocational decisions, the fulfillment of pilgrimage vows, questions about the Eucharist, and the manner of expelling demons. To each of these concerns Hildegard was able to transmit a message which she claimed came directly from her visionary experiences. Thus she portrayed herself—and was approached—as a channel of grace to those who sought her insight into their moral and spiritual problems.

The most common of all these requests was for prayers. Hildegard's prayers were seen as more efficacious than those of her contemporaries, and her visions increased her prestige as an intercessor before God. Some correspondents believed that Hildegard's direct access to God gave her privileged theological insights as well. Eberhard, bishop of Bamberg, wrote to Hildegard at St. Rupert to ask her to explain "according to what God has revealed to you" the relationship of the individual members of the Trinity.[43] In this request Eberhard hoped for ammunition in his Christological quarrel with Gerhoch of Reichersberg.[44] Odo of Paris, a *magister* of theology, wrote to her asking about one of the teachings of Gilbert of Poitiers, whether God's fatherhood and godhead were identical with God.[45] This issue was to be discussed at Gilbert's hearing at the Council of Reims. These requests for guidance reflect people's belief that, as Dronke puts it, Hildegard had "a means of judging different from and superior to normal methods of metaphysical inquiry."[46] In almost every case of a request for information, Hildegard's response contains the relation of a visionary experience, thus guaranteeing the orthodoxy of her response. Sometimes she wrote as the reporter of her experience, claiming, "In a true vision I saw and heard these words . . ." ("In vera visione haec verba vidi et audivi . . .") In more extreme cases, where extra emphasis might be needed, she might use the first person when referring to the divine message, as in the case, "I, the living fountain . . ." ("Ego fons vivus . . .").[47]

Quantitative Analysis of the Formula

The first part of Table 1 summarizes the incidence of visionary formulae described above which are included in Hildegard's letters. Hildegard uses some sort of visionary formula in two of every three letters. When we analyze the recipients of Hildegard's letters, we can gain some insight into the patterns of rhetorical strategy employed in the letters. The recipients of Hildegard's letters can be divided into three categories: monastic audience, lay audience, and ecclesiastical leaders. The majority of Hildegard's extant letters are addressed to members, especially leaders, of monastic communities. Fully 180 of 251 letters to known recipients were written to monastic figures, with 24 more addressed to clerics who may or may not have been living in religious communities. The second part of Table 1 shows the distribution of visionary formulae within this category of clerics, monks and nuns.

Thus, as a sort of control sample, we see that when writing to monastic

TABLE I: Incidence of Visionary Formulae in Hildegard's Letters

Type of formula	No. of times used	Percent of letters with formulae	Percent of overall letters
Overall audience			
None	93	—	33
Reportorial	80	42	28
Instrumental	19	10	7
Representative	92	48	32
Total	284	100	100
Monastic audience			
No formula	68	—	37
Reportorial	45	39	24
Instrumental	12	10	7
Representative	59	51	32
Total	184		100
Lay audience			
No forumla	11	—	44
Reportorial	7	50	28
Instrumental	0	—	—
Representative	7	50	28
Total	25		100
Hierarchical audience[48]			
No formula	5	—	12
Reportorial	7	19	16.5
Instrumental	7	19	16.5
Representative	23	62	55
Total	42		100
Unknown recipients			
No formula	9	—	27
Reportorial	21	87.5	64
Instrumental	0	—	—
Representative	3	12.5	9
Total	33		100

figures, Hildegard described a vision in over 60% of her letters. She used the representative formulation in the majority of those cases, thus invoking the greatest claim to authority.

These data are confirmed by an analysis of the visionary formulae which Hildegard used in the twenty-five extant letters to laypeople, both male and female (third part of Table 1). Again, although there is some slight variation, the proportion of letters including visions to those which do not is about 60–40. This time Hildegard uses the representative formulae slightly less than when writing to monastic figures.

These proportions break down significantly when we analyze the data on Hildegard's letters to members of the ecclesiastical hierarchy. Van Acker's critical edition contains thirty-seven letters to the papacy or to various bishops and archbishops, whose vision formulae are distributed as shown in the last part of Table 1. Fully 88% of Hildegard's letters addressed to hierarchical figures incorporate her visions in experiences that are specific to the message that she writes to these men. Further, of these letters which do include reference to a vision, 62% of them employ the boldest expression of these visions, in which Hildegard's voice and that of the source of her visions are combined. Members of the ecclesiastical hierarchy might have been more reluctant to recognize monastic figures without ecclesiastic titles in the teaching office. This reluctance is certainly heightened by Hildegard's gender. In addition, members of the hierarchy were in positions of authority through which they could limit or curtail Hildegard's ministerial activities. The higher percentage of representative formulae indicate that Hildegard's need to legitimate her role was thus more acute when dealing with such church officials.

A further analysis of the breakdown of Hildegard's formulae according to the gender of the recipient of her letters demonstrates that the issue is not solely one of authority but of gender as well. When we look for patterns in the prevalence of visionary formulae in the letters to men versus the letters to women, we see that Hildegard made greater use of these formulae in her letters to men. The breakdowns are shown in Table 2.

Table 2 demonstrates that Hildegard used visions more in her letters to men than in her letters to women. The ratio of 48% of letters with visionary formulae to 52% without in Hildegard's letters to women is far below the ratio for letters sent to men of 69% to 31%. Further, Hildegard's use of representative formulae is slight in her letters to women—just 13%—while it is 31% for men. Additionally, comparing the incidence of the representative formulae between the two audiences shows that Hildegard most com-

TABLE 2:   Incidence of Visionary Formulae in Letters by Gender

Type of formula	No. of times used	Percent of letters with formulae	Percent of overall letters
Letters to men			
No formula	64	—	31
Reportorial	56	33	23
Instrumental	21	11	7
Representative	64	56	39
Total	190		100
Letters to women			
No formula	26	—	52
Reportorial	14	62	28
Instrumental	1	4	2
Representative	9	34	16
Total	50		100

monly used this more forceful expression of authority to men rather than women (56% vs. 35%). These figures indicate that Hildegard felt not only a greater need to legitimate herself to her male audience, but also made bolder claims to men in order to do so.

An analysis of Hildegard's treatment of visions in her letters to her monastic audience provides further evidence of her impulse to legitimate herself to men. This comparison examines her interaction with men and women of approximately the same level of authority within the ecclesiastical structure. There are 144 extant letters which Hildegard wrote to male monastic figures and 40 which she wrote to female monastic figures. They use visionary formulae as shown in Table 3.

Table 3 demonstrates that, when writing to people of a similar monastic status, Hildegard still felt she had to legitimate her correspondence and message with visions more often with men than with women. Besides the differences between overall uses of visionary formulae (67% of her letters to monastic men vs. 45% of her letters to monastic women), there is a great difference in the percentages of times Hildegard used representative visionary formulae to men vs. to women (54% vs. 33%). Hildegard used the boldest claim she could in more instances with monastic men than with monastic women.

TABLE 3:   Incidence of Visionary Formulae in Letters to Monastics by Gender

Type of formula	No. of times used	Percent of letters with formulae	Percent of overall letters
Monastic men			
No formula	47	—	33
Reportorial	34	35	26
Instrumental	11	11	8
Representative	52	54	33
Total	144		100
Monastic women			
No formula	22	—	55
Reportorial	11	61	27
Instrumental	1	6	3
Representative	6	33	15
Total	40		100

If Hildegard uses these visionary formulae to establish her authority with the recipients of her letters, what does it mean to show that she uses them more in her correspondence with men than with women? Fundamentally, the level of discourse is different. In her correspondence with men, where questions of Hildegard's authority as teacher or visionary emerged as significant, there was a tension in the correspondence. Until Hildegard could demonstrate the inspired nature of her voice, there was always the possibility that men in higher ecclesiastical positions would challenge her ability to speak. Indeed, Hildegard is exceptional in that she *was* in fact accepted by her male contemporaries as authoritative. Although Hildegard had established some intimacy in her correspondence with men—particularly with Guibert of Gembloux—deeper relationships were possible with women, where equality could be assumed and credentials were not as important.

Conclusion

In this essay I have developed a method for analyzing the letters of Hildegard of Bingen. This method highlights the rhetorical strategies which the visionary incorporates in order to claim a voice in a contemporary ecclesiastical structure that was both hierarchical and androcentric. I propose that, as she wrote her letters, Hildegard made conscious decisions about the level of claims to authority that would be necessary both to promulgate her message and to gain credence in the eyes of the recipient. Hildegard responds to a hierarchical and androcentric environment by developing ways to phrase her visions which would match the level of authority of her audience. The formulae which Hildegard developed—reportorial, instrumental, and representative—formed part of an overall survival strategy for this woman who spoke her message of reform to a world not always prepared for the female prophet nor the strength of her words.

I would like to thank Barbara Newman for her review of earlier drafts of this essay. Also many thanks to Ulrike Wiethaus and Karen Cherewatuk for their helpful comments.

Notes

1. See, for example, Hildegard of Bingen, *Scivias*, trans. Columba Hart and Jane Bishop (New York: Paulist Press, 1990). See also Matthew Fox, ed., *Illuminations of Hildegard of Bingen* (Santa Fe, NM: Bear and Company, 1985).

2. For a preliminary study, see Barbara Newman, "Hildegard of Bingen: Visions and Validation," *Church History* 54 (1985): 163–75.

3. Newman, "Visions and Validation," p. 175.

4. For a summary of Hildegard's epistolary activity, see Peter Dronke, *Women Writers of the Middle Ages: A Critical Study of Texts from Perpetua (†203) to Marguerite Porete (†1310)* (Cambridge: Cambridge University Press, 1984), pp. 154–59, 165–71 and Sabina Flanagan, *Hildegard of Bingen, 1098–1179: A Visionary Life* (New York: Routledge, 1990), pp. 158–78.

5. In her *Scivias*, finished in 1151, Hildegard provided a description of her visionary calling, placing her experience in the context of the prophetic tradition. See discussion in Dronke, pp. 182–83 and Barbara Newman, *Sister of Wisdom: St. Hildegard's Theology of the Feminine* (Berkeley: University of California Press, 1987), pp. 15–18, 25–29.

6. Hildegard of Bingen, *Epistolarium,* ed. L. Van Acker, *Corpus Christianorum Continuatio Medievalis (CCCM)* 91:3.

7. Augustine creates the framework for a visionary epistemology in book 12 of *De Genesi ad litteram,* in which he identifies three types: corporal, spiritual, and intellectual. The corporal vision is perceived by the body and the senses; the spiritual vision includes a "spiritual image" as in 1 Corinthians 15:44; and the intellectual vision takes place within the mind. The intellectual vision is the most reliable; according to Augustine an intellectual vision does not err. (See book 12,

chapter 14, section 29.) *De Genesi ad litteram* is available in J. P. Migne, *Patrologia Latina (PL)* (Paris, 1887) 34:245–486.

8. See also her *vita* in *PL* 197:102c. For a discussion of Hildegard's experience of visions, see Dronke, *Women Writers,* pp. 160–70 and Newman, *Sister of Wisdom,* pp. 4–9.

9. Dronke, *Women Writers,* p. 252. Translation mine. For variant translations see also Dronke, p. 168 and Newman, *Sister of Wisdom,* p. 6.

10. Dronke, *Women Writers,* p. 252. Translation mine. See also translations in Dronke, p. 168 and Newman, *Sister of Wisdom,* p. 7.

11. See Flanagan, *Hildegard of Bingen,* pp. 44–45.

12. See the discussion of Hildegard's style in Newman, *Sister of Wisdom,* pp. 22–25.

13. This new study supersedes the epistolary collection in volume 197 of the *Patrologia Latina* and volume eight of Pitra's *Analecta Sacra.* For Van Acker's comparison of his own results with those of earlier letter collections, see L. Van Acker, "Der Briefwechsel der Heiligen Hildegard von Bingen: Vorbemerkungen zu einer kritischen Edition," *Revue bénédictine* 98 (1988):141–68; 99 (1989):118–55, esp. 99:137–50. Unfortunately, only the first volume has appeared in print and a manuscript of the second volume was unavailable. Thus only the data on the hierarchical recipients of Hildegard's letters are from Van Acker's first volume.

14. For more information, see Monika Schrader and Adelgundis Führkötter, *Die Echtheit des Schrifttums der heiligen Hildegard von Bingen* (Cologne and Graz: Böhlau, 1956), pp. 59–154.

15. See, for example, letter 20, *CCCM* 91:56; letter 13, 91:29; letter 22, 91:59; letter 31, 91:82; and letter 41, 91:105.

16. See letter 14, *CCCM* 91:31.

17. See letter 16, *CCCM* 91:48.

18. An analysis of the relationship between the functions of Hildegard's letters and the visionary formulae she uses is only possible on a general level, because many letters have several purposes. Thus categories that classify the functions of the letters are to a large degree artificial. However, it is certainly correct to say that Hildegard's use of visionary formulae is indeed related to the content and tone of her letters. Interestingly, there is no apparent correlation between the date of Hildegard's letters and her use of visionary formulae.

19. For examples of this reportorial formula see letter 16r, *CCCM* 19:49–51; letter 21, 91:58; and letter 23, 91:61.

20. See letter 2, *CCCM* 91:7.

21. See also the Prologue of the *Scivias.*

22. See above, pp. 47–48.

23. See, for example, letter 2, *CCCM* 91:7–8; letter 11, 91:26; and letter 25r, 91:71–72.

24. See letter 52r, *CCCM* 91:127. Hildegard's reference to the "living fountain" ("fons vivus") recalls Jesus' conversation with the Samaritan woman at the well in John 4.

25. See letter 8, *CCCM* 91:20. For other exhortations see letter 13r, 91:30; letter 40r, 91:103; letter 41r, 91:106; letter 52r, 91:127–30; and letter 64, 91:147–48.

26. See, for example, Jeremiah 2:4, 5:21.

27. See letter 81, *CCCM* 91:183. This same expression is used in letter 31r, 91:83 and letter 47, 91:116. In a similar formulation Hildegard writes, "The one who was, and who is, and who is to come . . . says . . ." ("Qui era, et qui est, et qui venturus est . . . dicit . . ."). See letter 15r, 91:34. See Revelation 1:8.

28. See especially Exodus 3:14 on the name of God.

29. Letter 9, *CCCM* 91:22.

30. For references to the living light see, for example, letter 2, *CCCM* 91:7; letter 20r, 91:57; letter 24, 91:67; and letter 36, 91:94–95. Kent Kraft has distinguished two types of visions based on this light. The first category includes visions from "the shadow of the living light," in which Hildegard "perceives images from the natural world, imaginative constructions, and human figures and artifacts projected upon a field of light which is her constant companion." The second type of visions stem directly from the "living light," which is at once healing and illuminating. Kraft identifies these types of visions in an Augustinian framework, associating the first type of vision with Augustine's *visio spiritualis* and the second with the *visio intellectualis*. See discussion in Kent Kraft, *The Eye Sees More Than the Heart Knows*, Ph.D. dissertation 1977, University of Wisconsin, pp. 62–72. While there is in Hildegard's letters a distinction between the "light" ("lux") and the source of the light ("lumen"), it is not clear that she meant two different sources.

31. See John 1:4–5, 9–10.

32. See Revelation 1:8.

33. For a complete discussion of Hildegard's understanding of the virtues, see Newman, *Sister of Wisdom*, esp. pp. 42–88.

34. See for example letter 25r, *CCCM* 91:71; letter 26r, 91:74; or letter 33, 91:90–91.

35. See letter 26r, *CCCM* 91:74–75. Hildegard's approach here regarding the role of women in the church is typically conservative. Women have a place as leaders only in the failure or absence of men. Indeed, in the *Scivias* women are portrayed as weak and unworthy of sacerdotal responsibilities: "So too those of the female sex should not approach the office of My altar; for they are an infirm and weak habitation, appointed to bear children and diligently nurture them" ("Sic etiam nec feminae ad idem officium altaris mei debent accedere, quoniam ipsae infirmum et debile habitaculum sunt, ad hoc positae ut filios pariant, et eos parientes diligenter enutriant"). Hildegard, *Scivias* (note 1), p. 278. Hildegard, *Scivias*, Book 2, Vision 6, in *PL* 197:545B.

36. See letter 37r, *CCCM* 91:96–97.

37. See, for example, letter 41r, *CCCM* 91:106–7; letter 37r, 91:96–97; and letter 32r, 91:89–90.

38. Dronke, *Women Writers* (note 4), p. 156.

39. See, for example, letter 15r, *CCCM* 91:34–44.

40. Pitra, letter 34, p. 520: "Dismiss them from their pastoral responsibility which carries with it shameful penalty; yet although some prelates may be overshadowed by their vicious habits, it is not fitting to depose certain prelates because of [the needs of] their subjects." ("Fugate illos de pastorali cura, quae poenam de

canibus portat; et quamvis quidam praelati sint obumbrati per vicissitudinem morum, tamen non decet quosdam praelatos propter quosdam subditos abjici")

41. See, for example, Hildegard's letter to Pope Anastasius, letter 8, *CCCM* 91:19–22.

42. See letter 19, *CCCM* 91:55. For the story of King Nebuchadnezzar's downfall, see Daniel 4:1–34.

43. See letter 31, *CCCM* 91:82.

44. See Newman, *Sister of Wisdom*, pp. 12–13.

45. See letter 127, *PL* 197:351–53.

46. Dronke, *Women Writers*, p. 149.

47. See Pitra, letter 3, pp. 334–36.

48. In many cases, more than one formula is used in a letter. For the most part, these formulae are within the same category, but in five of the thirty-seven letters written to hierarchical figures there are both instrumental and representative formulae used in the same letter.

Glenda McLeod

"Wholly Guilty, Wholly Innocent": Self-Definition in Héloïse's Letters to Abélard

The correspondence between Abélard and Héloïse has often and justifiably been studied as the continuation of one of the great love stories of the Middle Ages. Yet it also continued one of its great experiments in self-definition, the *Historia calamitatum*, broadening the enterprise to include Héloïse herself. Just as Abélard "turned inward in search of an explanation for his current state of affairs,"[1] so Héloïse was brought to the same point in her letters. Shaped by the *confessio peccatorium* and epistolary genres such as the *epistolae consolatoriae*, Héloïse's letters not only investigate and reinterpret Abélard's story but also help reveal the components of, and pressures surrounding, a twelfth-century woman's self-definition.

Such a claim assumes of course that Héloïse herself is responsible for at least some of the correspondence. Beginning with Orelli's 1841 edition of the *Historia calamitatum*, scholars have advanced various theories of forgery, most convincingly rejected by Étienne Gilson in 1938.[2] Despite recent arguments of several aspects of the case, many scholars today agree with Gilson. The collection may well be a redaction, as medieval letters often are, but even if we cannot prove their complete authenticity, we also have no compelling reason to doubt that the letters are Abélard's and Héloïse's. It seems prudent, then, to turn from investigations of authenticity to look at the letters themselves, a change in critical dialogue first recommended by Gilson and Peter von Moos and recently enacted in the work of Peter Dronke, Peggy Kamuf, and Linda Georgianna.[3] At the very least, such a change sheds light on one of the "two opposing and irreducible psychodynamisms" that dominate the letters."[4]

In connection with Héloïse, such an approach is rich in promise. Numerous studies exist of Abélard as autobiographer, but very few have studied the autobiographical impulse in Héloïse's letters.[5] Yet her first epistle describes a crisis of identity partly prompted by the *Historia calami-tatum*, a consolation that, as Héloïse puts it, is no consolation at all.[6] Such a disparity between form and content foreshadows Héloïse's self-perceived disparity between herself as abbess and wife, one of the impulses behind her letters. Although the conflict remains unvoiced in the first letter, her posi-tion as the abbess of the Paraclete makes a discordant background for much of what she has to say.

Letter One

In all the letters Héloïse switches between her roles as abbess and lover by switching the number of the speaking pronoun. First person singular indi-cates her private role as Abélard's wife; first person plural speaks as the more public abbess. The first epistle begins in the private first person singular but modulates subtly into a more public first person plural as Héloïse records responses to Abélard's autobiographical consolation. No person can read the story "dry-eyed" (110) ("cum siccis oculis" 68).[7] Héloïse's sorrows are renewed by "the detail" (110) ("singula" 68); likewise, the community—"all of us"—"are driven to fear and despair" (110) ("ut omnes . . . desperare cogamur" 68). The private Héloïse will often associate herself with the detail, the individual, the particular as she does here, leaving the more public role to the plural, the general, or, as in letter five, the species.[8] In her first transpositions between singular and plural, the levels do not apparently conflict as they do later.

Letter one's superscription testifies that while Abélard may regard the past as dead Héloïse experiences her life as a continuum. The address—"To her master, or rather her father, husband, or rather brother; his handmaid, or rather his daughter, wife, or rather sister; to Abélard, Héloïse" (109) ("Domino suo immo patri, coniugi suo immo fratri, ancilla sua immo filia, epsius uxor immo soror, Abaelardo Heloisa" 68)—embraces the whole history of their acquaintance, as Peter Dronke has noted.[9] The rapid changes in terms indicate her difficulties in defining their connection and her need to include all its aspects. Significantly, the inscription is not without a pattern. She moves from a public relationship where she is clearly the underling (master-handmaiden) to relationships progressively more familial and equitable (brother-sister).[10] By ending simply Héloïse and Abélard, Héloïse implies that all titles are needed to describe their connec-tion, thus linking for the first of many times public roles such as pupil and abbess to private ones such as wife and lover. Indeed, as letter one amply demonstrates, the connections between public and private are important to Héloïse and bespeak the different circumstances surrounding her entry and life in orders.

For Héloïse, the past, unmitigated by any experience of conversion such as Abélard claims to have had, colors the present and helps shape her life. This convergence is conspicuously suggested by her similar descriptions of herself and her community, the most eloquent of which occur in spatial metaphors. Such references to self are reiterated and modified throughout the correspondence.[11] Tied to classical rhetoric's science of memory, which taught students to remember famous personages by placing them in elaborate buildings, these metaphors also imply a concern with public reputation.[12] When Héloïse says Abélard is the "sole founder of this place" (111) ("huius . . . loci . . . solus es fundator" 69), she suggests both the Paraclete and herself, metaphorically claiming what she later says more explicitly, that her sense of identity remains rooted in him and their past. Perhaps most shocking, however, Héloïse reiterates the comparison by referring to the community as a "plantation" (111) ("plantatio" 70) in need of Abélard's irrigation, uniting not simply herself and the community but also a Biblical allusion (to 1 Corinthians 3:6) and a sexual connotation first noted by Dronke.[13] This sexual overtone is precisely what Héloïse's first letter memorializes and struggles to revive because, as the correspondence makes clear, her sexual past is still a key to her identity.

As she makes the letter's second shift from plural to singular, Héloïse evokes a sexual love "beyond all bounds" (113) ("immoderato amore" 70) that is responsible for both her loss of identity in Abélard and his corresponding debt to her. Of course, "debt" (113) ("debito" 70) would have implied marital coitus to a twelfth-century reader—the Pauline marriage debt that Abélard can no longer pay.[14] But while Héloïse cannot exact this debt, she models her request on its operation, claiming that a "deeper" (113) ("maiore" 70) and more endless debt of love *can* be called upon. This insistence echoes the superscription's move toward equality, for in canon law the sexual domain was unique in its accordance of equal rights to men and women. Characteristically, however, Héloïse bases the debt not only on the "marriage sacrament" (113) ("nuptialis . . . sacramenti" 70) but also on the "love I have always borne you" (113) ("quo te semper . . . immoderato amore complexa sum" 70), an affection whose nature is freer and whose consequences the letter now explores.

Around the letter's second, crucial change from "we" to "I," Héloïse clusters accusations that Abélard has misremembered his obligations as well as their history. Disingenuously arguing that his debt to the community can be discharged by repaying the greater debt he owes her (a claim also underlying letter five), she continues to merge the present and the past. Moreover, the convergence of public nun and private lover stems in part from Abélard himself. His songs had once publicized their private affair; although the *Historia calamitatum* was ostensibly addressed to an anonymous friend, Héloïse would have had every reason to suspect, as have generations of commentators, that it was intended for a wider audience.[15] As she notes several times, the "whole world" (113) ("omnes," 70) knows his interpretation of the story. But her role there and Abélard's misrepresentation of her arguments against marriage—he "kept silent about most of them" (114) ("plerisque tacitis" 71)—trouble her. Even more important, the affair and its aftermath have generated a personal crisis for Héloïse equal in magnitude to Abélard's but neglected and possibly unnoticed by him.

In letter three Héloïse calls this crisis her hypocrisy, but in letter one it is clearly expressed as a loss of identity. She has been bereft not just of Abélard or their love, but of herself. Everyone knows how Fortune's stroke "robbed me of my very self in robbing me of you" (113) ("me ipsam quoque mihi tecum abstulerit" 70). She in fact "destroyed" herself ("perdere" 70), her love rising "to such heights of madness that it robbed itself of what it most desired" ("amor insaniam . . . hoc ipse sibi sine spe recuperationis auferret" 70) when she changed "clothing along with . . . mind . . . to prove . . . [Abélard] the sole possessor of . . . body and will alike" ("habitum ipsa quam animum immutarem ut . . . tam corporis mei quam animi unicum possessorem ostenderem" 70). This emphasis on her willingness to undergo self-destruction confirms her love's disinterested nature, which letter one is at pains to prove.[16] But the self-destruction has also generated an aimlessness for which Abélard must bear partial responsibility, as the letter implies.

Héloïse's confession lies at the heart of letter one's self-analysis, yet, despite its importance, its wording is intriguingly vague. On one level, Héloïse is undoubtedly lamenting her loss of Abélard, but she does not specify exactly *when* she committed her act of self-destruction, of *what* she was depriving herself, or *whose* treachery occasioned the losses. Other interpretations are suggested, and these interpretations imply that Abélard not only overlooked but occasioned her losses. The letters indicate that he twice ordered her to do things against her wishes—on their marriage and on her entry into orders. Héloïse may well be referring to both in referring to her calamities, thus equating them with each other and possibly with Abélard's castration. Moreover, the starting point for her catastrophe, the "flagrant treachery" (113) ("nota proditio" 70), can be located in two different events. Abélard's castration is suggested by the words "one wretched stroke" (113) ("miserabili casu" 70) and "supreme act of flagrant treachery" (113) ("summa et ubique nota proditio" 70). But logically Héloïse can also be referring to Abélard's treachery against herself, an interpretation supported by ensuing charges that he is the "sole cause" of her sorrow (113) ("solus es in causa" 70) and that he never loved her at all.

Her reference to changing clothing also points to Abélard's, not Fulbert's, treachery. Héloïse changes clothing three important times in the letters—when she flees to Abélard's family in Brittany (precipitating the marriage), when she goes to live at Argenteuil (precipitating the castration), and when she takes the veil (sealing her entry into orders). But if she robs herself on these occasions, what does she lose? The castration, not Héloïse, has already taken or will soon take Abélard away in the last two instances. And how does she lose Abélard in marriage? Obviously, something else is displaced. From Abélard's own letters we know that his decision to marry Héloïse rose from his jealous possessiveness.[17] His distrust and his betrayal of *gratia*—a love freely given and based on chastity of the spirit—certainly constitute a treachery from Héloïse's point of view, for the marriage substitutes a love obligated by external constraint for one born of internal volition. What Héloïse loses thereby is more than simply Abélard. It is also her sense of dignity and self-worth, a sense that her relationship with him had conferred but that her marriage and entrance into orders had destroyed.

The "manner" (113) ("modo" 70) in which the loss occurred—a manner that she implies grieved her more than the loss itself—has a private and a public consequence for that sense of self. Gilson remarked in his magisterial study of the letters that Héloïse is especially tormented by her role as the causal agent of Abélard's downfall.[18] The implications of this role for her public reputation would not have been lost on a scholar such as Héloïse. Arguments attributed to her in *Historia calamitatum* demonstrate a deep acquaintance with the misogamous tradition, especially St. Jerome's *Adversus Jovinianum* and its excerpt from Theophrastus's *Aureolus liber de nuptiis*.[19] One of the most distinctive features of that text, a catalog of wicked wives, does not appear in Abélard's narrative, perhaps because, as Katharina Wilson and Elizabeth Makowski note, "Abélard was unlikely to put an inventory of female misbehavior in the mouth of his wise and responsible Héloïse."[20] But the catalog *does* surface in Héloïse's second letter, and her concern at joining Delilah, Eve, and others in the ranks of infamous spouses.

As she examines Abélard's memory of her disuasion against marriage, Héloïse uses her private judgment to refute this public assessment of herself. She bluntly tells Abélard he missed her main arguments against marriage. Her love's value was based on its disinterestedness, an equation modeled on the Ciceronian ideal of friendship described in *De amicitia*, which both lovers knew. Her self-disenfranchisement proves her love boundless, cognizant of neither the limits of self-interest nor the boundaries of self-hood. Love for Héloïse is thus "freedom" not "chains" (114) ("libertatem . . . vinculo" 77) and, in fact, constitutes a self-realization. For this reason "concubine" (113) ("concubinae" 71) or the even more shocking title of "whore" (113) ("scorti" 71) is sweeter than "wife" (113) ("uxoris" 71) because love freely given is innocent by Abélardian standards of pure intent. It can therefore serve as the basis of Héloïse's positive sense of herself, both in the past and present.

This vindication runs throughout letter one and apparently arises from Héloïse's reading of Abélard's *Historia*. Her first epistle demonstrates a concern not simply for her lost love but also for her lost self. She had argued the marriage would destroy *both* of them; Abélard, however, presents only the arguments concerned with his reputation.[21] While the *Historia*'s Héloïse claims that the title of mistress is dearer to her and more honorable to Abélard, the Héloïse of the letters neither hedges her terms nor leaves herself out. She was Abélard's "whore" (113) ("meretrix" 71), a title "dearer and more honorable" (114) to her ("carius . . . et dignius" 71) because of its integrity with her will. She enforces this paradoxical judgment with a reference to Aspasia, antiquity's famous courtesan, who advised Xenophon and his wife that people are never happy in their unions unless they believe they have the best of spouses. For Héloïse, these "saintly words" (114) ("sancta . . . sententia" 71) and their emphasis on internal judgment accord with the ideal of the chaste spirit which St. Augustine describes in *De bono coniugali*. And such *sententia* authorize Héloïse's former sense of identity and rectitude.[22]

In the past, public judgment accorded with this private estimate. The "world in general" (115) ("mundus universus" 71) acknowledged Abélard the most worthy of men in public and private spheres. His reputation exceeded that of kings and other philosophers (public power); "every young girl . . . queens and great ladies" (115) ("quae virgo . . . regina vel praepotens femina" 71) desired him in bed (private passion). Since Abélard publicized their love through songs, his reputation and hers rose together, bestowing an equal fame on Héloïse and arousing the envy of other women. In loving Abélard, then, Héloïse's actions were condoned by both interior and exterior sources; the public and private aspects of her identity were united.

Marriage divided this once seamless and whole self. "Wholly guilty though I am," she says, "I am also, as you know, wholly innocent" (115) ("quae plurimum nocens, plurimum, ut nosti sum innocens" 72). The repetition of "plurimum" emphasizes a signal move from singular to plural; Héloïse no longer has one self but two—public and private, guilty and innocent. The letters' associations between plural and species add other overtones. Héloïse lost the concreteness of her individual self in marriage, merging instead into the general species of wives, who always prove detrimental to the scholar. If she judges correctly—by inner intent (*affectus*) instead of outer effect (*effectus*)—she believes she is innocent. But it is precisely her inner intentions and her particular individuality that her marriage has obliterated and *Historia calamitatum* has neglected. This dilemma Héloïse asks Abélard to help resolve.

She presents her case logically, linguistically committing the public side to an Abélard who will judge "all" and "in everything" (116) ("cuncta . . . per omnia" 72). She also appeals to him as his private wife. To him who "alone . . . can judge" (116) ("solus . . . iudicare potes" 72), she sends the whole of the story, which she dares him to reinterpret. But she asks for something in return. Since she has given him all—the public stage—Abélard must tell her "one thing" (110) ("unum" 72) and so return her private estimate to herself. Why has he neglected her? This *omnia-unum* contrast, building on earlier public-private, singular-plural parallels, indicates a new conflict between public and private poles that letter three will explore in detail. In asking for one thing, Héloïse asks for the earlier self-image she claims was replaced by an estimate with "nothing personal or private about it" (116) ("non tam privata quam publica" 72). Many commentators have noted that although Héloïse asks Abélard to summon her to God at the end of the epistle, in letter one she seeks Abélard. But in seeking him she also seeks her own claim to her memories and a lost self.

Letter Two

Abélard's reply avoids the renewal Héloïse demands, but does so at the price of ignoring her crisis. Its opening superscription acknowledges only the monastic titles in Héloïse's opening, thus limiting the relationship to present, spiritual contexts. Héloïse is the "dearly beloved sister in Christ" (119) ("dilectissimae sorori suae in Christo" 73); Abélard is her "brother" (119) ("frater" 73) who will reply only "in matters pertaining to God" (119) ("in iis etiam quae ad Deum pertinent" 73). He entreats her prayers for "our many great aberrations" (120) ("nostris magnis et multis excessibus" 74) and thus insists upon their past as a defiled and defiling history. He also reiterates that he is in great danger and makes plans for his burial at the Paraclete, details that certainly provided Héloïse with nothing of what she sought.

But while Abélard gives no specific reply to Héloïse's questions, he surely noticed them, for in his pleas, he elaborates on her points with *exempla* of wifely concern. Applied to Héloïse, these *exempla* refute her identification as a wicked wife even while they misread her arguments against legally obligated obedience, the wifely system of debt in which women had no equal rights. In the most obvious of these *exempla* Abélard argues for the efficacy of wifely prayer by noting that Abigail successfully prayed for King David's mercy on her husband Nabal. She also married David, however, when God struck Nabal down, an aspect of the story that implies Héloïse should be content. She too wed a worthier husband—Christ—on the downfall of a less worthy one—Abélard himself. These Biblical *exempla*, allusions to texts such as the description of a good wife in Proverbs 31, and Abélard's editing of Héloïse's superscription Christianize the pagan, philosophical argument of Héloïse's own letter and call on her to focus on the present in continued and wifely obedience to Abélard.

Interestingly, the spatial metaphor applied to Héloïse and her community is similarly reworked. Instead of a place in need of irrigation, Abélard describes the Paraclete as "safe and salutary . . . fitting for Christian burial" (125) ("tutiorem ac salubriorem . . . Christianae sepulturae . . . rectius" 77). Refusing to address the differences Héloïse notes between his memories and hers, Abélard insists on the superiority of their present lives.

Letter Three

Still connected to the past, Héloïse responds in the only way she can. She never again reanalyzes her actions, but she does insist on the differences in her situation. Abélard assumes she has experienced the same conversion as he; her superscription emphasizes she has not. He is her "only one" (127) ("unico suo" 77) *after* Christ, but she can only be his "unica sua" (77) *in* Christ. For Abélard, Héloïse's past has been obliterated and Héloïse's present absorbed into the love of Christ, but Héloïse's private love for Abélard continues to impinge on her public role as the bride of Christ. In letter one, Héloïse explores her lost integrity and Abélard's past hypocrisy; in letter three, however, she explores her present hypocrisy and its connection to the integrity Abélard claims to have found. Such inversions thematically and structurally dominate Héloïse's second epistle where she describes her situation as a *mundus inversus* (world upside down).[23] She thus plays on the Latin word for conversion—*conversio* or *conversatio*, which translates literally as about face or inversion.[24] As letter three demonstrates, Abélard's conversion, which Héloïse has not experienced, has turned her world inside out, creating an existence of freakish impossibilities. Against the figure of the redeeming conversion, Héloïse invokes the random motions of Fortune's wheel as an emblem of her plight.

She begins by attacking not Abélard's editing of her salutation but his rhetorical reversals of it. In placing her name before his, he accords her undeservedly and unnaturally the superior position. A polemical element lurks in this reproach. In letter one, Héloïse bases her appeal to Abélard on her voluntary self-abnegation. Her complaints against a rhetorical transgression again use a claim to inferiority to press her case.[25] But the reversal also stresses Héloïse's sense of dilemma.

The continued use of sexually empowered language in letter three serves to define this dilemma. She asks for wise words, sharp as "nails driven home" which "cannot touch wounds gently but only pierce through" (135) ("clavi in altum defixi . . . vulnera nesciunt palpare, sed pungere" 82). The sayings are neither spiritual nor Christ-like, despite their evocations of the crucifixion; they have a broad, vivid, and Ovidian carnality suggested by the images of nails, wound, and piercing. Héloïse ties such injuries to her sexuality and lost identity, two aspects of self which have become linked for her. When she depicts herself as a mass of gaping wounds, she suggests both sexual longing and emptiness. A body so full of holes that "there is . . . no place left to take" another (129) ("nec . . . locum in me inveniret" 78) is scarcely a body at all. Moreover, the image of the wound itself destroys a distinction between public (exterior) and private (interior) dimensions. A wound pierces the exterior skin and reveals what's underneath, thus obliterating any difference between the two. Abélard's reversal of the *rectus ordo* thus has its corollary in her life. Because of love, she is living one-dimensionally, like a woman whose interior has suddenly become exteriorized.

This daring self-appropriation of the *mundus inversus topos* (and by extension its application to a God she describes as *crudelis*) illuminates her own experiences; she feels "all the laws of equity . . . were reversed" for her and Abélard (130) ("omnia . . . aequitatis iura pariter sunt perversa," 79). When guilty of "fornication" (130) ("fornicationi" 79), they were publicly spared. But once wed, they were publicly chastised. Chastity not unchastity, marriage not adultery, one not two were thus punished, and equality suggested by the word *aequitatis* was destroyed.

Now Héloïse feels she lives in a perpetual and unjust reversal. Because of the ruin their marriage has wrought, she appears as guilty as the wicked wives she goes on to cite in the third letter. But she knows herself innocent since "the tempter did not prevail on [her] to do wrong of [her] own consent" (131) ("quod . . . ille ut . . . in culpam ex consensu non traxit" 80). This claim had been the focus of letter one; here in letter three Héloïse expands it to her present situation. The same standard that exonerates her as Abélard's wife condemns her as Christ's bride, for she cannot give what she owes to God.[26] The abbess, not the whore, is culpable; Héloïse, not Abélard, is the delinquent debtor; the world appears random, ungoverned, without equity. While Abélard's individual "single wound" (133) ("una . . . plaga" 81) may have cured him, *all* her public wounds have paradoxically left her nothing—not Abélard, not her former identity, not even her present role, which is a hypocrisy.

In light of this inversion, Héloïse's catalog of wicked wives suggests an interesting interweaving of innocence and guilt in her self-concept. While Héloïse's *exempla* are dictated by tradition (although she does choose Biblical rather than pagan heroines), her treatment of these women is often quite original, as Dronke has noted.[27] Ostensibly, the catalog responds to Abélard's Biblical citations by aligning Héloïse with infamous Biblical wives. Her situation, however, often seems closer to the husbands', as her wording suggests. Like Adam, she was lured from paradise by her helpmate. Like Samson, she was led to self-destruction. Wise like Solomon, she was also driven "to . . . a pitch of madness" (131) ("in . . . tantam . . . insaniam," 79) that ended in a sort of idolatry, the substitution of Abélard for God as the object of her worship. Finally, like Job with whom she later equates herself in this letter, she is fighting her "last and hardest battle" (131) ("novissimam atque gravissiam . . . pugnam" 80) against her spouse who continually distracts her from God. In this marriage, Héloïse claims, she too was destroyed.

Throughout letter three and especially in letter five, Héloïse seeks some way to reassemble her parts into a new whole. She ends with another twist on the recurrent spatial metaphor which suggests new directions to this search. In letter three, she also imparts a sense of boundaries sharply antithetical to the boundless love implicated in her old sense of self-worth. She doesn't need a martyr's crown; she will be satisfied "in whatever corner of heaven God shall place" her (136) ("quocumque me angulo coeli Deus collocet" 82).

Letter Four

Abélard's reply in letter four, longer and more thoughtful than the one in letter two, partly seeks to give Héloïse a sense of her role as nun. But in doing so he draws solely on the nun's metaphorical position as the bride of Christ. Héloïse is thus retained in the innermost recesses of the metaphorical divine house—more specifically, the bedchamber.[28] The metaphor—carnal and yet not carnal—not only redefines Abélard's relationship with Héloïse but also impoverishes both public and private aspects of her identity, thus reenacting the circumstances of her marriage.

The movement is mediated through Christ, Abélard's lord and Héloïse's husband, who now divides and unites them both. As usual, the salutation sets the stage for the argument. Héloïse is "sponsae Christi" (82); Abélard is "servus eiusdem" (83). Héloïse's earlier claims to Abélard's attention had rested on her protests of inferiority; they must be invalidated. While as Christ's servant he is obligated to Héloïse, Christ's bride, and while she as the wife of his Lord is indeed his lady, that relationship does not exist in the sense that Héloïse longs for. The result is a diminished role for both the nun and Héloïse.

In the ensuing letter, as Abélard compares Héloïse to the black bride of *Canticum Canticorum*, the limits of being a bride of Christ become quite clear.[29] Drawing not so much on dialectics as on biblical exegesis, Abélard reverses Héloïse's complaint. Where she had claimed her outer appearance did not correspond to her inner defiance, Abélard's reply differentiates between the bride's outer and "less lovely" (138) ("deformior," 84) appearance and the "lovelier" (138) ("formosior" 84) because virtuous interior. Literally divested of flesh, it is compared to the whiteness of bones and teeth.

Oddly, this spiritual metaphor is the most erotic passage in Abélard's letters, but as in other passages it strongly suggests Abélard's rather than Héloïse's experiences. As Peggy Kamuf has remarked, the secret and hidden

relationship between Christ and the bride resembles Abélard's and Héloïse's clandestine marriage.[30] Moreover, the bride longs for the private world
because of the "disfigurement of the blackness" (140) ("nigredinis defor-
mitas" 85), a comparison that recalls Abélard's reaction to his castration
more forcefully than Héloïse's feelings on entering the convent. Finally, the
metaphor recenters Héloïse's life through the very marriage model she had
resisted before, compromising any personal autonomy by relegating her to
a private existence.

In the details of his explication, Abélard also modulates and transforms
Héloïse's references to wounds. The afflictions that blacken the bride's skin
make it softer and "more suitable for private than public enjoyment" (140)
("earum voluptas secretis gaudiis quam publicis gratior" 83). As Kamuf has
pointed out, this detail brings what is inside (virtue) to the surface of the
skin, making both the exterior and interior subject to the bridegroom's
touch.[31] But while Héloïse also evoked this blurring between outer and
inner, she associated it with the loss and pain of a wound. Abélard endows
it with a positive, spiritual value resident in Christ's ownership of the bride,
an ownership that in turn recalls the mystical absorption of the soul into the
Godhead.

Abélard's spiritual ambitions for Héloïse are thus great, but they leave
Héloïse with little room for herself. Yet she should be content, Abelard
argues. Picking up the spatial metaphor again, he reminds her that while at
the convent of Argenteuil they made use of a "corner of the refectory" (146)
("parte . . . refectorii" 88) to satiate their lust. This "shameful business"
(146) ("impudentissime" 88) refutes Héloïse's claim they had lived chastely
and apart after the wedding. The emphasis on corner and small, reminiscent
of the small bedchamber of the king as well as Héloïse's hoped for corner of
heaven, responds to her modest hopes for salvation. Size does not correspond to importance, as her last letter implied. A small and constricted
space can be the site of great sin as well as great virtue.

Letter Five

No denial of the past could have been firmer or more absolute, as Héloïse
understood. Her fifth letter and the *Problemata* she later sent Abélard come
from Abélard's spiritual daughter or disciple rather than his wife. Yet, as
several critics have noted, these documents continue themes expressed in
the earlier letters.[32] Héloïse not only clings vigorously to the importance of

her inner voice but also continues to seek a public context for its growth. In this project she may well be responding to a phrase in Abélard's second letter. There, immediately after the bridal metaphor, he defines the true hypocrite as one who lives not by "rule" but by "custom" (142) ("regula," "consuetudinem" 85). Within the monastic context, *regulus* and *consuetudo* carry very specific meanings derived from Augustine's affirmation that Christ said he was the truth, not the custom. The rule, as Abélard understood it, concerned matters of spiritual principle; customs are things of outward observances. In fact, the *consuetudines* of the Paraclete clashed with Abelard's rule in many particulars; Abélard in making this distinction is thus referring to an extant and honored monastic rhetoric. However, his observation carries other shades of meaning, especially in consideration of the marital metaphor of his letter. Custom was the ruling agency of the private family; rule or law, however, belonged to the public sphere.[33]

For Héloïse, public existence is related to her vocation, the subject of letter five. Her last, cryptic, and richly suggestive superscription has helped fuel a continuing debate on whether or not she experienced a true conversion to this vocation.[34] But the superscription itself can perhaps best be seen as both a salutation and self-definition, one implying relationships with Abélard and God and defining Héloïse as both individual and species, private and public being. The relationships thus defined are problematic to say the least: "Domino specialiter, sua singulariter" (241) can be translated two ways, as the translations of Betty Radice and Peter Dronke show. To begin with, the word *dominus* can take on three meanings: the Lord (that is, God), one's feudal lord, or one's husband. All three are appropriate to the context of the letter. If taken to mean "God's own in species, his own as individual" (155), Héloïse's last self-identification links her to both God and Abélard, continuing the letters' association between the singular and the private wife and the plural and the public abbess. But if translated "To him who is especially her lord, she who is uniquely his" (155), Héloïse insists on the primacy, even exclusivity, of her relationship to Abélard. God is not mentioned and, despite the elaborate bridegroom metaphor, she affirms she is Abélard's alone.

Even if one takes the first translation as definitive, the salutation clearly accords Abélard an important and insisted-upon place. The word "specialiter" bears a philosophic meaning perhaps pertinent to the question of universals, a keenly debated topic in the twelfth century concerning the degree of reality or significance adherent in the individual as opposed to the species.[35] Abélard played an important part in this debate, arguing against

William of Champeaux, who maintained that the nature of a being (its species) was "essentially and wholly present at one and the same time in every individual."[36] Such a position destroyed the individual, Abélard maintained, by eliminating particularity; he proposed instead that both the individual and the universal hold reality and significance but that reality is more distinctive in the individual. While the word for the universal bears meaning, only individuals objectively exist in Abélardian dialectics.

Héloïse's association between her role as wife and her existence as an individual is thus telling. As a concrete, physical individual, she belongs to Abélard and not to God. Such a gesture is richly ironic since, as Georgianna has pointed out, Abélard has been denying Héloïse's particularity throughout the correspondence.[37] Yet only in the less specific sense of species—a nun—is she the Lord's.[38] As demonstrated by the parallel structure of the superscription's two parts, these two levels are not unconnected, however.

Whichever meaning the author intended—she may well have intended both—each stresses a continuing, definitive allegiance to Abélard and a need to define the connection. Indeed, the interactions possible between Héloïse and her respective *domini* are precisely the areas letter five addresses. Her reform of the Rule of St. Benedict uses Abélard's own ethics to ground love of God in the *affectus* of the individual, the same source as her early love of Abélard. The nature of that new love differs, however, in the degree of personal autonomy it provides both to the nuns and to Héloïse personally. Indeed, in letter five, Héloïse seeks the freedom of the Gospels ("evangelicae libertati" 251) just as she based her love of Abélard on her free intention. Her proposed love of God is not the selfless love Abélard describes, a self-absorption into the Godhead. Nor is it a spiritualized version of her passion for Abélard. Rather, it is an experience of self-realization that Héloïse wants but has yet to find, a self-realization that preserves her individual self and yet implicates love.

While the bulk of letter five is devoted to speculations on the Rule, love is still Héloïse's subject. In the opening passage she continues to speak of her private love of Abélard. Because she never again adopts the tones of letters one and three, some have read her opening words as proof that she underwent a true conversion. The salutation suggests not, and nothing in Héloïse's ensuing discussion explicitly supports such an interpretation.[39] Indeed, the alternations between "I" and "we" in this opening paragraph express Héloïse's continuing connection to her private love. On one hand, she won't be "disobedient" (155) ("inobedientia" 241), but the heart isn't "under our control" (159) ("in nostra . . . potestate," 241) and "we are forced to obey it" (159) ("eique . . . obedire cogimur" 241), a plural that may indicate Héloïse the abbess, Héloïse and Abélard, the community of nuns, or the species of humankind. The conflicts between hand and tongue, heart and hand reinforce the gap between "I" and "we." The individual "I" moves to obey, but the more general "we" cannot control the heart. Indeed, as her reforms demonstrate, Héloïse will obey Abélard as wife but must respect her inner judgment in matters pertaining to her profession as nun.

The shift from personal to spiritual matters is presented as a remedy for grief, even though the change will not "entirely remove" the problem (159) ("non hunc omnino possis auferre" 241–42). In a simile from Cicero,[40] Héloïse explains that the new subject will drive out the old as "one nail drives out another hammered in" (155) ("enim insertum clavum alius expellit" 242). This pagan source implicitly challenges Abélard, whose last letter had used only two passages from pagan authors, Virgil and Lucan, and then only to exemplify inappropriate behavior.[41] In contrast, Héloïse's letter also cites only two pagans, Cicero and Persius, but both support her most important points. Cicero refers to the change of subject; the quotation from Persius's *Satires*, "Do not look outside yourself" (176) ("Ne te quaesiveris extra" 251), sums up her reform's emphasis on the individual. Finally, the image of the hammered nail, besides recalling the earlier sexual nuances of Héloïse's metaphors, also recalls letter three, in which she had compared a nail to wise words and linked these words to her wounds. Paradoxically, the nails seal that wound and thus restore integrity to the body's structure, if not without pain. Clearly just as the past lingers in the abbess, so it will shape her responses.

Using the first person plural, Héloïse goes on to make two requests which echo her preceding letters. The first, historical in nature, asks Abélard to "teach us how the order of nuns began" (159) ("nos instruere velis unde sanctimonialium ordo coeperit" 242), a parallel to her opening investigation of her personal history. The second request for a new rule roughly recalls her plea that Abélard summon her to God. Rather disingenuously, however, Héloïse, proceeds to outline the reform herself, going far beyond her original brief to present a general Rule applicable to both sexes.

Her complaints against the Rule of St. Benedict often resemble her earlier personal disagreements with Abélard. To show how unsuitable the Rule is for women, she adduces a wealth of concrete, supporting detail that emphasizes precisely the sort of individual difference Abélard ignored when giving her advice.[42] She explores a vast range of social, physical, and sexual details. Because they menstruate, women find it more difficult than men to wear wool close to the skin. Likewise, men do not face the same conflict or public scandal that Héloïse and her sisters face in having a male abbot come to read the Gospel to them. In letter four, Abélard had specifically designated the bride's place as the bedroom, not the table. Should an abbess then offer pilgrims and guests the hospitality of her table "where gluttony and drunkenness are rife"? (160) ("ubi crapula dominatur et ebrietas" 242). And how shall nuns preserve their chastity but not offend men whose services are needed? These practical concerns revolve around individual situations, but taken together they indict the Rule as a whole.

The theological point that Héloïse raises from the Epistle of James and raised again in her *Problemata*, strikes to the heart of this relationship between part and whole, singular and plural. It also echoes the origin of her conflict between personal self and public persona and reaffirms her connections between singular and plural, species and individual. If one breaks "one single point" (161) ("uno factus," 243) of the law, does one not break "all of it" (161) ("omnium reus," 243)? To illustrate the problem, she points to James's own examples. One can be innocent of adultery and yet guilty of murder and thus a law-breaker. She too has been faithful to Abélard and thus wholly innocent of adultery, but her self-destruction has made her live the wholly guilty life of a nun not devoted to God. The problem, directly related to her hypocrisy, differs from letter three's discussion only in its situation within the public context of the Rule rather than the private one of Héloïse's marriage.

As the point from the Epistle of James suggests, the new rule would restore internal struggle as the focus of Héloïse's and the monastic life. For Héloïse " . . . those who are true Christians are wholly occupied with the inner man, so that they may adorn him with virtues and purify him of vices . . . they have little or no concern for the outer man" (174) ("quicumque sunt vere Christiani sic toti circa interiorem hominem sunt occupati ut eum scilicet virtutibus ornent et vitiis mundent, ut de exteriori nullam vel minimam assumant curam" 250). The Rule as it now stands pays excessive attention to this outer man just as Abélard pays excessive attention to Héloïse's outer semblance. She feels the law governing a religious community should free the mind from excessive attention to such "indifferent matters" (170) ("indifferentia" 248) and give the nuns a public order within which inner nature is respected and may thrive. She argues that any monk or nun "who adds the virtue of continence to the precepts of the Gospel will achieve monastic perfection" (164) ("quisquis evangelicis praeceptis continentiae virtutem addiderit, monasticam perfectionem implebit" 245).

As Georgianna has pointed out, this questioning of the Rule sympathizes with other reform movements of the time, movements that frequently called for a return to the Gospel.[43] Interestingly, however, Héloïse's reform also returns to an earlier Christian egalitarianism subverted by such notions as the marriage model Abélard uses. In letter five, she begins her examination of the Rule by protesting that it overlooks women's frailty and infirmity. Yet she not only elaborates on past concessions to men's frailty in the Rule, but she also reiterates that those who are "equal in virtue . . . deserve equally of him [that is, God]' (174) ("quicumque virtutibus pares sunt . . . aequaliter ab ipso promereri" 250). Finally, the Rule she advocates applies to both sexes. It accords nuns equal participation in the Abélardian doctrine of pure intention and thus helps to restore the laws of equity she saw reversed in her affairs.

In essence, then, Héloïse's review of past and present leads her to a love that offers individuals the choices which for medieval men and women were self-defining. Both of Héloïse's two roles are grounded in love; however, the love proposed as the goal of monastic life differs significantly from her boundless passion for Abélard. This love Héloïse rejects by agreeing with St. Jerome: "virtues which exceed all bounds and measures are . . . to be counted among the vices" (162) ("virtutes excedentes modum atque mensuram . . . inter vitia reputari convenit" 243). Like the small corner of heaven envied by no one, the love of God that Héloïse seeks is not immoderate and not without boundaries. Indeed, Héloïse presents it as dependent on a defined, individual self. Subject to reason, this love isn't likely to reach the heights of madness and self-destruction that her other passion did. So Christ the bridegroom, who controls the bride's bedchamber and owns her virtue through his caress, has no place in letter five. Here the love of God springs only from the heart which "we are forced to obey" (159) ("obedire cogimur" 241).

To see this dialectic between inner and outer, singular and plural, as an interaction between public and private, one should take into account what the terms "public" and "private" might have implied in the twelfth-century. Among others, historian Georges Duby has equated the latter with "family life," noting that the "cement that held the group together" was "friendship."[44] This is the model Héloïse uses for her love affair with Abélard. Public power, on the other hand, was much more diffuse since "feudalization should also . . . be seen as a fragmentation" of that power.[45] Duby maintains a public-private distinction existed throughout the Middle Ages even if the line between the two was fluid, and he associates the public side with law, the area most often evoked in Héloïse's descriptions of her religious life.

While medieval men and women usually saw monastic life as a "res familiaris,"[46] for Héloïse, the private family is Abélard while her family in Christ is her more public role. The private family was typically governed by custom, not law. Abélard himself, who brings up the question of custom in letter four, discards it as an unacceptable standard for the Christian. Héloïse builds on this gesture. In asking for a history of nuns, she asks what "authority there is for our profession" (159) ("nostrae sit professionis auctoritas" 242), and thus seeks some public roots for her vocation. In asking for a rule for the community, she seeks to avoid custom and define the public sphere thus authorized. The letters themselves support such an association. Her own references to the monastic life make little use of familial parallels such as Abélard's. She depicts God juridically, as a "witness" ("testem" 71), or a judge who "searches our hearts and loins and sees in our darkness" (133) ("cordis et renum probator est, et in abscondito videt" 81). As Héloïse creates her Rule, however, she takes care to define a public order that does not invalidate, dominate, or appropriate her sense of interior self. The self's primacy she religiously maintains, and its importance she jealously guards as the font of her public, monastic life.

It is thus significant that at the end of letter five, Héloïse once more takes up the recurring spatial metaphor for self. Echoing her own words from letter one, Héloïse notes Abélard is "after God . . . the founder of this place, through God . . . the creator of our community, with God . . . the director of our religious life" (178) ("post Deum huius loci fundator, tu per Deum nostrae congregationes es plantator, tu cum Deo nostrae sis religionis institutor" 253). The ending "with" equates God and Abélard as co-directors just as the superscription makes them the twin poles of Héloïse's life. Moreover, the description invokes a well-known Trinitarian formula that heightens the identification between Abelard and God. But the "solus" used with these phrases in letter one is now missing. Héloïse still owes obedience to Abélard and God, but here, unlike the other letters, she reserves some room for herself and ascribes the singular "solus" to neither of her *domini*. Paradoxically, she thus constructs a private space by asserting her place within a public one.

As might be expected in the twelfth century, Héloïse's sense of individuality expresses itself as a conflict between competing networks of allegiance: one to God and one to Abélard, one public and one private. The dominance of the private aspect is entirely consonant with the privatization of life in the feudal epoch. Conducted through letters, Héloïse's self-fashioning occurs through a unique, open-ended dialectic with her *dominus*, whose authority Héloïse is able to challenge from within her vows of obedience. In her desire for wholeness, she proves herself a child of her century. Her unflinching need to exclude nothing—not past experiences, not present difficulties, not public duties, not private doubts—testifies to her integrity. But the letters also show that for Héloïse, integrity was an enterprise that balanced, even depended upon, an acknowledged duality. Beginning in a search for personal autonomy, her letters inexorably end in a definition of public boundaries. As the image of the wound demonstrates, the integrity of self required defining both an inner and outer, a public and private domain.

Notes

1. Chris Ferguson, "Autobiography as Therapy: Guibert de Nogent, Peter Abelard, and the Making of Medieval Autobiography," *Journal of Medieval and Renaissance Studies* 13 (1983): 199.

2. See Étienne Gilson, *Héloïse et Abélard*, 2nd ed. (Paris: Libraire Philosophique J. Vrin, 1948), esp. pp. 150–71. The authenticity of the correspondence has never been conclusively established, but neither has its forgery, despite frequent, often fierce, debate. The principal arguments against authenticity are found in Ludovic Lalanne, "Quelques doutes sur l'authenticité de la correspondance amoureuse d'Héloïse et d'Abélard," *La correspondance littéraire* 1 (1856): 27–33; Bernhard Schmeidler, "Der Briefwechsel zwischen Abaelard und Heloise: eine Fälschung," *Archiv für Kulturgeschichte* 11 (1913): 1–30; Schmeidler, "Der Briefwechsel zwischen Abaelard und Heloise dennoch eine literarische Fiction Abaelards," *Revue bénédictine* 52 (1940): 85–95; and Charlotte Charrier, *Héloïse dans l'historie et dans la légende* (Paris: Champion, 1933). For the most recent forgery theories see John Benton, "Fraud, Fiction, and Borrowing in the Correspondence of Abélard and Héloïse," in *Pierre Abélard—Pierre le Vénérable: Les courants philosophique, littéraires et artistiques en occident au milieu du XIIe siècle*, Colloques Internationaux du Centre National de la Recherche Scientifique, no. 546 (Paris: Éditions du Centre National de la Recherche Scientifique, 1975), pp. 469–512 and the ensuing discussion on pages 507–11. Benton retracted this theory and proposed a much more elaborate one suggesting Abélard wrote Héloïse's letters. See "A Reconsideration of the Authenticity of the Correspondence of Abelard and Heloise" in *Petrus Abaelardus (1979–1142): Person, Werk und Wirkung*, ed. Rudolf Thomas et al., Trierer Theologische Studien, no. 38 (Trier: Paulinus-Verlag, 1980), pp. 41–52. (This last volume will hereafter be referred to as *Trier 1980*.) The most important rebuttals are found not only in Gilson but more recently in Peter Dronke, *Abelard and Heloise in Medieval Testimonies*, W. P. Kerr Memorial Lecture, no. 26 (Glasgow: University of Glasgow Press, 1976) and

"Excursus: Did Abelard Write Heloise's Third Letter?" in *Women Writers of the Middle Ages: A Critical Study of Texts from Perpetua (†203) to Marguerite Porete (†1310)* (Cambridge: Cambridge University Press, 1984), pp. 140–43. Although not concerned directly with the correspondence, another rebuttal to Benton is to be found in S. Jaeger, "The Prologue to the *Historia calamitatum* and the 'Authenticity Question'," *Euphorion* 74 (1980): 1–15.

3. Linda Georgianna, "Any Corner of Heaven: Heloise's Critique of Monasticism," *Mediaeval Studies* 49 (1986): 221–53; Peggy Kamuf, "Marriage Contracts: The Letters of Heloise and Abelard" in *Fictions of Feminine Desire: Disclosures of Heloise* (Lincoln: University of Nebraska Press, 1982); and Peter Dronke, "Heloise," in *Women Writers of the Middle Ages* have followed the advice given by Gilson and by Peter von Moos, who discussed this problem in "Was kommt nach der Authenzizitätsdebatte über die Briefe Abaelards und Heloises?" *Trier 1980*, pp. 19–39.

4. Jean Leclercq, "Modern Psychology and the Interpretation of Medieval Texts," *Speculum* 48 (1973): 484.

5. On the subject of Abélard as autobiographer, see, for example, Chris Ferguson, "Autobiography as Therapy" (note 1); Jean Leclercq, "Modern Psychology and the Interpretation of Medieval Texts," *Speculum* 48 (1973): 476–90; and Mary McLaughlin, "Abelard as Autobiographer," *Speculum* 42 (1967): 463–88.

6. See Ferguson, "Autobiography as Therapy," pp. 200–201.

7. For this essay, I have used J. T. Muckle's edition of the Latin letters found in "The Personal Letters between Abelard and Heloise," *Mediaeval Studies* 15 (1953): 47–94, and "The Letter of Heloise on Religious Life and Abelard's First Reply," *Mediaeval Studies* 17 (1955): 240–81. Translations are from Betty Radice, *The Letters of Abelard and Heloise* (Baltimore: Penguin, 1974). Further references to these editions appear solely in the text. Heloise's letter to Abelard is numbered letter 1 in these comments; the numbers do not include, as is sometimes the case, the *Historia calamitatum*.

8. For a sensitive and perceptive commentary on this distinction see Georgianna, "Any Corner of Heaven" (note 3) pp. 239–40. Georgianna's commentary is rich in stimulating and insightful perspectives on Héloïse's letters. One should note, however, that *species* also carries other meanings than the antonym of individual (*singularis*). It can also refer to the genus and commonly has the meaning of appearance as opposed to substance, and even pretense. In these latter usages, it obviously supports Héloïse's confessions that her life is hypocritical.

9. Dronke, *Women Writers of the Middle Ages*, p. 112.

10. In her discerning exploration of the imagery of these letters, Kamuf also notes a shift from "hierarchial terms . . . to terms in which only the masculine/feminine distinction is pertinent." See Kamuf, "Marriage Contracts," p. 9.

11. Danielle Régnier-Bohler discusses this spatialization of the self through the later Middle Ages in "Imagining the Self: Exploring Literature" in *Revelations of the Medieval World*, vol. 2 of *A History of Private Life*, ed. Philippe Ariès and Georges Duby, trans. Arthur Goldhammer (Cambridge, MA: Harvard University Press, 1988), pp. 311–94. While she limits her discussion to the thirteenth, fourteenth, and fifteenth centuries, the use of space to express individual states of being also occurs

earlier. An interesting example of the metaphor in another medium is Abbé Suger's use of the Gothic cathedral to spatialize an inner experience of God.

12. For a discussion of this science, see Frances Yates, *The Art of Memory* (Chicago: University of Chicago Press, 1966).

13. Dronke, *Women Writers of the Middle Ages*, (note 2) p. 116.

14. For a discussion of the Pauline debt see James Brundage, "Sexual Equality in Medieval Canon Law" in *Medieval Women and the Sources of Medieval History*, ed. Joel Rosenthal (Athens: University of Georgia Press, 1990), pp. 66–79; Elizabeth Makowski, "The Conjugal Debt and Medieval Canon Law," *Journal of Medieval History* 3 (1977): 99–114; and John T. Noonan, "Marital Affection in the Canonist," *Studia Gratiana* 12 (1967): 479–509.

15. See, for example, McLaughlin, who argues that *Historia calamitatum* was primarily a public letter in "Abelard as Autobiographer" (note 5), p. 468.

16. Dronke, *Women Writers of the Middle Ages* (note 2), p. 117; Radice, Introduction to *The Letters of Abelard and Heloise*, p. 18; and Étienne Gilson, *Héloïse et Abélard* (note 1), p. 62 all discuss this point.

17. He wrote that "I desired to keep you whom I loved beyond measure for myself alone" (149) ("cuperem te mihi supra modum dilectam in perpetuum retinere" 90). This same jealous possessiveness may well have lain behind his command that Héloïse enter orders, as Radice notes in her Introduction, *The Letters of Abelard and Heloise*, pp. 22–23.

18. Gilson, *Héloïse et Abélard* (note 2), p. 73.

19. For a discussion of this tradition see Katharina M. Wilson and Elizabeth Makowski, *Wykked Wyves and the Woes of Marriage: Misogamous Literature from Juvenal to Chaucer*, SUNY Series in Medieval Studies 1 (Albany: State University of New York Press, 1990). On *Adversus Jovinianum* and its long legacy, see Philippe Delhaye, "Le Dossier anti-matrimonial de l'*Adversus Jovinianum* et son influence sur quelques écrits Latins du XIIe siècle," *Mediaeval Studies* 12 (1951): 65–86.

20. *Wykked Wyves and the Woes of Marriage*, p. 80.

21. Kamuf also discusses this misrepresentation of Héloïse's remarks with a different emphasis. See "Marriage Contracts" (note 3), pp. 14–15. In a more general review, Leclercq remarks that Abelard has "a narcissism which continues to be naive and childish . . . [;] . . . he speaks of hardly anything but his own person." See LeClercq, "Modern Psychology and the Interpretation of Medieval Texts," (note 5), p. 484.

22. Both Abélard and Héloïse quote from Augustine's book—Abélard in letter six, Héloïse in letter five.

23. Dronke speaks of this inversion in "Heloise's *Problemata* and *Letters*: Some Questions of Form and Content" in *Trier 1980*, pp. 53–73. He connects the reversals with the "human reversals, in the *ordo naturalis rerum*" (p. 59). For a discussion of the *mundus inversus topos*, which was most frequently used in satiric verse, see Ernst Curtius, *European Literature and the Latin Middle Ages*, Bollingen Series, no. 36, trans. Willard Trask (Princeton, NJ: Princeton University Press, 1973), pp. 94–98.

24. Both Abélard and Héloïse use these two terms for conversion interchangeably in the letters. Georgianna, "Any Corner of Heaven" (note 3), p. 228 n. 24, discusses the different types of conversion—one a dramatic change of heart, the other simply the entry into the monastic life.

25. For a detailed discussion of this battle for second place among the lovers see Peggy Kamuf, "Marriage Contracts," pp. 9–10.

26. This standard of pure intent that pervades Héloïse's arguments comes from Abélard's *Ethica*, written around the same time as the *Historia calamitatum*. See *Peter Abelard's Ethics: An Edition with Introduction*, D. E. Luscombe (Oxford: Clarendon Press, 1971), especially pp. 44–46.

27. See Dronke's discussion in *Poetic Individuality in the Middle Ages: New Departures in Poetry 1000–1150* (Oxford: Clarendon Press, 1970), pp. 123–39, where he deals in detail with Héloïse's treatment of Samson. He shows how her view of Samson's destruction of the Temple (presented as a self-destruction) is especially innovative.

28. In literary texts, this "chamber was a place for isolating and protecting women," as noted by Danielle Régnier-Bohler in "Imagining the Self," (note 11), p. 140. Abélard's own letter draws a private/public contrast between the world of the bedchamber and the more public world of the table, which would have been situated in the hall. Héloïse is thus confined to the areas of the metaphorical house linked to the lord's private existence.

29. Many exegetical interpretations of the *Canticum Canticorum* were produced in this century, often associating the bride with the Virgin, the soul, or the Church. Among those who composed such glosses are Honorius Augustodunensis, Rupert of Deutz, and Alain de Lille. Bernard of Clairvaux in his homilies to the Virgin, "Super Missus est," also draws heavily on this biblical book as he compares the bride to the Virgin Mary. See E. Ann Matter, *The Voice of My Beloved: The Song of Songs in Western Medieval Christianity* (Philadelphia: University of Pennsylvania Press, 1990) and Ann Astell, *The Song of Songs in the Middle Ages* (Ithaca, NY: Cornell University Press, 1990).

30. Kamuf, "Marriage Contracts," p. 30.

31. Kamuf, "Marriage Contracts," p. 30.

32. The continuation of themes has been discussed by Georgianna, "Any Corner of Heaven," 221–53; Dronke, *Women Writers of the Middle Ages*, and "Heloise's *Problemata* and *Letters*" in *Trier 1980*; and Peter von Moos in "Le Silence d'Héloïse et les idéologies modernes" in *Pierre Abélard—Pierre le Venerable*, pp. 425–68.

33. For a discussion of this association, see Georges Duby, "Private Power, Public Power" in *Revelations of the Medieval World*, (note 11), esp. pp. 7–8.

34. On the subject of whether Héloïse truly converted there have been many opinions. D. W. Robertson in *Abelard and Heloise* (New York: Dial Press, 1972) proposes that the work is an *exemplum* of conversion, an argument attacked very persuasively by Dronke in *Abelard and Heloise in Medieval Testimonies* (note 2). For a good review of various readings of Héloïse's silence and its relationship to the question of her conversion, see von Moos, "Le Silence d'Héloïse et les idéologies modernes," *Colloques*, pp. 425–30.

35. Dronke, *Women Writers of the Middle Ages*, pp. 127–28 also notes this possible implication, as does Georgianna, "Any Corner of Heaven" (note 3).

36. David Knowles, *The Evolution of Medieval Thought*, p. 112.

37. "Any Corner of Heaven" (note 3), p. 240.

38. Gilson interprets the last superscription in this way in *Héloïse et Abélard*,

(note 2), pp. 110–11. For other interpretations, see Dronke, *Women Writers of the Middle Ages* (note 3), pp. 122–28; Radice, Introduction to *The Letters of Abelard and Heloise* (note 17), p. 159 n. 1; and Georgianna, "Any Corner of Heaven," pp. 238–39, who suggests some fascinating implications from Héloïse's associations between herself and the particular.

39. Georgianna suggests that while this letter "does not offer evidence of a conversion in any conventional sense," it does suggest that she is seeking a conversion which is " . . . an intellectual, emotional, and spiritual process, slow and painful at times, whose success is always reversible and always in doubt." See "Any Corner of Heaven," p. 229.

40. Muckle identifies the source as Cicero in "The Letter of Heloise on Religious Life and Abelard's First Reply," *Mediaeval Studies* 17 (1955): 242 n.12, but Dronke has suggested Jerome's *Epistulae* 125.14 in *Women Writers of the Middle Ages*, p. 305 n. 39.

41. Both passages rebuke Héloïse for aspects of her behavior toward Abélard. The first comes from Virgil's *Eclogues* and erects a pseudo-comparison between Héloïse and the nymph Galatea who seeks to attract her lover by fleeing from him. The second comes from Lucan's *Pharsalia* and suggests that if she continues to lament Abélard will think she loved his fortune more than him. See Kamuf, "Marriage Contracts," pp. 33–35 for a discussion of the comparison with Galatea.

42. Georgianna, "Any Corner of Heaven," pp. 238–40.

43. Georgianna, "Any Corner of Heaven," pp. 232–33.

44. Duby, "Private Power, Public Power," p. 8.

45. "Private Power, Public Power," p. 9.

46. "Private Power, Public Power," p. 7.

Karen Scott

"*Io Catarina*": Ecclesiastical Politics and Oral Culture in the Letters of Catherine of Siena

It is May 6, 1379. Rome is divided by a civil war into camps supporting two contending Popes, Urban VI and Clement VII. The mercenary soldiers of the Company of St. George have just succeeded in recapturing the Castel Sant'Angelo for Urban VI after a long siege. Soon the Antipope Clement VII will have to flee Rome and establish his court in Avignon.[1] That day Catherine of Siena dictated at least four letters concerning the events of the Schism. She sent two letters to supporters of Urban VI—the city government of Rome and the Captain of the Company of St. George; and she sent two letters to the supporters of Clement VII—Queen Giovanna of Naples and King Charles V of France.[2] She had been in Rome since late November 1378, called there officially by Urban to help him reunite the Church, and now she was busy doing so through her prayer, her verbal persuasion, and her voluminous correspondence.

Among Catherine's many activities at the time of the Schism, one must count her attempt to bring to Rome a contingent of holy men to assist Urban VI, her exhortation of the college of cardinals in Rome to remain faithful to him, and her desire to travel to Naples to convince Queen Giovanna to support him.[3] She sent over sixty letters relating to the Schism, most of them to the protagonists of the conflict. But she had too little time for her plans to bear fruit. Catherine would die on April 29, 1380, worn out by her work for Church unity; the Schism continued well into the fifteenth century.

If the Pope called on Catherine of Siena, an uneducated *popolana* of the artisan class and a lay Dominican tertiary, for help in the arduous task of ending the Schism, it was because by 1379 she was Italy's most famous holy woman, known not only for her fasts and her visions but also for her active desire to effect political and ecclesiastical reform. In 1376 Catherine had traveled to Avignon to convince Pope Gregory XI to make peace with a League of Italian cities and to return the seat of his government to Rome; with Papal approval she had preached peace in the Sienese countryside in 1377; and in 1378 she had spent several months trying to persuade the Florentines to end their war with the Papacy. By 1379 she had finished dictating the theological masterpiece which she called her *Libro* or Book, and which later editors entitled *Il Dialogo della divina provvidenza* (*The Dialogue of Divine Providence*).[4] She also had already sent the majority of her 382 letters to prominent politicians, Church prelates, and ordinary people.

Catherine's correspondence is characterized by a combination of didactic content, personal tone, and passionate concern to affect public matters and people's lives. Her prolific writings manifest her wide circle of human relations, her deep caring for temporal peace and ecclesiastical reform, and her desire to present spiritual issues in thoughtful and convincing ways. Through her epistles she hoped to inspire her correspondents to take specific actions. An overview suggests that Catherine's letters might best be analyzed as examples of female activism and raises the question of how she might have obtained such an outspoken and confident voice in public affairs.[5] This essay argues that the answer to that question lies in the oral culture in which Catherine lived. Significantly, however, recent studies have not emphasized Catherine's actual apostolic endeavors, her self-image as a person called to travel and preach "for the honor of God and the salvation of souls," or her dictation of letters as a means of furthering her political and ecclesiastical causes. Two other interpretations have drawn the most scholarly attention and will need to be examined carefully: first, the letters have been viewed as examples of early Italian literature; and second, they have been considered "prophetic" and "mystical" texts.

The *Epistolario* as Literature

Because it cannot boast a modern critical edition and has not yet been translated in its entirety into English, the *Epistolario* is often neglected today as a source for Catherine's life and thought.[6] This neglect continues a trend in Catherine studies which began in the Renaissance. Since the sixteenth century scholars who have paid attention to her letters have concentrated not on her apostolic activities, but on her place in the development of the Italian language. The key to Catherine's literary reputation is the first printing of the complete *Epistolario* in 1500 by the influential Venetian humanist Aldus Manutius. Though he did not publish the letters for their stylistic merit, the fact that he had published them at all brought them to the attention of prominent humanists.[7]

By the middle of the sixteenth century Catherine's *Epistolario* was the only letter collection by a woman to be included in the literary canon set up in Anton Francesco Doni's *Libraria*, a list of books which he believed a scholarly humanist should have in his private library. Doni listed Catherine's name several times, most notably in the category of writer of "Translated letters" (as if she had originally written her letters in Latin, and then had had them translated into Italian):

> Cicerone / Ovidio / Fallaride / Seneca /
> Di diversi: Plinio, Petrarca, Pico, Poliziano e altri / San Cipriano / Marsilio Ficino / Papa Pio / Battista Ignazio / San Girolamo / Santo Agostino / Santa Catarina.[8]

By being associated with admired Latin authors from the ancient Roman, early Christian, and Renaissance periods, Catherine acquired the reputation of being a valid and solid literary figure. Her Italian letters could then be appropriated as real stylistic models seminal to the formation of the modern Italian language.

Catherine's inclusion in such sixteenth-century lists of valued letter collections in the vernacular ensured her a prominent place in Italian literary debates. In the early eighteenth century her letters became the focus of an intense controversy in Tuscany, when the Sienese scholar Girolamo Gigli published her complete works and argued in his *Vocabolario cateriniano* that her Sienese language was superior to the Florentine tongue. This claim brought down on him the wrath of the Florentine Academia della Crusca. The Grand Duke of Tuscany had the *Vocabolario* banned and burned, and Gigli was forced into exile.[9]

In more recent literary studies, Catherine's letters have attained dubious honor. The *Epistolario* is included among the earliest examples of vernacular Italian literature—Catherine is still considered the first important woman writer in Italy—and then critiqued and practically dismissed, this time not because of its Sienese dialect, but because of its very "imperfect" style. Beginning with pre-determined literary standards about "serenity" and "harmony," clear structure, stylistic variety, grammatical correctness, and sobriety in the use of imagery and redundancy, scholars such as Giovanni Getto and Natalino Sapegno have found Catherine's prose to be far less "artful" than the "genuine" masterpieces by Dante or Petrarch.

For example, Sapegno wrote that her letters were works of political propaganda and mysticism, written with a practical and didactic, and not a valid "poetic" intent. He called her style "strange" and "flowery," "spontaneous," and "colloquial" (*dialettale*). Typical is his judgment of the imagery Catherine used so often to make her thinking more appealing: "the mystic's glimmering and carnal metaphor is one thing, and the poet's limpid metaphor . . . is quite another" ("Altra cosa e la metafora fremente, carnale . . . del mistico, e altra la metafora limpida . . . del poeta").[10] Paradoxically, then, Catherine's inclusion in the humanist canon both ensured the survival of her letters, considered basic to the development of Italian literary discourse, and led to their discredit because of their lack of poetic quality, their confused style, and their mystical, didactic, and political content.

Although it is important to evaluate the literary quality of early vernacular letters like Catherine's in order to determine their place in the history of the Italian language, the type of analysis proposed by Getto and Sapegno is misleading and anachronistic. What Italian literary critics since the sixteenth century have not considered sufficiently is that Catherine's letters were oral documents dictated by an uneducated and, at best, only partly literate person whose goals were anything but stylistic or literary. Moreover, these scholars have not focussed on the fact that this author was a woman, in fact the only one included in their anthologies of fourteenth-century Italian literature. It has been argued that religious women, whose culture was still predominantly oral, played an important part in the development of the various vernacular literatures of the late Middle Ages, and that their style of writing reflected their particular background.[11] For Catherine, the question that needs to be posed is not why her style was so "deficient" and "unliterary", but how this uneducated woman was able to develop her particular kind of style and voice.

Catherine's Voice as Supernatural: Holy Women and Hagiography

Catherine's remarkable success as a writer of letters leads one to wonder what factors enabled her to overcome the many obstacles facing women in Trecento Italy and what factors made possible such an extroverted and active epistolary "career." One often assumes that persons such as herself, an uneducated lay woman of the artisan class, had few opportunities to know about or affect decisively the politics of their commune or the life of the Church. They had no official channels to political or religious power. Confessors advised women who desired holiness to live humbly in solitude or in cloistered communities, to pray, and to do penance. Women were usually not encouraged to make political and ecclesiastical affairs the focus of their spirituality, to preach, or to write.[12] Moreover, the fourteenth century was an age of improved literacy in both Latin and the vernacular. In Tuscan cities schooling was relatively common, and Italian society was increasingly dependent on the written word.[13] Modern scholars often assume that people who remained illiterate or barely literate functioned with difficulty within this literate and more bureaucratic system. Such an assumption would seem especially true of lay women like Catherine who had much less access to formal education than did men.

How were Catherine and other uneducated women able to find a voice and exert public influence? One answer scholars have given is that the prophetic and supernatural quality of their speech made their words acceptable to their audiences and gave them the courage to act. From this perspective, women in a patriarchal society and church can acquire an acceptable voice and exert power in religious matters only if the words they speak are considered to be God's words and not their own. Such an approach to Catherine tends to minimize her desire to shape Church and state affairs in a practical way and stresses the more narrowly defined ascetic and mystical sides of her life.[14]

The interpretation of Catherine which emphasizes the supernatural dimension of her life is based less on an analysis of her letters than on the abundant hagiographical sources for her life, especially the *Legenda Major*, written several years after her death by her former confessor Raymond of Capua to help bring about her canonization by the Church. It is important to examine the evidence in this Saint's life because it contains important information about Catherine's composition of the letters and because its portrait of her as a mystic prepared for the establishment of her cult. Moreover, though Catherine's self-presentation in her own letters differs significantly from Raymond's stylization of her, as we shall see, it is his view that has most fascinated devotees and recent historians.

In the *Legenda* Raymond attributes to Catherine a kind of semi-literacy, noting her ability to read certain prayers of the divine office in Latin but not to read ordinary texts or write in Italian or in Latin.[15] His main message is that she was taught all she knew directly by the Holy Spirit and consequently did not attend school or learn anything from teachers or books. Although she worked hard to learn to read in the ordinary way by mastering the alphabet, the task proved impossible. In the context of a story about her custom of walking about her little room praying the Psalms out loud, literally, with Jesus at her side, Raymond inserts an account of how Catherine was miraculously instructed by the Holy Spirit, and learned to "read" the Canonical Hours in Latin "very fast" (*velocissime*). He specifies that her ability to read the Office was truly remarkable because after the miracle occurred she could still not speak Latin, read by separating syllables, or distinguish the letters.[16] Though Raymond's intent is to stress the miraculous dimension of the event and to reinforce his mystical portrayal of her, and not to give precise information concerning her ability to read, this account leads one to doubt whether Catherine really achieved the skills one normally associates with literacy.[17]

In addition, by implying that Catherine did not use her miraculous gifts to peruse books other than the prayers of the Office, Raymond may be hinting that she was unable to read anything she had not heard chanted out loud in a liturgical setting.[18] Another possible interpretation of his remarks is that he is using this story to protect her from a male ecclesiastical audience who assumed that interest in doctrinal matters on the part of uneducated lay women would be easily tainted with misunderstandings and heresy.[19] He wants to make clear that she read out of a desire only to pray better, not to seek special doctrinal instruction or entertainment. Consequently, he implies also, the content of her writing and preaching could not be based on information gained from books but only on divine inspiration.

In his Prologue to the *Vita* Raymond addresses the issue of Catherine's importance as a writer and affirms that she dictated all her letters with God's direct assistance. The fact that she spoke so quickly and self-confidently and could keep in mind what she wanted to say to three or four secretaries at a time, each taking down a different letter, is a sign to him that her writing was a real miracle:

> She dictated these letters quickly and without any interval for thinking, however small; she spoke as if she were reading out of a book placed before her. . . . Many who knew her before I did have told me that very frequently they had seen her dictating to three or four writers at the same time, and with that same speed and power of memory; for me, that this occurred in the body of a woman so weakened by vigils and fasting points more to a miracle and a super-celestial infusion than to any natural capacity of hers.

Has autem epistolas ita dictabat velociter absque cogitationis inter-
vallo etiam modico, ac si legeret in aliquo libro ante se posito quidquid
dicebat. . . . Responsum est mihi per plures qui eam noverant ante me,
& frequentius viderant eam dictantem, quod aliquando tribus, aliquando quatuor scriptoribus similiter dictaverat, ut dictum est, & cum
celeritate, necnon & memoriae firmitate; quod in corpore muliebri,
tam macerato vigiliis & inedia, potius dat mihi signum miraculi &
infusionis supercaelestis, quam cujuscumque naturalis virtutis.[20]

Raymond finds Catherine's writings to be especially remarkable and
filled with supernatural power because they were dictated effortlessly. Perhaps his awe at her capacity to compose letters so easily reflects his inability,
as a highly literate man, to understand the process of oral composition.
Catherine may have dictated her letters at the speed of oral discourse, one
that was ordinary to her, but too quick to be comprehensible to Raymond,
accustomed to the laborious process of written composition. In any case,
this account of her dictating letters reveals that Raymond is following a
supernatural model of holiness that attributes all of the saint's achievements
to God's miraculous intervention. Raymond makes the same point when he
expresses admiration that the *Epistolario* was authored by a holy person so
terribly worn down and weakened by ascetic practices. Only divine help
could account for the energy she exhibited in the act of dictating so many
letters.

Raymond reinforces his emphasis on God by pointing out that it was a
mere "woman" who produced these texts. Elsewhere in the *Legenda* Raymond maintains that though women are "ignorant and fragile by their very
nature" ("feminas, de sui natura ignorantes & fragiles"), God sometimes
chooses them to ensure the success of His salvific mission. Completely
"filled" with God because they are by nature so "empty", these female saints
teach divine doctrine and reform the hearts of men, "especially those who
consider themselves well-educated and wise" ("potissime illorum, qui lit-
teratos & sapientes se reputant"). These women are "fragile but chosen
vessels" ("vasa fragilia sed electa"), "gifted with divine power and wisdom,
to confound the temerity [of proud men]" ("virtute & sapientia divina
dotatas, in confusionem temeritate eorum").[21] Raymond emphasizes Catherine's natural female weakness so as to give all the credit for her achievements to God alone.

As a further proof of the divine origin of Catherine's speech, Raymond pays her the very high compliment of saying that if one were to translate her Italian idiom into Latin, her style would be comparable to the Latin prose of St. Augustine and the Apostle Paul. Modern literary critics do not share this view, but it is nonetheless important that Raymond attributes to her words a kind of supernaturally infused literary style which had Latinate qualities.[22] Though he may have been the first commentator on Catherine to emphasize the beauty of her style and lead readers to think of her as a literary figure, he does so not in order to attribute her success as a writer to her own natural gifts or hard effort to communicate well, but rather to prove that given her low level of instruction and literacy, only God Himself could have been the author of her letters.

Finally, Raymond states in his Prologue that all Catherine's words were so astonishingly wise for a woman as to constitute a sign that God was speaking through her:

> The Lord gave her a most erudite tongue, so that she knew how to utter a speech in every place, and her words burned like flames; and there was no one hearing her who could completely hide from the warmth of her fiery words. . . . Who from these signs would not see that the fire of the Holy Spirit lived in her? What other proof does one need that Christ spoke in her? . . . Where did this little woman get such wisdom? . . . She held the key to the abyss, that is to the depth of supernatural wisdom, and by illuminating darkened minds, she opened to the blind the treasure of eternal light.

> Dominus emim ei dederat linguam eruditissimam, ut sciret proferre sermonem ubique verbaque ipsius ardebant ut faculae; nec erat quicumque audiens eam, qui se a calore ignitorum verborum ejus totaliter posset abscondere. . . . Qui per haec signa non videat ignem Spiritus sancti habitanti in ea? Quis aliud quaerat experimentum ejus qui loquebatur in ea Christus? . . . Unde huic mulierculae sapientia tanta? . . . Clavem habebat abyssi, profunditatis scilicet sapientiae supernaturalis: & mentes illuminans tenebrosas, aperiebat caecis thesaurum lucis aeternae.[23]

Ultimately Raymond links Catherine's success as a writer to the warmth of her spoken words, and not her literary talents. He attributes the effective-

ness of those words to the fire of the Holy Spirit and the very power and
wisdom of God which lived in this fragile female "vessel."

In the narrative sections of the *Legenda* Raymond uses accounts of
Catherine's effective speaking to reiterate his theology of female weakness
and divine inspiration. In particular, he tells a significant story about her
preaching at the beginning of the Schism to the Pope and his cardinals in
Rome. After listening to Catherine's exhorting them to trust in divine
providence and not fear for the future of the Church, Raymond says, Urban
VI spoke these words to his cardinals:

> "This little woman shames us. I call her a little woman not out of
> contempt for her, but as an expression of her female sex which is by
> nature fragile, and for our own instruction. This woman by nature
> ought to fear, while we ought to be secure: and yet while now we
> tremble, she is without fear and comforts us with her persuasive
> words. A great shame must arise in us now." And he added: "What has
> the Vicar of Jesus Christ to fear, even if the entire world opposes him?
> The omnipotent Christ is more powerful than the world, and it is not
> possible that He abandon His holy Church".

> Haec muliercula nos confundit. Mulierculam autem voco, non in
> contemptus ejus, sed in expressionem sexus feminei, naturaliter fra-
> gilis, & ad nostrem instructionem. Ista siquidem naturaliter timere
> deberet, etiam quando nos essemus bene sicuri: & tamen ubi nos
> formidamus, ipsa stat absque timore, suisque persuasionibus nos con-
> fortat. Magna hinc nobis debet oriri confusio. Et subjunxit: Quid
> debet timere Vicarius Jesu Christi, etiam si totus mundus se contra
> eum opponeret? Potentior est mundo Christus omnipotens, nec est
> possibile quod derelinquat Ecclesiam suam Sanctam.[24]

Raymond does not conclude from the empirical evidence of Catherine's strength that the female nature might not be so naturally fragile as he
had been led to believe. Instead, Urban's surprise at Catherine's superb
performance as a preacher reflects Raymond's view that a female voice can
emerge only if it is totally controlled by the divine. Under such conditions,
however, he hints that even Popes may be converted. "Instructed" by her
exceptional and miraculous example and words, Urban can now fulfill the

properly male and papal role and confidently exhort his cardinals himself. One notes in passing that Raymond implies that Urban's bold speech is normal, not exceptional or supernatural like Catherine's. Though ending the story with the Pope's words may help Raymond assert the dominance of ecclesiastical over charismatic power and highlights Catherine's obedience to the Church, it also underlines her miraculous effectiveness in her mission of humbling, or "shaming" proud men.

Catherine's Letter to the Government of Rome

If one turns from a study of the hagiography to Catherine's own writings and her references to herself as a letter writer and speaker, one finds that she projects a sense of self that is rather different from Raymond's. First, her correspondence shows that being an uneducated woman may very well have been less of an obstacle to her developing a public apostolate and finding a strong voice than Raymond and subsequent historians imagined. Her letters are self-confident and natural, as if advising important people about spiritual, ecclesiastical, and political affairs were the most normal activity for a simple lay woman. Her presentation of self displays none of Raymond's careful apologetic focus. The *Epistolario* indicates that Catherine was well-informed about the main events of her day and formed opinions about them. When she saw an urgent need to find solutions to problems, she had the courage to speak about what she thought and to send letters to the main protagonists telling them what they should do to bring about Church reform and peace.

Second, though she believed that obeying the divine will was essential in any Christian life, including hers, and though she often expressed gratitude to God for her gifts and achievements, rarely did Catherine give a supernatural or prophetic flavor to her statements about her relationship with Him. The tone of most of her letters is so mundane that they hardly qualify as "mystical" or "literary" texts. Rather, her tone most resembles that of other Italian Trecento letters sent by ordinary people about ordinary things.[25] This similarity in tone suggests that Catherine viewed her writing of letters as part of her broader active vocation, which for her was one of ordinary speech and oral communication, and not prophetic or supernatural speech.

Among the letters which Catherine dictated on May 6, 1379, the one she sent to the city government of Rome ("A' Signori Banderesi e quattro

Buoni Uomini mantenitori della Repubblica di Roma") is particularly interesting as an example of her epistolary strategy and her degree of involvement in public affairs during the Schism. It shall serve as a starting point for a discussion and explanation of her importance as a writer of letters.[26] The letter begins with a set of formulas which recur often, with slight variations, in all of her correspondence: "In the name of Jesus Christ crucified and sweet Mary. Dear brothers and earthly Lords, in sweet Christ Jesus. I Catherine, slave of the servants of Jesus Christ, write to you in His precious blood, with the desire to see you be grateful . . ." ("Al nome di Gesù Cristo crocifisso e di Maria dolce. Carissimi fratelli e signori in terra, in Cristo dolce Gesù. Io Catarina, schiava de'servi di Gesù Cristo, scrivo a voi nel prezioso sangue suo; con desiderio di vedervi grati . . .").

After this introduction, Catherine devotes the main part of the letter to a long religious lesson on the spiritual and social consequences of ingratitude and gratitude to God. Her message is relatively simple and straightforward. People who are ungrateful to God, she says, offer the love they owe Him to their own sensuality and turn the love they owe their neighbor into hatred, envy, malicious gossip, and injustice. Deprived of charity, their hearts are so narrow that there is no place for God or neighbor within them. With characteristically blunt and passionate language Catherine accuses the ungrateful person "of contaminating justice and selling the flesh of his neighbor. . . . Not only does he blaspheme and speak ill of other creatures; but his mouth treats God and His Saints no better nor worse than he might do with his feet" ("contaminando la giustizia e rivendendo la carne del prossimo suo. . . . Non tanto che bestemmi e dica male delle creature, ma egli pone bocca a Dio e a' Santi suoi nè più nè meno, come se lo avesse fatto co'piedi").[27]

On the contrary, Catherine says that people who are grateful to God look to Christ's humility and purity, and to the abundance of blood He shed out of love for humanity, and they broaden their hearts to offer assistance to all.

> Such a person lives honestly, helping his neighbor in his need whether he be subordinate or lord, . . . small or great, poor or rich, according to true justice. He does not lightly believe in a neighbor's failing, but with a prudent and mature heart he examines very carefully who speaks [about that failing] and who the person is that is spoken of [accused]. He is grateful to who serves him: because he is grateful to God, he is

grateful to him. And he does not serve only those who serve him, but he loves and is merciful to whoever disserves him.

Vive onestamente, sovvenendo al prossimo suo, o suddito o signore che sia, in ogni sua necessità . . . ; fa ragione al piccolo come al grande, e al povero come al ricco, secondo che vuole la vera giustizia. Egli non è leggiere a credere un difetto del suo prossimo; ma con prudenzia e maturità di cuore ragguarda molto bene colui che dice, e di cui egli dice. Egli è grato e cognoscente a chi 'l serve; perchè egli è grato a Dio, però è grato a lui. E non tanto che egli serva chi 'l serve, ma egli ama e fa misericorddia a chi l'ha disservito.[28]

Following this didactic section, the last quarter of the letter shifts in tone to a strongly worded request that the Roman officials apply her general moral principles about gratitude to the situation of the moment, and therefore adopt certain policies. The government, she writes with her firm, almost imperious *voglio* ("I want you to . . ."), should recognize that the papal victory is God's doing. Officials should institute public rituals to thank God for saving Rome from danger: they could imitate Urban VI's humble procession barefoot through the streets of the city. The government should also organize better care for the soldiers of the Company of St. George, especially for those who were wounded in the battle for Castel Sant'Angelo, because these men were Christ's instruments and because a show of genuine gratitude would keep these mercenaries on Urban's side.[29]

Furthermore, Catherine asks the government of Rome to put an end to some negative talk about Giovanni Cenci, the Senator who organized the Pope's victory, and to thank him more fully for his selfless and prudent contributions:

I would not want him or anyone else who is serving you to be treated in this way [with ingratitude and slander], because it would be greatly offensive to God and harmful for you. For the entire community needs wise, mature, and discreet men with a good conscience. No more of this, for the love of Christ crucified! Take whatever remedy your Lordships think best, to keep the simple-mindedness of the ignorant from impeding what is good.

Non vorrei che si facesse così nè di lui nè di veruno altro che vi servisse; perchè sarebbe offesa di Dio, e danno a voi. Che tutta la communita ha bisogno di uomini savi, maturi e discreti e di buona conscienza. Non si faccia più così, per l'amore di Cristo crocifisso! Poneteci quel rimedio che pare alla Signoria vostra, acciocchè la semplicità degl'ignoranti non impedisca il bene.[30]

Finally, at the very end of the letter, fearing that her words might have sounded too outspoken, and perhaps knowing that in a time of civil war her suggestions would not be popular with everyone in Rome, Catherine suggests that her correspondents ought to listen to her because she is truly disinterested, caring, and sincere. This closing assumes a quite personal tone:

I say this to you for your own good, and not out of self-interest, for as you know I am a foreigner and I speak to you for your good, because I value all of you and him [Cenci] as much as my own soul. I know that as wise and discreet men you will look to the affection and purity of heart with which I write to you. And so you will forgive the presumption, with which I presume to write.

Questo dico per vostra utilità, e non per veruna affezione; che voi sapete che io son peregrina, parlandovi per lo buono stato vostro; perchè tutti insieme con lui, tengo che siate l'anima mia. So che, come uomini savi e discreti, ragguarderete all'affetto e alla purità del cuor mio, con che io scrivo a voi. E così perdonerete alla mia presunzione, che presumo di scrivere.[31]

The letter concludes with a set of formulas which recur very often in the correspondence: "I say no more. Remain in the holy and sweet love of God. Be grateful to God. Jesus sweet, Jesus love" ("Altro non dico. Permanete nella santa e dolce dilezione di Dio. Siate, siate grati e cognoscenti a Dio. Gesù dolce, Gesù amore").[32] In her letter to the government of Rome Catherine gives very practical advice and moves from an abstract to a more personal tone.

The *Epistolario*: An Overview

Catherine's remarkable *Epistolario* is composed of 382 extant letters dictated and sent to a total of about 220 individuals and 25 groups (governments and religious communities) over the span of about eight years. She engages her correspondents well enough to elicit written answers from some of them and to exchange letters with them over a period of several years.[33] These letters generally follow the pattern exemplified in the one she sent to the government of Rome. An overview of the correspondence allows one to discern the epistolary strategy which Catherine used to persuade people to take the actions she deemed desirable. These letters also carry something of her original voice, and thus they can serve as an introduction to the personality and concerns of the historical Catherine.

The opening formulas ("In the name of Jesus Christ crucified and of sweet Mary" and "I Catherine, servant and slave of the servants of Jesus Christ") indicate that Catherine desires to communicate her views with great authority, both in God's name and in her own. The wording of these formulas is her own, reflecting her Christocentric spirituality and her self-image as loving "servant" to both God and neighbor. These idiosyncratic introductions may function as the equivalent of signatures confirming the authorship of her letters.[34] From the very beginning Catherine also creates intimacy with her correspondents by addressing them as her spiritual relatives—as her "sons" or "daughters" if they are her disciples, and as her "mothers" or "fathers" if they are rulers or members of the clergy to whom she must express respect.[35]

Catherine leaves to a comparatively short end section any mention of the concrete action which she wants to inspire her correspondents to take, and she spends most of each letter teaching in a reasoned and rather impersonal way the spiritual lessons that should persuade them to do as she wishes.[36] She structures these didactic sections around a discussion of a main virtue which she wishes her correspondents to understand and practice better—gratitude, charity, obedience, humility, patience, and so on—or a vocation which she believes they need to live more fully—priest, cloistered nun, pope, knight, political leader, son or daughter of God, and so on. Christ is the central model and theological focus of her teaching, and she relies heavily on imagery of all sorts to make her thinking accessible and appealing.[37] The moral and doctrinal content of her teaching is conventional, ordinary, and mostly unoriginal. The tone is simple and straightforward—usually not mystical or visionary, theological or philosophical, or stylistically artful.

What is more remarkable about these didactic sections, if one examines the entire *Epistolario*, is their variety. Catherine has at her disposal a vast repertoire of suggestions and arguments, and her letters advocate and defend many different callings.[38] On the one hand, she writes a community of enclosed nuns in Perugia to do everything to avoid social contact: they should flee the parlor, keep to their cell, and converse only with God.[39] Likewise she advises a prominent Florentine politician to keep away from the Chancery and the Palace, to refuse any new office, and to stay at home to avoid becoming entangled in the world.[40] On the other hand, Catherine can portray in glowing terms the heart-warming joys of good conversation among ordinary God-fearing people.[41] Moreover, she spends much energy attempting to persuade prelates to become less reclusive and to pay attention to Church reform. Since the shepherds of the Church are asleep in their own selfishness, she says, they hardly notice that their sheep are being stolen by infernal wolves. So she exhorts one prelate to awake and cry out with a hundred thousand tongues, and she tells a Cardinal to roar like a lion.[42]

Catherine adapts her spiritual and moral teachings and the imagery she uses to convey her points to her particular audiences. Even her portrayals of Christ can vary: for some correspondents He is the loving bridegroom, while for others He is the immaculate Lamb shedding salvific blood on the cross. He can be a model of humble silence and patience, the spiritual Master, or the eternal Truth and Word of God the Father. This variety reflects Catherine's desire to make her letters personal and unique: she sends her correspondents individually tailored sermons containing those spiritual lessons which she believes they most need to hear or read. The diversity of content in the *Epistolario* also means that one should be careful not to generalize about her moral and spiritual thought from what she wrote in any one letter.

In the end sections of her letters Catherine abandons the general approach of the didactic portions and applies her theoretical teachings to the particular circumstances of her correspondents. She usually highlights the distinction between the two main sections of her letters by inserting the customary phrase "I have nothing more to say" ("altro non dico") at the end of her lesson. She implies that she is beginning the least formal and most personal portion of her text. Her tone becomes very ordinary and intimate, especially when she deals with matters pertaining to her "family" of spiritual disciples in Siena.

For example, she writes this message to invite her young friend Neri Pagliaresi into her spiritual family: "You asked me to receive you as my son: so though I be unworthy, lowly, and wretched, I have already received you, and I receive you with affectionate love" ("Domandastemi, che io vi ricevessi per figliuolo: onde io, poniamochè indegna misera e miserabile sia, v'ho già ricevuto e ricevo con affettuoso amore").[43] Another disciple, Francesco Malavolti, has left her group and engaged in a life of sin, and she sends him this note: "I write to you with the desire of putting you back in the sheepfold with your companions. . . . Console my soul; and do not be so cruel to your own salvation as to deny me a visit. Do not let the devil trick you with fear or shame. Break this knot; come, come, dearest son" ("Io scrivo a te con desiderio di rimetterti nell'ovile con li compagni tuoi. . . . Consola l'anima mia; e non essere tanto crudele per la salute tua, di far caro d'una tua venuta. Non ti lassare ingannare, per timore nè per vergogna, al dimonio. Rompi questo nodo; vieni, vieni, figliuolo caris-simo").[44] Thus Catherine reassures her friends that she loves them and prays for them.

When her friends are ill, imprisoned, bereaved, or suffering economic difficulty, Catherine writes to express affection and consolation. Her advice manifests a certain concern with the practical side of life. For example, she suggests that the sick temper their ascetic practices. She says to Daniella of Orvieto, "If the body is weak and sick, one should not only stop fasting, but also eat meat; and if once a day is not enough, then four times a day. If one cannot stand up on the ground, then one should go to bed; and if one cannot kneel, then one should sit or lie down if necessary" ("Se il corpo è debile, venuto ad infermità, debbe non solamente lassare il digiuno, ma mangi della carne: e se non gli basta una volta il dì, pigline quattro. Se non può stare in terra, stia sul letto; se non può inginocchioni, sia a sedere e a giacere, se n'ha bisogno").[45] In other letters, Catherine's desire to assist her friends is reflected in her offer to intervene with the prefect of Rome to ask that he free a prisoner without exacting an enormous ransom, and in her request that friends visit another prisoner.[46] She begs financial assistance for poor nuns, and she tells a prostitute from Perugia that her brother has promised to support her if she renounces her profession.[47]

Because of her focus on the apostolate, Catherine rarely indicates that it is *she* who needs assistance, but on a few occasions she does insert short phrases indicating that she misses the companionship of a friend. Raymond of Capua, her confessor and disciple, was the person whose absence caused her most hardship at the end of her life when her attempts to help resolve the Schism were not meeting with success. She suggests in a parenthetical aside that her apostolic work would be easier if he were present: "I, a wretched slave, put in this field where blood is shed for love of [Christ's] blood (and you have left me here, and have gone off with God), will never stop working for you" ("Io vile schiava, che son posta nel campo, ove è sparto il sangue per amore del sangue (e voi mi ci avete lassata, e setevi andato con Dio), non mi ristarò mai di lavorare per voi").[48] In her last letter to Raymond Catherine expresses again her need for his friendship, but she sets his work for Church unity as a higher priority: "Do not be afflicted because we are physically separated from each other, for though it would be a very great consolation for me [to see you], the joy of seeing the fruit you make in the holy Church is a greater consolation" ("E non pigliate pena perchè corporalmente siamo separati l'uno dall'altro; e poniamochè a me fusse di grandissima consolazione, maggiore consolazione è l'allegrezza di vedere il frutto che fate nella santa Chiesa").[49]

It is usually in these end sections that Catherine discusses events in her own life and places other autobiographical materials, especially issues related to her apostolic activities. In a little less than half of the extant letters (about 160), the end sections show that Catherine's main goal in writing is to persuade her correspondents to take concrete political or ecclesiastical actions.[50] She sent these letters to advance the great causes which she held dear, such as peace in Italy, a crusade, Church reform, or the return of the Pope to Rome. Many of the letters she wrote between November 1378 and her death in April 1380 reflect her strong desire to end the Schism and her search for practical solutions.

For example, it is with reasoned arguments and outright threats that Catherine begs Urban's supporters to remain faithful and his opponents to return to the fold. She sends her disciples on mission to Genova and Naples. She asks nuns, bishops, and members of confraternities to say special prayers. Catherine suggests that Urban VI create good bishops and keep faithful friends at his side and she sends many letters to convince her more "spiritual" followers and acquaintances to join her in Rome for that purpose. In these sections of her letters, her tone also becomes self-assured and uncompromising. Catherine's individual voice emerges distinctly because she highlights the personal quality of her views with such words as *io* and *voglio*.

It is here that she shifts occasionally from offering her strongly opinionated advice to mentioning quite unapologetically her own participation as a protagonist in public affairs, especially her conversations with political and ecclesiastical officials. Particularly significant is her account of her first meeting with Pope Gregory XI in Avignon several years before the beginning of the Schism, when she worked to mediate a conflict between Florence and the Papacy. She writes the Florentines,

I have spoken with the holy Father. He heard me graciously, by God's goodness and his own, showing that he has an affectionate love for peace. . . . He took such a special delight in this that my tongue can hardly narrate it. After I had talked a good long time with him, at the conclusion of these words he said that if what I had put before him about you was true, he was ready to receive you as his sons and to do whatever seemed best to me.

Ho parlato al santo Padre. Udimmi, per la bontà di Dio e sua, graziosamente, mostrando d'avere affettuoso amor della pace. . . . Quanto egli ebbe singolare letizia, la lingua mia non il potrebbe narrare. Avendo ragionato con lui buono spazio di tempo, nella conclusione delle parole disse, che, essendo quello che io gli ponevo innanzi, di voi; egli era acconcio di ricevervi come figliuoli e di farne quello che ne paresse a me.[51]

Catherine usually keeps such autobiographical materials for the end sections of her letters. An important exception to this rule is a series of short narratives about her personal spiritual experiences which she inserts in the didactic portions of some twenty-five of her letters. Significantly, when she discusses these encounters with God, it is usually not to draw attention to her own uniqueness or supernatural powers; instead, her goal is to teach and encourage her correspondents to accomplish whatever they need to do for their own spiritual progress. While Raymond's *Legenda* highlights all that was miraculous and exceptional about Catherine's life with God, as we saw above, in her letters she describes her own experiences as simple, quite unspectacular dialogues between God and "a soul" or "a servant of God".[52]

In these dialogues God and Catherine talk about mainstream moral, theological, and spiritual matters. For example, Catherine begins a letter to "a great prelate" with an abstract exposition of the idea that the pain of Christ's desire to save humanity was greater than any physical suffering He endured. Then she inserts this more autobiographical passage to confirm and reinforce her idea:

This reminds me of what the sweet and good Jesus once manifested to a servant of His [Catherine]. She saw in Him the cross of desire and the cross of His body, and she asked: "My sweet Lord, what caused You greater pain, the pain of the body or the pain of desire?" He responded sweetly and benignly, and said, "My daughter, do not doubt. . . . As soon as I, the incarnate Word, was sown in Mary's womb, I began the cross of My desire to obey My Father and fulfil His will for man, that man be restored to grace and receive the end for which he was created. This cross brought Me greater suffering than any other physical pain I endured. . . ."

Questo mi ricordo che il dolce e buono Gesù manifestava una volta ad una serva sua. Vedendo ella in lui la croce del desiderio e la croce del corpo, ella dimandava: "Signore mio dolce, quale ti fu maggiore pena, o la pena del corpo, o la pena del desiderio?". Egli rispondeva dolce e benignamente, e diceva: "Figliuola mia, non dubitare. . . . Come io, Parola incarnata, fui seminata nel ventre di Maria, mi si cominciò la croce del desiderio ch'io avevo di fare l'obbedienza del Padre mio, e d'adempire la sua volontà nell'uomo; cioè che l'uomo fusse restituito a Grazia, e ricevesse il fine pel quale egli fu creato. Questa croce m'era maggiore pena che veruna altra pena ch'io portassi mai corporalmente. . . ."

This conversation continues for several pages. Then Catherine shifts back to the general lesson she wants the prelate to learn:

So you see well, reverend Father, that the sweet and good Jesus Love, He dies of thirst and hunger for our salvation. I beg you for the love of Christ crucified to take the hunger of this Lamb as your object. This is what my soul desires, to see you die from a holy and true desire, that is from the affection and love which you will have for the honor of God, the salvation of souls, and the exaltation of holy Church.

Adunque ben vedete, reverendo padre, che il dolce e il buono Gesù amore, egli muore de sete e di fame della salute nostra. Io vi prego per l'amore di Cristo crocifisso che voi vi poniate per obietto la fame di questo Agnello. Questo desidera l'anima mia, di vedervi morire per santo e vero desiderio, cioè che per l'affetto e amore che voi arete all'onore di Dio, salute dell'anime ed esaltazione santa Chiesa.[53]

Though Catherine revealed a great deal about herself throughout the *Epistolario*, she conveyed above all a strong identification with her varied apostolates. Even when she inserted personal dialogues with God in her letters, she wanted less to explore the intricacies of the self, or to write formal autobiography, than to present the self as a general model and source of encouragement to others. Such an extroverted self-portrait is essential also to Catherine's interpretation of her role as a writer of letters. Further analysis will show that Catherine developed her epistolary voice out of a deep need to communicate to others her experience of God and her views about political and ecclesiastical affairs. She believed that God had bestowed upon her a mission to speak. Undoubtedly the oral culture in which she lived facilitated her practice of that call.

"I Catherine write to you": Writing and Orality

Catherine's letters reflect a late fourteenth-century culture that was aware of the literate world but still essentially and self-consciously oral. Access to the public sphere, in her case, was facilitated by her reliance on an epistolary genre that partook of both the oral and the written. Far from representing a serious obstacle to her apostolate, her lack of education in such a context may well have constituted an advantage. Catherine's oral culture sharpened her capacity for speech and helped her to formulate ideas, opinions, and advice in a blunt, passionate, and articulate manner. Moreover, viewed as the written version of spoken words, letters held many advantages for someone like Catherine who felt a strong desire to influence other people. When her words were dictated to secretaries, they became letters which could reach extended audiences. Finally, such letters constituted an important meeting place of literate and oral cultures. Since both educated and uneducated people in the Middle Ages often dictated their letters, this genre enabled Catherine to enter the public sphere and to communicate with political and ecclesiastical leaders almost on a footing of equality.

Moreover, letters of the sort that Catherine sent were considered so ephemeral by her society as to be uncontroversial; they were personal and private documents, neither threatening nor as legally binding to their recipients, unlike official Latin or Italian epistles.[54] The private, oral, and momentary nature of Catherine's kind of letter writing was especially beneficial to women, who were forbidden official channels of communication and influence, but who could not be stopped from sending personal messages. Significantly, while Catherine's writings contain important evidence that her travels and unofficial preaching were criticized in her own day, there is no hint that anyone ever questioned her sending of letters, or that she felt the need to defend the legitimacy of her epistolary activities.[55] Rather, she indicates that dictating her correspondence is an enjoyable and worthy task that is obviously on a continuum with other forms of ordinary speech meant to benefit her neighbors.

In her statements about herself in the *Epistolario* Catherine specifies some of the ways in which letter writing was personally rewarding for her. Letters allow her "refreshment" ("recreazione") from the labors of the apostolate.[56] When she is suffering from physical ailments, dictating letters "distracts" her from her pain ("spassare le pene").[57] After she experiences union with God, writing about what she has learned helps her "unburden her heart" ("sfogare il cuore").[58] The most common sentiment which Catherine expresses about her motivations for writing, however, is that letters allow her to express love for her neighbor and that God Himself wants her to help save souls and resolve the problems of her day through her correspondence. For example, this is how she justifies the outspoken nature of a letter to the Queen of Naples: "Because I love you, I have been moved to write you, out of a famished desire for the salvation of your soul and body. . . . Now I have unburdened my conscience" ("Perchè io v'amo, mi sono mossa dall'affamato desiderio della vostra salute dell'anima e del corpo a scrivere a voi. . . . Ho scaricata la coscienzia mia").[59] Catherine's conscience bothered her equally for the Queen's adversary Pope Urban VI. She explains to him that she has written him with such "strong assurance" ("sicurtà") because she "was constrained by the divine Goodness, the general need, and the love I bear for you" ("costretta dall divina Bonta, e dal bisogno che si vede, e dall'amore ch'io porto a voi").[60]

Catherine's statements about herself as a writer reflect an apostolic, not a literary sensitivity. The closest she comes to expressing self-conscious pride in her writings is a note in the last letter she wrote as she was dying in Rome, probably in February 1380, to her confessor Raymond of Capua: "I also ask you to get your hands on my Book [the *Dialogue*] and every other writing of mine that you can find [presumably her letters], and do with them whatever will best serve the honor of God" ("Anco vi prego che il libro e ogni scrittura la quale trovaste di me . . . ; e fatene quello che vedete sia più onore di Dio").[61] That Catherine wants her works to be preserved and distributed by her confessor and friends reflects her awareness of their value and potential usefulness. But when she states that she hopes to further "the honor of God" she implies that her goal in writing is not literary but religious: she wants her letters to help save souls.

Catherine's lack of formal education ensured that her basic mentality remained that of an illiterate person. Though she was aware of the effects that literacy and study can have on people, Catherine consistently disapproved of these effects or downplayed them. For example, in several letters she delights in the fact that literacy is not a requirement for salvation. Christ crucified is the only "Book" one needs to read, she says. This "Book" was "written" with blood, not ink, and its large illuminated letters [*capoversi*] are Christ's wounds. The content of this Book is Jesus' virtues of humility and meekness. With such a Book, "who will be so illiterate with so low an understanding, that he will not be able to read it?" ("Quale sarà quello idiota grosso, di si basso intendimento che non lo sappia leggere?")[62]

Likewise, Catherine advises people to prefer the spiritual direction of "a humble and unschooled person who has a holy and upright conscience to that of a proud scholar who studies with much knowledge" ("Unde ti dico che molto meglio è ad andare per consiglio della salute dell'anima a uno idioto umile con santa e diritta coscienza, che a uno superbo letterato studiante con molta scienza").[63] Her distrust of formal education is reflected also in her condemnation of excessively rhetorical preaching. In a passage about bad priests in the *Dialogue*, Catherine writes that God said to her: "Their sermons are set up to please men and give pleasure to the ear, rather than give honor to Me; for they study not a good life, but very elegant speech" ("Le loro predicazioni sono fatte più a piacere degli uomini e per diletta-re l'orecchie loro che ad onore di me; e però studiano non in buona vita, ma in favellare molto pulito").[64]

The *Epistolario* provides important evidence that Catherine "wrote" through dictation, and that letters were an oral medium for her. First, her letters name several of her secretaries. In a letter to the Podestà of Siena, she says: "My female companions who used to write for me are not here now, and so it has been necessary for me to have Frate Raimondo write" ("Non ci sono ora le mie compagne che mi solevano scrivere: e però è stato di bisogno che io abbia fatto scrivere a frate Raimondo").[65] At the end of a letter to her disciple and friend Stefano Maconi, her secretary of the moment adds: "May the negligent and ungrateful writer be recommended to you" ("Il negligente e ingrato scrittore ti sia raccomandato").[66] Many other letters include similar greetings, often somewhat humorous and self-deprecating, which name Catherine's friends who served as her secretaries: "Alessa grassotta" (fatty Alessa Saracini), "Cecca perditrice di tempo (Francesca the time waster), "Giovanna Pazza" (crazy Giovanna Pazzi), "Francesco cattivo e pigro" (naughty and lazy Francesco Buònconti), "Neri del quattrino" (wealthy Neri Pagliaresi), and "Barduccio cieco" (blind Barduccio Canigiani).[67]

Second, some of the language which Catherine uses at the end of her letters to soften her reproofs of church prelates reflects the fact that she was writing with her tongue and her mouth—that is, that she was dictating. In a letter to Pope Urban VI a few months before her death she refers to her mouth: "Forgive me, most sweet and holy Father, if I say these words to you. . . . Do not despise or disdain them because they come out of the mouth of a most unworthy woman" ("Perdonatemi, dolcissimo e san-tissimo Padre, che io vi dica queste parole. Confidomi, che l'umiltà e benignità vostra è contenta che elle vi sieno dette, non avendole a schifo nè a sdegno perchè elle escano di bocca d'una villissima femmina").[68] In a cryptic message of a letter to Raymond of Capua concerning the beginning of the Schism and her opinion of Urban VI, she uses an odd mix of language about the mouth and the hand: "Now keep silent, my soul. I do not want to try my hand, dearest father, at saying that which I could not write with a pen or say with my tongue; but let my being silent manifest to you what I want to say" ("Or tieni silenzio, anima mia, e non parlare più. Non voglio mettere mano, carissimo padre, a dire quello che con penna non potrei scrivere nè con lingua parlare; ma il tacere vi manifesti quello ch'io voglio dire").[69] Catherine's wording shows that writing for her was simply a form of speaking.

Third, she views her letters as the written record of an oral discourse of hers which will be delivered orally to her correspondent by a messenger or carrier.[70] She asks Raymond of Capua to "announce to the Pope what I write in this letter, as the Holy Spirit will inspire you to do" ("annunziategli quello che io vi scrivo in questa lettera, secondo che lo Spirito Santo vi ministrerà").[71] Her Sienese disciple Sano di Maco receives a letter containing her request that he "read this letter to all my children" ("Voi prego, Sano, che a tutti i figliuoli leggiate questa lettera").[72] Catherine sends Stefano Maconi a note telling him to read two other letters she had enclosed, to give them to their addressees, that is, to the Government of Siena and to the members of a confraternity, and "to speak to them fully about this matter which is contained in the letters" ("Parla loro pienamente sopra questo fatto che si contiene nelle lettere").[73] In all these cases the written text is actually an oral medium, a means for her message to travel from her mouth to her friend's ear.

Fourth, for Catherine the writing of letters was really a form of speech, in continuity with other kinds of words which she believed God called her to utter, and that is, informal preaching and prayer. At the beginning of the Schism she writes Pope Urban VI about what she sees as the three compo-nents of her vocation: "As long as I live, I shall never stop spurring you on with my prayer, and with my live voice or my writing" (Io non mi resterò mai di stimolarvi coll'orazione, e con la voce viva o con scrivere, mentre che io viverò").[74]

Finally, Catherine said to many of her correspondents that she would have preferred direct oral discourse with them to dictating and sending written letters to them. For example, during the Schism she writes King Charles V of France, "It is love for your salvation that makes me say these things; I would much rather say them to you with my mouth and with my presence than in writing" ("L'amore della vostra salute mi costringe a più tosto dirvele a bocca con la presenzia, che per scritta").[75] "Let it not seem hard if I sting you with words, for it is the love of your salvation which has made me write you", she says to three schismatic cardinals. She then adds, "I'd rather sting you with my live voice, if God were to allow me to do so" ("Non vi parrà duro se io vi pungo con le parole, che l'amore della salute vostra m'ha fatto scrivere; e più tosto vi pungerei con voce viva, se Dio m'l permettesse").[76] Letters were only a poor substitute for the warmth of the human voice. Catherine clearly believes that her action would be far more effective if she could visit Urban VI's opponents, see their situation first hand, and address them directly with whatever tone and advice they seemed to need most.

Catherine's emphasis on speech brought her to reflect a great deal on the power and the morality of words, her own and those of her contemporaries. In her view words carry power, not because God grants supernatural effectiveness to the words of a few chosen individuals, but because words which represent strong personal emotions are always effective and persuasive. For her this is as true of the words of sinners as it is of the words of saints. For example, she attributes much of the urban violence she witnessed around her to the inflammatory power of hateful speech. God tells her: "As a result of words you have seen and heard of revolutions, the destruction of cities, and many evils and murders. For the word entered the center of the heart of the person to whom it was said; it entered where the knife could not have passed" ("Per le parole avete veduto e udito venire mutazioni di stati, disfacimento delle città e molti altri mali e omicidi; perchè la parola entrò nel mezzo del cuore a colui a cui fu detta: intrò dove non sarebbe passato il coltello").[77] Insults such as "You are a brute animal" cause an escalation of anger: "One word seems like a knifing, and if they do not answer with four words, they feel their heart will explode with poison!" ("Una parola gli pare una coltellata; e se essi non ne rispondono quattro, pare che il cuore scoppi veleno!").[78] "Sometimes this gives birth to injurious words, and these words are often followed by murder" ("Alcuna volta partorisce parole ingiuriose, dopo le quali parole spesse volte seguita l'omicidio").[79] In Catherine's experience, evil words almost inevitably lead to evil consequences.

Likewise, words that are good and holy cannot fail to pierce and convert the heart of their listeners. The key to holy words is their speaker's sincerity and godliness of purpose. Catherine explains that a sincere and open heart is one which "everyone can understand, for it does not demonstrate one thing on the face and the tongue, while it has another thing inside" ("Ogni uno el può intendere perchè non dimostra una cosa in faccia e in lingua, avendone dentro un'altra").[80] The "voice of the heart" is as effective a force for good as words of hatred are a force for violence and murder. When Catherine writes to the Romans that they should listen to her words because of the "affection and purity of heart with which I write to you" she is really expressing her trust that her letter will bear good fruit in the souls of those who hear it.[81]

Catherine's model for the power of good speech is the Apostles after Pentecost. As she writes to a Dominican preacher, "When the fire of the Holy Spirit came upon them, they climbed into the pulpit of the holy cross, and there they could feel and taste the hunger of the Son of God, and the great love he had for us; and so the words came out of them like a fiery knife out of the furnace, and with this warmth they pierced the hearts of those who listened" ("Perchè il fuoco dello Spirito Santo fu venuto sopra di loro, essi salsero in su'l pulpito dell'affocata croce, ed ine sentivano e gustavano la fame del Figliuolo di Dio, e l'amore che portava all'uomo: onde allora escivano le parole di loro, come esce il coltello affocato dalla fornace; e con questo caldo fendevano i cuori degli uditori").[82] Catherine explains the Apostles' success as preachers through the power of their deep identification with Christ's salvific love for humanity. The fire within their hearts becomes a fire potent enough to pierce through all obstacles in the hearts of their audience. Such is the fire which she wants her Dominican correspondent to communicate through his holy words.

Catherine does not believe that God gives this fire only to priests, however. She calls Mary Magdalene *apostola* and *discepola*, and she identifies personally with Christ's male and female apostles.[83] This apostolic fervor is echoed in a letter which she wrote her mother in 1377 to defend her own informal preaching mission in the Sienese countryside. Catherine asked her mother to treat her with the same understanding which Mary showed her Son's Apostles after Pentecost: "The disciples, who loved her without measure, actually leave joyfully and sustain every pain [of the separation] to give honor to God; and they go among tyrants, bearing many persecutions. . . . You must know, dearest mother, that I, your miserable daughter, have not been put on earth for anything else: my Creator elected me to this" ("I discepoli che l'amavano smisuratamente, anco, con allegrezza si partono, sostenendone ogni pena per onore di Dio; e vanno fra i tiranni, sentendo le molte persecuzioni. . . . Sappiate, carissima madre, che io miserabile figliuola, non son posta in terra per altro. A questo m'ha eletta il mio Creatore").[84] Fortified by the example of the Apostles, Catherine too is willing to travel, preach to the "tyrants" of her day, and bear many "persecutions," for she is convinced that it is her vocation to utter relentlessly earnest, passionate, and ultimately persuasive words.

Catherine's approach to speech provides the key to how she explained her success as an apostle and a writer of letters. She is convinced that if one's words are inspired by a sincere and humble desire to obey the promptings of the Holy Spirit and to help bring salvation to souls, then one's speech cannot fail to effect good. For Catherine this holds true for all kinds of speech: oral discourse is especially effective, but letters are influential to the degree that the power of her original voice dictating those words can be transmitted onto the written page. Moreover, this power and influence are present not only in the exceptional words of a few saints, but also in the ordinary words of all kinds of people, including Popes, ordained priests, politicians, and even well-intentioned lay women like herself.[85]

Conclusion: Women and Oral Culture

It is Catherine's trust that her sincere words would bear fruit in the hearts of her various audiences that propelled her, a woman, into the public sphere as a writer of letters, and that explained, at least to her satisfaction, whatever measure of influence and success she enjoyed in her apostolic work. This understanding of herself is significantly different from the portrayal of her in the hagiographical literature. One recalls that Raymond of Capua emphasized the supernatural quality of her life, including the miraculous components of her writing letters, in order to defend her sanctity as an ignorant and weak female vessel completely filled with divine power. Her being a woman was one of the issues which concerned Raymond the most. Though this view of Catherine may reflect how many of her contemporaries explained the impact of her voice and why they were willing to listen to her, it does not explain how she became confident enough to speak, because this was not her self-understanding.

Catherine did not focus on whatever might have been exceptional in her life. Her main desire was to love her neighbor and advance her various political and ecclesiastical causes through ordinary written and oral speech. Perhaps the most significant characteristic of her approach is her silence about the fact that she was a woman engaging in these activities. Catherine does not mention even once in the *Epistolario* that her apostolate was controversial because of her gender. Among the social categories she discusses, male and female distinctions have no place. She does not reflect on what a female "nature" might be: if she believes herself to be a sinner in need of divine mercy and assistance, she does not attribute her failings to a particularly "female weakness." Though it is known that at the time of the Schism she suggested a mode of life somewhat like her own to at least one other woman, she did not found a religious community of female activists.[86] Unlike her near contemporary Christine de Pizan, Catherine did not feel the need to defend the female sex from attack in any way.[87]

Why did Catherine not talk about herself as a woman? Faced with the paradox of an influential activist woman who did not write about gender, one must conclude that she was relatively indifferent to gender, and that God and the success of her apostolic causes mattered to her more. It is likely that Catherine's oral culture was one reason for that indifference. The feminist consciousness of a writer such as Christine de Pizan arose out of a clearer awareness of the classical and medieval intellectual tradition of misogyny than Catherine could ever have achieved. Christine begins her *Book of the City of Ladies* by describing herself seated in her study and in a state of considerable discomfort because she perceives that throughout history so many learned men have insulted women in their books. Her interest in defending women comes from the realization that they have been unjustly attacked. Catherine may have been less vulnerable to negative views of women because she was not used to reading books. Her lack of education may have shielded her from the more virulent and debilitating theories of misogyny prevalent in her time. Instead, she saw other urgent needs in her world and her Church, and she spoke her mind about them in a manner which was very much her own creation.

Notes

1. For an analysis the events of the Schism and Catherine's participation in them, see Arrigo Levasti, *S. Caterina da Siena* (Turin: U.T.E.T., 1947), pp. 414–500;

Giles Meerseman, "Gli amici spirituali di S. Caterina a Roma alla luce del primo manifesto urbanista," *Bulletino Senese di Storia Patria* 69 (1962): 83–123; André Vauchez, "La sainteté mystique en Occident au temps des papes d'Avignon et du Grand Schisme," in *Genèse et débuts du Grand Schisme d'Occident: Avignon, 25– 28 septembre 1978* (Paris: Éditions du Centre National de la Recherche Historique, 1980), pp. 361–68.

2. The edition of Catherine's letters that I have used here is *Le Lettere di S. Caterina da Siena*, ed. Piero Misciatelli (Florence: Giunti, 1940), 6 vols. The letters Catherine sent on May 6, 1379 are numbers 347, 348, 349 and 350, in *Lettere*, vol. 5, pp. 165–87. All translations in this paper are my own.

3. In addition to Catherine's letters, one can find much information about her activities during the Schism in her main *vita*, Raymond of Capua's *Legenda Major*. This text is published under the title of *De S. Catharina Sensensi virgine de poenitentia S. Dominici*, in *Acta Sanctorum Aprilis*, vol. 3 (Antwerp, 1675), pp. 853– 959. A recent English translation of the *Legenda* is *The Life of Catherine of Siena*, trans. Conleth Kearns (Wilmingon, DE: Michael Glazier, 1980).

4. S. Caterina da Siena, *Il Dialogo della divina provvidenza ovvero Libro della divina dottrina*, ed. Giuliana Cavallini (Rome: Edizioni cateriniane, 1980). The most recent English translation is *The Dialogue*, trans. Suzanne Noffke (New York: Paulist Press, 1980).

5. For a full presentation of the evidence, see Karen Scott, "Not Only With Words, But With Deeds: The Role of Speech in Catherine of Siena's Understanding of Her Mission" (Doctoral dissertation, University of California, Berkeley, 1989).

6. A modern critical edition exists only for the first eighty-eight letters which Catherine sent between the early 1370s and the end of 1376: S. Caterina da Siena, *Epistolario*, ed. Eugenio Dupré Theseider (Rome: Tipografia del Senato, 1940). This volume has been translated recently into English: *The Letters of Catherine of Siena*, trans. Suzanne Noffke (Binghamton, NY: Center for Medieval and Early Renaissance Studies, 1988). Antonio Volpato of the University of Rome is currently working to complete Dupré Theseider's critical edition.

7. Amadeo Quondam, "Dal 'Formulario' al 'Formulario': cento anni di 'Libri di lettere'," in *Le "carte messaggiere." Retorica e modelli di comunicazione epistolare: per un indice dei libri di lettere del Cinquecento* (Rome: Bulzoni, 1981), pp. 13–156, esp. p. 60. See also Carlo Dionisotti, *Gli umanisti e il volgare fra quattro e cinquecento* (Florence: F. Le Monnier, 1968), pp. 3–5; and Gabriella Zarri, "Le sante vive. Per una tipologia della santità femminile nel primo Cinquecento," *Annali dell'Istituto storico italo-germanico in Trento* 6 (1980): 408–9.

8. Anton Franceso Doni, *La Libraria*, ed. Vanni Bramanti (Milano: Longanesi, 1972), p. 195. Doni also included Catherine's letters and the *Dialogue* in another list of titles, in the category of texts available in the vernacular: *La Libraria*, pp. 208, 210. The only other female writers mentioned in that second list are Angela of Foligno, Tullia, Olimpia, Terracina, and Isabella Sforza. For a short study of Doni's work, and Catherine's mention in it, see Quondam, "Dal Formulario," p. 59.

9. *L'Opere di Santa Caterina da Siena, nuovamente pubblicate da Girolamo Gigli* (Siena, 1707–1726). The *Vocabolario cateriniano* constitutes volume 5 of Gigli's

work. See Augusta Theodosia Drane, *The History of St. Catherine of Siena and Her Companions* (London: Longmans, Green, 1915), p. xviii.

10. N. Sapegno, *Il Trecento* (Milan: Vallardi, 1966), p. 495; Giovanni Getto, *Saggio letterario su S. Caterina da Siena* (Florence: G. C. Sansoni, 1939).

11. An early study of the link between vernacular writing and women is Herbert Grundmann, *Religiöse Bewegungen im Mittelalter* (1935); see also the Italian translation *Movimenti religiosi nel Medioevo* (Bologna: il Mulino, 1974), esp. Ch. 8. For an illuminating discussion of stylistic aspects of medieval women's writings, see Elizabeth Alvida Petroff, "Introduction" to *Medieval Women's Visionary Literature* (New York and Oxford: Oxford University Press, 1986), pp. 3–59.

12. There is a growing historiography on women, politics, and religion in late medieval Italy. See for an example Christiane Klapisch-Zuber, *Women, Family, and Ritual in Renaissance Italy*, trans. Lydia Cochrane (Chicago and London: University of Chicago Press, 1985). For a review of the literature see Scott, "Not Only With Words" (note 5), pp. 117–25, 139–48.

13. Recent studies of the growth of Italian literacy include Franco Cardini, "Alfabetismo e livelli di cultura nell'età comunale," *Quaderni storici* 13 (1978): 488–522; Peter Burke, "The Uses of Literacy in Early Modern Italy," in *The Historical Anthropology of Early Modern Italy: Essays on Perception and Communication* (Cambridge: Cambridge University Press, 1987), pp. 110–31; and Paul F. Grendler, *Schooling in Renaissance Italy: Literacy and Learning, 1300–1600* (Baltimore: Johns Hopkins University Press, 1989).

14. Though Catherine's historical significance as an activist and writer has not been explored in depth in recent historical scholarship, her life has usually been subsumed under the category of prophecy and visionary activity. For example, Rudolph Bell, Anna Benvenuti Papi, Caroline Bynum, John Coakley, Richard Kieckhefer, and André Vauchez have recently noted Catherine's extreme fasting, rigorous ascetic practices, and mystical religious experiences, and have used them to explain how she gained fame as a holy woman: see Rudolph M. Bell, *Holy Anorexia* (Chicago and London: University of Chicago Press, 1985), pp. 22–53; Anna Benvenuti Papi, "Penitenza e santità femminile in ambiente cateriniano e bernardiniano," in *Atti del simposio internazionale cateriniano—bernardiniano, Siena, 17–20 aprile 1980*, ed. Domenico Maffei and Paolo Nardi (Siena: Accademia senese degli intronati, 1982), pp. 865–78, esp. 872; Caroline Walker Bynum, *Holy Feast and Holy Fast: The Significance of Food to Medieval Women* (Berkeley and Los Angeles: University of California Press, 1987), pp. 165–80; John Wayland Coakley, "The Representation of Sanctity in Late Medieval Hagiography: The Evidence from *Lives* of Saints of the Dominican Order" (Th.D. dissertation, Harvard University, 1980); Richard Kieckhefer, *Unquiet Souls: Fourteenth Century Saints and Their Religious Milieu* (Chicago and London: University of Chicago Press, 1984); and André Vauchez, "Les Représentations de la sainteté d'après les procès de canonization médiévaux (XIII–XVe siècles)," in *Convegno internazionale. Agiografia nell'occidente cristiano, secoli XIII–XV, Roma (1–2 marzo 1979)* (Rome: Accademia nazionale dei lincei, 1980), pp. 31–43.

15. Like Raymond of Capua, Catherine's second most important hagiographer Thomas Caffarini believed that she miraculously learned to read and dictated

her letters. However, unlike Raymond he stated that toward the end of her life Catherine learned to write in her own hand through a further divine miracle. He limited this claim, though, by stating that she herself had written only two letters, the concluding part of the *Dialogue*, and a prayer, and thus by implying that on the whole she continued to function most comfortably within her oral culture. See *Il Processo Castellano*, ed. M.-H. Laurent, Fontes Vitae S. Catharinae Senensis Historici, vol. 9 (Milan: Bocca, 1942), pp. 51, 62; and *Libellus de Supplemento: Legenda prolixe virginis Beate Catharine de Senis*, ed. Giuliana Cavallini and Imelda Foralosso (Rome: Edizioni Cateriniane, 1974), pp. 77–79. Caffarini's views may be based on Catherine's L. 272, in *Lettere*, vol. 4, p. 172.

16. *Legenda*, p. 881, col. 1: "Verum, quia mentio facta est hic de psalmodia, scire te, lector, volo, quod virgo haec sacra litteras quidem sciebat, sed eas homine viatore docente nequaquam didicerat: & dico literas, non quod sciret loqui Latinum, sec scivit legere literas & proferre." Unable to learn to read in an ordinary way, Catherine asks God for a miracle: "Antequam de oratione surgeret, ita divinitus est edocta, quod postquam ab ipsa surrexit, omnem scivit litteram legere, tam velociter & expedite, sicut quicumque doctissimus. Quod ego ipse dum fui expertus, stupebam: potissime propter hoc, quod inveni, quia cum velocissime legeret, si jubebatur syllabicare, in nullo sciebat aliquid dicere: imo vix literas cognoscebat: quod aestimo pro signo miraculi ordinatum a Domino tunc fuisse" (*Legenda*, p. 881, col. 1–2).

17. Overall, the story sounds similar to the achievement of small children who have heard their parents read stories to them so often that they memorize the words and can pretend to read as they recite what they know by heart.

A further indication that Raymond considered Catherine's Latin literacy weak is the fact that though she could "read" Latin in that particular way, she could not use this language fluently for prayer, writing, or direct speech. Throughout her life, he said, she loved to repeat the prayers which begin the divine Office, but she did so not in Latin but in the vernacular. See *Legenda*, p. 881, col 2: "Verbum psalmi, per quod quaelibet hora incipitur, scilicet: Deus in adjutorium meum intende, Domine ad adjuvandum me festina: quod in vulgari reductum, frequentius repetebat." Raymond also mentioned that when Catherine visited Avignon to speak with Pope Gregory XI in 1376, he had to serve as her interpreter because she spoke no French or Latin: *Legenda*, p. 925, col. 2 and p. 956, col. 2. He did not comment at all on any ability of hers to read or write Italian.

18. *Legenda*, p. 881, col. 2: "Coepit libros quaerere divinum Officium continentes, & in ipsis legere psalmos, hymnos, & reliqua quae pro canonicis Horis sunt deputata."

19. See Grundmann, *Movimenti religiosi*, pp. 156, 281; and comments by Jean Gerson quoted by Caroline Walker Bynum, "Jesus as Mother and Abbot as Mother: Some Themes in Twelfth-Century Cistercian Writing" in *Jesus as Mother: Studies in the Spirituality of the High Middle Ages* (Berkeley, Los Angeles and London: University of California Press, 1982), pp. 134–35.

20. *Legenda*, "first prologue," p. 854, col. 2.

21. See *Legenda*, p. 883, col. 1–2. For an analysis of the place of these passages in the *Legenda* as a whole, see Scott, "Not Only With Words", pp. 161–81. For the

view that medieval interpretations of women viewed their "natural" vulnerability and weakness as the female avenue to power and strength, see Bynum, *Holy Feast*, and Barbara Newman, *Sister of Wisdom. St. Hildegard's Theology of the Feminine* (Berkeley and Los Angeles: University of California Press, 1987). I shall argue below that Catherine did not share Raymond's or Hildegard's "theology of the feminine."

22. *Legenda*, First Prologue, p. 854, col 2: "Quamvis enim proprio sermone vulgari loquatur in eis, quia non cognovit letteraturam: quia tamen introivit in potentias Domini cum clavi profunditatis profundae, stylus eius (si quis diligenter advertit) potius videtur Pauli quam Catharinae, melius alicujus Apostoli quam cujuscumque puellae"; and "Sententiae sunt tam altae pariter & profundae, quod si eas in Latino perceperis prolatas, Aurelii Augustini putes potius fuisse quam cujuscumque alterius."

23. *Legenda*, p. 885, col. 1.

24. *Legenda*, p. 937, col. 1–2. Raymond also discusses Catherine's desire to travel to Naples to persuade Queen Giovanna to support Urban VI. His intent in describing her activities during the Schism may be to portray her life as a model for the *vita apostolica*. He mentions that her group of followers in Rome lived together in voluntary poverty, and "chose to travel and beg with the holy virgin" ("eligentes magis cum sacra virgine peregrinari & mendicare"; *Legenda*, p. 937, col. 1.) He gives no hint that such a mode of life involving mendicant itinerant preaching was controversial for lay women and men in his time; he may have had in mind the observant reform he was promoting among friars as Master General of the Dominican Order at the time he was composing the *Legenda*. For Raymond's use of Catherine's life to promote the Urbanist Papacy and his own observant reform, see Coakley, "The Representation of Sanctity," pp. 86–90.

There is another interesting account of Catherine "preaching" to men. Raymond writes that at some unspecified time the prior of the Carthusian monastery on the island of Gorgona, near Pisa, invited her and some twenty companions to come to the island and speak to his monks. The entire community walked to the lodging where she and her female companions (*socia*) were staying. The prior "cunctos Fratres duxit ad eam, rogans aedificationis verbum pro filiis. . . . Tandem aperuit os suum, & locuta est prout Spiritus sanctus dabat . . ." (*Legenda*, p. 927, col. 1).

25. For example, see the letters published by Lodovico Zdekauer in his *Lettere familiari del Rinascimento senese (1409–1525)* (Siena, 1897) and *Lettere volgari del Rinascimento senese* (Siena, 1897); *Le Lettere di Giovanni Colombini*, ed. Dino Fantozzi (Lanciano, n.d.); "Le Lettere di Margherita Datini a Francesco di Marco," ed. Valeria Rosati, *Archivio storico pratese* XLX (1974): 4–93.

26. L. 349 in *Lettere*, vol. 5, pp. 219–25. This is one of the few letters of the *Epistolario* which is dated. The rubrics which are found in the first letter collections and were printed in the first editions indicate also that the letter was dictated while Catherine was in a state of ecstacy: "A dì 6 Maggio 1379. In astrazione fatta."

27. L. 349, p. 177.

28. L. 349, p. 178.

29. L. 349, pp. 178–79. Raymond of Capua suggests in the *Legenda* that Urban's decision to walk barefoot in a procession of thanksgiving was due to Catherine's direct influence: see *Legenda*, p. 940, col. 1.

30. L. 349, pp. 179–80.

31. L. 349, p. 180.

32. L. 349, p. 180.

33. Catherine indicates that she is answering a letter from a correspondent in sixty-six of her letters. She mentions receiving sixty-nine letters from a total of fifty different people or groups of people. Her politically prominent correspondents were Pope Gregory XI, Niccolò Soderini of Florence, Bernabò Visconti the Duke of Milan, Queen Giovanna of Naples, and the governments of Siena and Bologna. None of the letters which Catherine mentions having received is to be found among the four extant letters which were sent to her (by Tommaso Caffarini, Bernabò Visconti's daughter-in-law Elizabeth of Bavaria, the Prior of the Carthusian monastery of Gorgona, and the Abbot of Monte Oliveto); see *Lettere*, vol. 6, pp. 45–53.

34. Catherine's formula is her original variation on the ordinary salutation one finds at the beginning of other Trecento letters: "In God's name. Amen" ("Al nome di Dio. Amen"). The formulas with which she ended all of her letters are similarly her own.

35. On the epistolary form as it was used in the Middle Ages, see Giles Constable, *Letters and Letter Collections*, Typologie des sources du Moyen Âge occidental, fasc. 17 (Turnhout: Brepols, 1976); and James J. Murphy, *Rhetoric in the Middle Ages. A History of Rhetorical Theory from St. Augustine to the Renaissance* (Berkeley and Los Angeles: University of California Press, 1974), pp. 194–268. For late medieval Italian letters see Nicola De Blasi, "La lettera mercantile tra formulario appreso e lingua d'uso," *Quaderni di retorica e poetica* 1 (1985): 39–47. In contrast to most medieval writers of letters who used their opening salutations to emphasize the differences in social level of their correspondents, Catherine kept her opening salutations very simple.

36. Though the content of Catherine's didactic sections is conventional and similar to that found in letters by other religious figures of the Middle Ages, both men and women, the division of each letter into two distinct parts—general and personal—and the ordered structure of the didactic section seem more idiosyncratic.

37. For example, self-knowledge and humility are a "treasure" one should "buy" and "possess." One should dwell in the "shop," "cavern," "cell," "house" of self-knowledge and love of God. Humility is also one's "armour" and "sword" in the "battle" against spiritual "enemies"; or it is "clothing," a "belt," a "pin." Humility is the charity's "wetnurse" or "mother"; self-knowledge "feeds" the "hungry" soul. It is a "deep abyss," or a "fertile" "ground" upon which all the virtues are "planted." For a "dictionary" of Catherine's imagery, see Gabriella Anodal, *Il linguaggio cateriniano* (Siena: Edizioni Cantagalli, 1983).

38. For examples of how Catherine's spiritual advice can differ from one letter to another, see Karen Scott, "La tolleranza religiosa nel pensiero di Santa Caterina da Siena," *Nuovi studi cateriniani* 2 (1985): 97–111; and "La pratica della tolleranza religiosa da parte di S. Caterina," *Nuovi studi cateriniani* 3 (1987): 5–26.

39. L. 217 in *Lettere*, vol. 3, p. 257.

40. L. 258 in *Lettere*, vol. 4, pp. 96–97.

41. L. 190 in *Lettere*, vol. 3, p. 143.

42. L. 16 in *Lettere*, vol. 1, pp. 54–56; and L. 177, vol. 3, pp. 92–93.

43. L. 99 in *Lettere*, vol. 2, pp. 117–18.

44. L. 45 in *Lettere*, vol. 1, pp. 180–182.

45. L. 213 in *Lettere*, vol. 3, p. 233.

46. L. 89 (XIV) in *Lettere*, vol. 6, p. 36; and L. 254, in *Lettere*, vol. 4, p. 82.

47. For letters about poor nuns, see L. 88, 129, 170, 198; L. 276 is addressed to the prostitute from Perugia.

48. L. 344 in *Lettere*, vol. 5, p. 155.

49. L. 373 in *Lettere*, vol. 5, p. 292.

50. An even greater proportion of Catherine's letters than this probably contained practical suggestions for political or ecclesiastical action. It is known that some of her early editors cut out the more practical end sections of the letters and published only the moral and spiritual lessons which they considered more useful for the general religious edification of the faithful. It would be a mistake to conclude from this that the early editors sustantially altered the content or the wording of those sections of Catherine's letters which they did publish, for the evidence is that they left the didactic lessons intact.

To reconstruct Catherine's political and ecclesistical activities from her *Epistolario* is not an easy task. Unfortunately for modern scholars, most of her letters were probably not dated: only three of the eight originals are dated. However, even when dates were originally included, they were usually placed at the end of the end sections, and thus some dates were probably cut out. See Robert Fawtier, *Sainte Catherine de Sienne: Essai de critique des sources*, vol. 2 (Paris: E. de Boccard, 1930), Ch. 7–8.

Five of the original letters are preserved in Ms. T.III.3 of the Biblioteca Comunale of Siena: L. 298, 320, 319, 329, and 332. The other letters are preserved in a Sienese Confraternity (L. 365); at the monastery of San Rocco in Arcireale (L. 192); and at Saint Aloysius church in Oxford. This last letter is not numbered; Robert Fawtier published it in "Catheriniana," *Mélanges d'archéologie et d'histoire* 34 (1914): 31–32.

51. L. 230 in *Lettere*, vol. 3, p. 312.

52. Significantly, Catherine uses a very similar dialogue form to convey important theological and spiritual insights in her masterpiece called, appropriately, the *Dialogue of Divine Providence*.

53. L. 16 in *Lettere*, vol. 1, pp. 52–53.

54. The fact that only eight of Catherine's original letters survived may reflect the difficulties of the Trecento postal system, as well as the private nature of such an *epistolario*.

55. See below for examples of Catherine's response to criticism of her itinerant preaching.

56. L. 373 in *Lettere*, vol. 5, p. 291.

57. L. 119 in *Lettere*, vol. 2, p. 190.

58. L. 272 in *Lettere*, vol. 4, pp. 171–72.

59. L. 312 in *Lettere*, vol. 5, p. 14.

60. L. 364 in *Lettere*, vol. 5, p. 251.

61. L. 373 in *Lettere*, vol. 5, p. 291.

62. L. 309 in *Lettere*, vol. 4, p. 294. See also L. 316 and 318. Catherine's letters show that though she is aware the Christian Scriptures are actually written texts, the Bible she is familiar with is the oral text proclaimed and preached in church. She knows the provenance of certain phrases: "Taste and see" ("Gustate et vedete") comes from the Psalter, and "Come beloved bride" ("Vieni, diletta sposa mia") is part of the Song of Songs ("Cantica"). She has heard of the Old Testament ("Testamento vecchio"). She mentions the "Gospel" quite often, and she notes once that St. Paul communicated in "letters" ("pistola") (*Dialogo*, XI, p. 27). Still, for Catherine Scripture mostly takes the form of short pithy sayings; she does not comment on long Biblical texts or differentiate among the evangelists as writers. She is interested in what Jesus said, or in what God's trumpeter ("banditore") Paul said, not in where and how those spoken words were written.

63. *Dialogo* LXXXV, pp. 194–95. Significantly, two centuries later the literate Teresa of Avila would advise the opposite to her nuns. See *The Life of Teresa of Jesus. The Autobiography of St. Teresa of Avila*, trans. E. Allison Peers (Garden City, NY: Image Books, 1960), Ch. XIII, pp. 144–47.

64. *Dialogo* CXXV, p. 316.

65. L. 135 in *Lettere*, vol. 2, p. 257.

66. L. 320 in *Lettere*, vol. 5, p. 60.

67. I have counted over thirty letters with probable references to secretaries. The question of how much these men and women influenced the content of Catherine's letters as they took her dictation or made clean copies of the texts is important and difficult. They certainly controlled details of spelling and punctuation, and it is likely that they inserted something of their own here and there. But they also revered Catherine as their spiritual teacher, and they would have felt that altering her words was sacrilegeous. The opening and closing formulas bear Catherine's personal mark; her style and use of imagery are equally idiosyncratic. Overall, the letters do seem to convey Catherine's voice.

68. L. 370 in *Lettere*, vol. 5, p. 272.

69. L. 330 in *Lettere*, vol. 5, p. 87.

70. In some cases Catherine entrusted the carrier with an oral message that was too important to be written down. See L. 295 in *Lettere*, vol. 4, p. 243: "Lasso questo e l'altre cose dire a Cristofano."

71. L. 267 in *Lettere*, vol. 4, p. 147.

72. L. 294 in *Lettere*, vol. 4, p. 239.

73. L. 368 in *Lettere*, vol. 5, p. 265.

74. L. 364 in *Lettere*, vol. 5, p. 252.

75. L. 350 in *Lettere*, vol. 5, p. 187.

76. L. 310 in *Lettere*, vol. 4, p. 306.

77. *Dialogo*, p. 217.

78. L. 318 in *Lettere*, vol. 5, p. 52.

79. *Dialogo*, p. 15.

80. S. Caterina da Siena, *Le Orazioni*, ed. Giuliana Cavallini (Rome: Edizioni cateriniane, 1978): Orazione III, p. 88.

81. L. 349 in *Lettere*, vol. 5, p. 180.

82. L. 198 in *Lettere*, vol. 3, p. 172.

83. Karen Scott, "St. Catherine of Siena, '*Apostola*'," *Church History* 61 (March 1992): 34–46.

84. L. 117 in *Lettere*, vol. 2, p. 185.

85. See also Sharon Farmer, "Persuasive Voices: Clerical Images of Medieval Wives," *Speculum* 61 (1986): 517–43.

86. L. 316 in *Lettere*, vol. 5, pp. 37–41.

87. Christine de Pizan, *The Book of the City of Ladies*, trans. Earl Jeffrey Richards (London: Pan Books, 1983).

Diane Watt

"No Writing for Writing's Sake": The Language of Service and Household Rhetoric in the Letters of the Paston Women.

An exchange of private letters creates an ongoing dialogue between writer and recipient. From them the critic can analyze the character of the writer, her or his relationship with and attitudes to the recipient, and their respective social roles and positions. The letter can be on the one hand conventionalized and influenced by the writer's culture and on the other an expression of the writer's individuality and immediate personal experience.[1] The epistolary form is capable of allowing greater self-analysis than almost any other medieval literary mode (except perhaps the "confession"); this potential is exemplified in the correspondence of Héloïse. Yet, although most of the Paston letters are written for a limited and private audience, they contain little inner reflection. On reading Gairdner's edition of the Paston letters, Virginia Woolf commented, "in all this there is no writing for writing's sake; no use of the pen to convey pleasure or amusement or any of the million shades of endearment and intimacy which have filled so many English letters since."[2] Woolf's evaluation is too harsh—both self-conscious artistry and expressions of emotion are found in this collection—but while the letters of Héloïse to Abélard describe so evocatively the writer's own longing, need and suffering, there is no place in the Paston correspondence for such extended self-examination.

The Paston letters include the largest collection of personal writings by one woman in Middle English—the correspondence of Margaret Paston.[3] Historians and philologists have long been aware of the Paston correspondence, but its potential has been given inadequate recognition by literary critics, despite the dearth of writing by women in the Middle Ages.[4] Medieval women authors seldom wrote for literary reasons and the fifteenth-century Paston letters are a case in point. The correspondence as a whole is concerned with domestic and business matters and the letters were not intended for publication—in fact, one letter from Margaret Paston carries the instruction (which was evidently ignored): "Lete this letter be brent whan ye haue vnderstond it" (no.213).[5] Such caution was at times necessary because of the local hostility generated by the swift rise to prominence of the Paston household during the Wars of the Roses. When John Falstoff, a wealthy Norfolk knight, made his friend and trustee John Paston I beneficiary under his will, the inheritance was disputed and a long period of conflict followed. John Paston I, his father, wife (Margaret) and heirs (the brothers John II and John III) preserved much of their correspondence as potential evidence for future legal disputes; John Paston I is said by Margaret to have "in hys trobyll seson set more by hys wrytyngys and evydens than he dede by any of his moveabell godys" (no.198).

The Paston women write most frequently either as householders in their own right or as their absent husbands' representatives.[6] John Paston I entrusts his wife with "the god gouernaunce of my housold and guydyng of other thynges touchyng my profite" (no.72). The women write business letters, keep their husbands informed about the running of the estates, and maintain contact between different members of the household. Obviously the collection of letters as it stands represents only a part of the original correspondence; some drafts and letters were not preserved in the first place, while over the centuries others have been lost or destroyed. For these reasons it is more than likely that many letters written by or to the Paston women have not survived. There are no letters written by Margaret Paston's two daughters and only two by Elizabeth, the sister of John I. These may have been kept because one relates to her marriage and the other to her inheritance of her husband's estate.

The existing letters of the Paston women may seem localized in their concerns, even rurally domesticated; Norman Davis described Margaret Paston as "old-fashioned, or provincial, or both."[7] Margaret certainly spent less time away from the family estates than her husband, but she did travel around Norfolk and was not isolated from the centres of political and economic control which, in the fifteenth century, were still largely based in the great households of the localities.[8] Unfortunately, there is no one full account of the rhetoric of the late medieval household. However, an examination of the backgrounds of the main writers in the Paston family and the context of the correspondence will reveal that the letters of the Paston women, far from being parochial, were written in a style appropriate to their function as household correspondence. Furthermore, the letters reveal that the women at times dominated the domestic sphere and even confronted local political power: Margaret Paston in particular emerges as a courageous and forceful woman, dedicated to augmenting the honor of the family into which she had married.

Education and Background

> Grammar, and nonsense, and learning.
> —Oliver Goldsmith

The four most prolific letter writers are respectively Margaret, her sons John II and John III, and her husband John I. Previous studies have suggested that Margaret, to whom are attributed 107 out of the 421 letters and papers written by members of the family, received very little if any formal schooling, while it is known that John I was given an extensive education: he went to Trinity Hall and Peterhouse, Cambridge, and completed his studies at the Inner Temple.[9] Norman Davis has contended that Margaret Paston and her mother-in-law Agnes were probably illiterate, basing his argument on the claim that none of their letters are written in their own hands.[10] Against this position it ought to be noted that John Paston I, who obviously could write, frequently relied on a secretary, as only three of his letters are entirely autographic. Even if one accepts the proposition that neither of these women was able to write, it should not be assumed that they were completely illiterate. Two of the Paston women are known to have had books in their possession: Agnes borrowed a copy of *Stimulus Conscientiae* and her daughter Anne owned a copy of *The Siege of Thebes*. Although these books may have been read to the women rather than by them, other evidence suggests that Agnes, who at times took full responsibility for the running of the household, may have been at least partially literate. Her dying husband entrusted her with the variation of his will and she records that "inmediatly after my husbondys decesse I hopynd and declaryd to John Paston and al the other excectorys of my husbond, desyeryng hem to haue performyd it" (no. 32).[11]

The Pastons regarded a knowledge of the law as crucial to the education of men. Agnes Paston gave this advice to her second son Edmond: "(I) avyse yow to thynkke onis of the daie of yowre fadris counseyle to lerne the lawe; for he seyde manie tymis that ho so euer schuld dwelle at Paston schulde have nede to conne defende hymselfe" (no.14). Experience had shown that the Paston estates, an indication of the family's social status, could be more adequately protected at law than by force. Furthermore the legal profession was financially rewarding, and with money the Pastons could buy and marry their way up the social hierarchy. Although, as in the case of Margaret Paston, there are no records of the schooling of John II or John III, both would probably have attended a grammar school where they would certainly have been taught Latin, one of the languages of the Common Law, and possibly even basic business studies.[12] Both brothers, like their father before them, received judicial appointments and sat in the House of Commons. Understanding of the law was not, however, the prerogative of the men. The letters sent and received by the women of the family clearly demonstrate that they had acquired considerable legal acumen. In 1465, for example, Margaret Paston took the initiative in the recovery of property at Drayton seized by the Duke of Suffolk. While household servants attempted to hold court at Drayton manor, Margaret attended the shire court in person and successfully entreated the judges to intervene in the dispute (no.189). At the same time Margaret was entrusted by her husband to deliver writs and obtain warrants to enable the recovery of livestock lost in the feuding (no.74). The extent of the women's familiarity with legal terminology and their understanding of the legal issues which they had to address in the course of running the household and estates provides evidence of their learning, if not of their formal education.

It is possible to identify more significant influences on the development of the personal styles of the main writers than their schooling, about which so little is known. Children of wealthy families were placed in the households of the nobility so that they could learn the manners and customs appropriate to their class, and at the same time receive the patronage of those in a position of power: Agnes Paston wrote a memorandum that she must "sey Elyzabet Paston that che must vse hyr-selfe to werke redyly as other jentylwomen don, and sumwhat to helpe hyr-selfe ther-wyth" (no.28). John I's daughter Anne was also sent into service with a "good lady" (no.201). John III was initially given a position in the household of the Duke of Norfolk, but for the politically ambitious, the Royal Court, "the house of houses principal in England,"[13] was the place to be. Increasingly in this period the power of a household did not depend solely on the strength of the retinue but on royal favor. John Paston II was sent to the Royal Court in the hope that he would benefit the family as a whole. Court society was highly competitive—one had to be noticed. Clement Paston thus analyses his nephew John II's failure at court: "[he] is not ȝet verily aqweyntyd in þe Kyngys howse. . . . [and] not bold y-now to put forthe hym-selfe" (no.116), and John I echoes these words four years later in one of his criticisms of his eldest son for his inability to "put hym-self foorth to be in favour or trust with any men of substauns þat myght forther hym" (no.72).

In contrast, John III was much more successful in his attendance at the Court, but political life in the fifteenth century was very unstable. In the dangerous times of civil war, warnings like John II's to John III, "be ware . . . þat fro hense forthe by yowr langage noo man parceyue þat ye fauor any person contrary to þe Kynges plesure" (no.263) are especially potent. David Starkey suggests a growing self-awareness and agitation among courtiers at the close of the Middle Ages,[14] and John III reflects on the fragility of his position and the political uncertainty of his day, when he quotes to his brother: "But Fortune wyth hyr smylyng contenans strange / Of all our purpose may mak a sodeyn change" (no.350).[15] Although it is not known that Margaret Paston ever entered service herself, she was aware of the risks taken by those who relied on the patronage and protection of others. She warned John III: "Trost not mych vp-on promyses of lordes now a days that ye shuld be the suerere of þe favour of þer men" (no.213).

The Rhetoric of Service

> Youre termes, youre colours, and youre figures,
> Keepe hem in stoor til so be ye endite
> Heigh style, as whan that men to kynges write.
> *The Clerk's Prologue*

Although it is easy to exaggerate the extent to which the letters are characterised by the known or hypothesized differences in education of the main writers, without doubt the skills which John III learnt and the sort of letters which he had to write as a courtier set his more polished writings apart from much of the other correspondence. Nonetheless, given that the hierarchical and patronage-based social structure of the Royal Court was fundamentally the same as that of the smaller households, it may perhaps be worth digressing to look at the courtly letters of John Paston III in order to compare the rhetoric of the court to the conventional and formal language which is found in the household correspondence generally, and which colors the letters of the Paston men and women alike.

The Royal Court and the great households of England had their own "language" or vocabulary through which was expressed the social relationship of service, one of the most important forms of political and social allegiance in England. The hierarchical social structure is formalized in conventions of address. Written appeals for patronage and protection ("good lord/ladyship") are formal and deferential, reflecting both the obsequious language spoken at court and the influence of the *ars dictaminis*. Included in the documents written in the hand of John Paston III is a poem of complaint to an unidentified lord.[16] The opening lines take the form of a petition:

> My ryght good lord, most knyghtly gentyll knyght,
> On-to your grace in my most humbyll wyse
> I me comand, as it is dew and ryght,
> Besechyng yow at leyser to aduyse
> Vp-on thys byll, and perdon myn empryse
> Growndyd on foly for lak of prouydence
> On-to your lordshep to wryght wyth-owght lycence. (no.351)

No Middle-English letter-writing manuals survive, but Norman Davis has shown that official and private letters written in English in the later Middle Ages conformed to certain precepts. These conventions were regularized in France, where the *ars dictaminis* was applied to letters written in the vernacular. With only minor variations, certain words and phrases follow an established sequence: this verse epistle opens with the word "right" which is only found in English letters, but the writer's commendation and declaration of humility closely correspond to the French formulae "se recommande" and "treshumblement."[17]

The greater the social divide between writer and recipient, the more exaggerated the formality of the language and the more extreme the writer's appeal to the condescension of the recipient. Having apologised for the presumption of writing, the suitor in the verse epistle goes on to describe the anguish suffered in the absence of the lord and entreats for the opportunity to wait attendance upon him.[18] The rhetorical skill of John Paston III allows him to exploit the conventions of this language. He humorously petitions Lord Fitzwalter for a dozen rabbits, describing himself in exaggerated self-deprecation as "your dayly seruaynt and beedman John Paston, more kayteff than knyght" and claiming that his own property is inadequate for his needs, "More lyeke a pynnefold then a parke" while theft is impossible from Fitzwalter's well-protected estates (no.390).

Well-rehearsed in court circles was the ability to promote oneself while at the same time reinforcing the self-esteem of one's patrons. John III expresses deference and loyalty to a superior through lavish praise "of þe most corteys, gentylest, wysest, kyndest, most compenabyll, freest, largeest, and most bowntefous knyght . . . he is on the lyghtest, delyuerst, best spokyn, fayirest archer, deuowghtest, most perfyght and trewest to hys lady of all the knyghtys that euer I was aqweyntyd wyth" (no.352).[19] Such rhetoric was often criticised by contemporaries as insincere; the poet Hoccleve condemns the flattery of courtiers: "Many a seruant vnto his lord seith þat al the world spekith of him honour, / Whan contrarie of þat is soothe in feith."[20] Margaret Paston advises her son to be wary of the deception of those whose support he solicited too extravagantly, "for though ye haue nede thei wull not be right redy to help you of there owyn" (no.210).

The Paston women were not unacquainted with court and political life. John III is certain that if his mother were to attend the Duchess of Norfolk during her confinement, Paston affairs will be furthered (no.371). Several years later his wife Margery offers to speak to the Duchess on her husband's behalf, arguing that, "on word of a woman shuld do more than the wordys of xx men" (no.418). Margaret Paston was even present during a visit of the Queen to Norfolk, but the excitement with which she describes the event reveals that this was for her a rare glimpse of court life. Margaret's cousin actually spoke with the Queen, but Margaret complains that she herself did not even have a necklace fit to be worn "among so many fresch jantylwomman as here were at þat tym" (no.146). Under normal circumstances the Paston women, unlike more privileged members of their sex, did not have the opportunity to attend the Royal Court and had only limited access to its culture. Consequently, the sophistication of court rhetoric and the creative self-consciousness so typical of the letters of John Paston III occur rarely in the correspondence of the women.

However, the language of service did infuse the vocabulary and imagery of many other social relations including the discourse of love and the rhetoric of the household. John III asks his elder brother to recommend him to Sir John Parre "wyth all my seruys, and tell hym by my trouthe I longyd neuer sorer to se my lady then I do to se hys mastershepe. And I prey God that he aryse neuer a mornyng fro my lady his wyff wyth-owght it be ageyn hyr wyll tyll syche tyme as he bryng hyr to Ouyr Lady of Walsyngham" (no.352).[21] By means of romantic playfulness, John III is able to express his esteem for his lord's wife with the deference appropriate to a retainer. Such eloquence suggests that he may well have been experienced in the courtly pastime of lover's conversation, termed "luf-talkyng" by the Gawain-poet.

The same relationship of service is invoked in his private love letters. John III humbly offers life-long obedience to a potential bride:

> Mastresse, thow so be that I, vnaqweyntyd wyth yow as yet, tak vp-on me to be thus bold as to wryght on-to yow wyth-ought your knowlage and leue, yet, mastress, for syche pore seruyse as I now in my mynd owe yow, purposyng, ye not dyspleasyd, duryng my lyff to contenu the same, I beseche yow to pardon my boldness and not to dysdeyn but to accepte thys sympyll bylle. (no.373)

He is willing to withdraw his attentions if they become burdensome, "for I wyll no ferther labore but to yow on-to the tyme ye geue me leue and tyll I be suer that ye shall take no dysplesure wyth my ferther labore." Yet, despite his protestations of honor, his letters betray insincerity. He begs one 'Mastresse Annes' to "let me not be forgotyn when ye rekyn vp all your seruauntys, to be sett in the nombyr wyth other" (no.362), but elsewhere describes her as "þe thyng" (no.363). On hearing of his sister's marriage he writes to his brother, "I prey yow aspye some old thryffty draffwyff in London for me" (no.369). These flippant remarks indicate that John III accepts the prevalent attitude of the time that marriages should be socially or economically advantageous—he includes a wealthy widow on his long list of possible brides. It is not surprising that John II cynically remarks to John III and a friend, "Yit weere it pyte þat suche craffty wowerys as ye be bothe scholde speede weell but iff ye love trewly" (no.287).

When Margery, John III's future wife, found herself separated from her fiancé while the families negotiated the dowry, she was justifiably concerned about her father's financial reticence. She appealed to her lover as a petitioner ("bedewoman"), describing the pain which she suffered as a result of their separation, and humbly pleading with him to accept her:

> yf þat ȝe cowde be content wyth þat good and my por persone, I wold be þe meryest mayden on grounde. And yf ȝe thynke not ȝowr-selfe so satysfyed, or þat ȝe myght hafe mech more good, as I hafe vndyrstonde be ȝowe afor, good, trewe, and lovyng Volentyne, þat ȝe take no such labure vppon ȝowe as to com more for þat mater; but let it passe, and neuer more to be spokyn of. . . . (no.416)

Like so much of John III's own writing, Margery's letter is consciously creative—part of the letter is written in rhyming prose.[22] As a betrothed woman rather than a lover's "mistress," Margery happily accepts the sovereignty of her future husband, and instead of holding herself aloof, she promises that, despite any opposition from her friends, "yf ʒe commande me to kepe me true where-euer I go / Iwyse I will do all my myght ʒowe to love and neuer no mo" (no.415) The social convention which made John III "servant in love" combined with the law of church and state to make him "lord in mariage."[23] There is no suggestion in any of the surviving letters that in the years to come Margery ever seriously challenged the authority of the man who remained her "owyn swete hert" (no.418).

Address was formalized both in the extended household and within the family unit.[24] The Paston women as well as the men were addressed with humility by their employees and dependants. While Richard Calle, the trusted and respected family bailiff, addressed both his master and mistress quite informally, one Piers, a servant who had been imprisoned for theft, had to plead for favours, placing himself entirely at Margaret Paston's mercy (nos.714, 715, 169). John Paston I had certain expectations of his household: "euery gentilman that hath discrecion waytith that *his ken and seruantis þat levith be hym* and at his coste shuld help hym forthward" (no.73). The symbiotic relationship of patronage and service even infiltrated the heart of the household—the nuclear family. As patrons, householders would protect the interests not only of their retainers, domestic servants and tenants, but also of their children. John II had to strive to regain John I's "good faderhood" after a period of friction (for example, no.178). Margaret Paston describes her cousin's dilemma over his mother's proposed marriage; he has done all he can to dissuade her but runs the risk of losing "hyr gode modyrchep" (no.152). Such a loss would indeed be serious. Margaret's daughter forfeited the "good ore helpe ore kownfort" of her family and friends by marrying Richard Calle against their wishes, and Margaret went so far as to ban her from the house (no.203). Family patronage extended beyond the relationship of parent and child. The head of the household also had a certain amount of responsibility for her or his younger siblings: Margaret asks her husband to be a "gode brothere" to his sister Elizabeth in furthering negotiations for her marriage (no.145).

In return for parental patronage, children were expected to show obedience and honor. When John II seeks his father's forgiveness, he complains of "the peyn and heuynesse þat it hathe ben to me syn yowre departyng owt of thys contre" and begs for grace:

> I beseche yow of yowre faderly pyte to tendre þe more thys symple wryghtyng, as I schal owt of dowght her-afftere doo þat schal please yow to þe vttermest of my powere and labore. And if there be any servyce þat I may do, if it please

yow to comaund me or if I maye vnder-stonde it, I wyl be as glad to do it as any thyng erthely, if it were any thyng þat myght be to yowre pleasyng. (no.234)

John III's younger brother Edmond apologizes to his mother for his neglect in similar terms: "And it plese ȝow to be so good and kynde modyre to forgeue me and also my wyffe of owur leude offence þat we haue not don owur dute, whyche was to haue seyn and ave waytyd vp-on ȝow ore now" (no.399). Edmond recognises that he must attend his mother just as a courtier is obliged to attend the sovereign.

Household Rhetoric and Plain Style

> Speketh so pleyn at this tyme, we yow preye,
> That we may understonde what ye seye.
> *The Clerk's Prologue*

Despite the pervasiveness of at least some degree of formality in the Paston correspondence, the predominant style which characterizes the letters as a whole is a plain one. According to medieval *ars rhetorica*, style ought to reflect context; "high" style characterized by formal language and complex grammar was appropriate, as the Host observed to the Clerk, "whan that men to kynges write." In contrast, a "plain" style would be fitting for general household correspondence. The sixteenth-century letter-writing manual of William Fulwood advises against "rare and diffused phrases," recommending rather "the common and familiar speache" of the vernacular.[25] This style could be described as "colloquial," bearing a striking resemblance to, and having its origins in the spoken idiom.[26]

The often dramatic prose of Margaret Paston has many features of oral narrative. In one of her most lively letters, she describes an attack on the family chaplain which occurred while he was walking home from the town. The attacker, John Wymondham, stood at his gate with some of his men, while another man stood on the road "by þe canell side":

> And Jamys Gloys come with his hatte on his hede betwen bothe his men, as he was wont of custome to do. And whanne Gloys was a-yenst Wymondham he seid þus, "Couere thy heed!" And Gloys seid ageyn, "So I shall for the." And whanne Gloys was forther passed by þe space of iii or iiij strede, Wymondham drew owt his dagger and seid, "Shalt þow so, knave?" (no.129)

Margaret's own intervention in the brawl is signaled by a shift away from dramatic direct speech into indirect discourse:

And with þe noise of þis a-saut and affray my modir and I come owt of þe chirche from þe sakeryng; and I bad Gloys go to my moderis place ageyn, and so he dede. And thanne Wymondham called my moder and me strong hores. . . . And he had meche large langage, as ye shall knowe herafter by my mowthe.

Such a movement from third-person to first-person narrative is characteristic of informal speech. In her analysis of the passage, Janel Mueller notes that by means of this grammatical transition Margaret controls the narrative, just as she took charge when she came upon the fight.[27] Margaret may have felt that she was invulnerable to assault. She mentions in her letter that the attack took place while she was in the church, exactly at the moment of the elevation of the host. According to popular belief, seeing the elevated host could protect one from dying suddenly and unprepared.

The colloquialism found in the writing of Margaret Paston could be explained by the fact that she dictated her letters to a secretary, were it not for the appearance of a similar narrative style in the autograph correspondence of the other writers. John III, who is capable of writing an 18-line complex sentence in one short letter of petition (no.359), slips into a much simpler style when writing of a family disagreement to his elder brother:

Many qwarellys ar pyekyd to get my brodyr E. and me ought of hyr howse. We go not to be vnchedyn lyghtly. All þat we do is ille doon, and all that Syr Jamys and Pekok dothe is well deon. Syr Jamys and I be tweyn. We fyll owght be-for my modyr wyth "Thow prowd prest" and "Thow prowd sqwyer", my modyr takyng hys part, so I haue almost beshet þe bote as for my modyrs house. (no.353)

In this letter Margaret is portrayed as a matriarchal figure dominating the household. John III expresses in energetic prose his anger at the abuse which he is forced to endure and at his own sense of powerlessness. The spontaneity of the tense-switching is analogous to the grammatical fluidity of spoken narrative.[28] To the modern reader, such apparent inconsistency stands out in a written context as ungrammatical.

Apart from syntactic characteristics, certain features of vocabulary and phrasing within the letters, in particular proverbs, idioms and neologisms (such as "beshit the boat," meaning "to make oneself unwelcome")[29] are indicative of a colloquial style.[30] Such speech-like forms are not merely typical of the women's writing but are found throughout the collection. One of the most striking examples of a proverbial style is seen in a letter written by Agnes Paston to her eldest son, following a period of strained relations. Agnes begins in somber tones offering him her blessing: "þat blyssyng þat I prayed ȝoure fadir to gyffe ȝow þe laste day þat euer he spakke, and þe blyssyng of all seyntes vndir heven, and myn." She goes on:

> ȝoure fadyr sayde, "In lityl bysynes lyeth myche reste." Þis worlde is but a þorugh-fare and ful of woo, and whan we departe þer-fro, riȝth nouȝght bere wyth vs but oure good dedys and ylle. And þer knoweth no man how soon God woll clepe hym, and þer-for it is good for euery creature to be redy. Qhom God vysyteth, him he louyth. (no.30)

The gnomic wisdom of Agnes's husband is confirmed by the authority of the New Testament reminders of the transitory nature of earthly things (1 Tim. 6:7), the inevitability yet unpredictability of death (Matt. 24:44), and the consolation of God's greater wisdom (Heb. 12:6).[31] The passage has the measured control of a medieval sermon and belies any suggestion that Agnes Paston is uneducated. For medievals, proverbs were expressions of *communis sententia*. When John II finds occasion to lament the instability of the world, he uses a similar expression of piety: "God hathe schewyd hym-selffe marvelouslye, lyke hym þat made all and can vndoo ageyn whan hym lyst" (no.261).[32]

The greatest number of proverbs are found in the letters of John II and John III, and even the most cursory study reveals that idioms and neologisms are scattered throughout the Paston letters. It may be that the most prolific letter-writers were not self-conscious when writing or dictating and as a result, their writing style resembled more closely their every-day speech; as Karen Scott has shown in this volume, although Catherine of Siena dictated some 382 epistles, she still considered letters merely to be written speech, an extension of orality. It is also probable that proverbs and other "colloquial" features were considered appropriate to the rhetoric of household correspondence. The sixteenth-century Lord Keeper, Sir Nicholas Bacon, was renowned for both his courtly rhetoric and his sententious plain speaking, and he too expressed himself in homely proverbs in letters to his family.[33]

Woman's Authority in the Paston Household

> On word of a woman shuld do more than the wordys of xx men.
> Margery Paston

The plain and didactic prose used by all the main letter writers allows women as well as men an authoritative voice. Indeed, the rhetoric of the household acknowledges the possibility of a woman having "maistrye." Margaret, representing her husband in the dispute over the Paston manor of Cotton, was accorded by her son the respect appropriate to her position. John III apologises to his lord the Duke of Norfolk for his inability to act in the matter, explaining "þat at that tyme I had *my mastyr* wyth-in þe maner of Cotton, *whyche was my modyr*, and in-to the tyme þat I had spook wyth hyr I cowd geue none answer" (no.324). Although the *Middle English Dictionary* gives only metaphorical or derogatory examples of the application of "maister" to women, there is no sense of irony in John III's description of his mother.[34] Margaret considered herself to be ultimately answerable to her husband in all that she did, assuring him that "it is not my will no þer to do ne sey that shuld cawse yow for to be displeasid" (no.148); nevertheless she acted with full authority in the household during his frequent absences. Even after John II's inheritance of his father's estate, Margaret dominated the lives of her sons; she did not hesitate to criticise John II for overspending or to speak out angrily when she feared that his profligacy undermined the honor of the family. Margaret objects in the strongest terms to John II's plans to sell part of his inheritance because "if it were knowyn shuld cause bothyn your elmyse and your frendes to thynk þat ye dede it for right gret nede, or ell þat ye shuld be a wastour and wuld wast your lyvelode" (no.214). In her last surviving letter she reproached John II because twelve years after his father's death, he had not built him a tomb (no.228).

When John Paston II praises his brother as "a good huswyff" for helping him to solve his financial problems (no.274), he also acknowledges, if only in jest, the importance of the woman's role in the domestic sphere. From the evidence of the letters, Margaret arranged for the education of the children, found them places in service and looked for suitable marriage partners, supervised servants, organised the buying and selling of provisions, and oversaw the maintenance of the estates and collection of the rents.

The Paston women not only managed practical and economic matters but also acted in the social and political affairs of the household. Margaret Paston fostered support for the family among tenants and local nobility while passing on information to her husband and sons about recent events in the area. Her duties as a housewife were not only varied and often arduous, but on occasion even dangerous. In one letter, Margaret directs her husband to buy provisions for the household, which, in addition to almonds, sugar, and cloth, included: "crosse bowis, and wyndacis to bynd þem wyth, and quarell, for ȝwr hwsis here ben so low þat þere may non man schete owt wyth no long bowe þow we hadde neuer so moche nede. . . . And also I wold ȝe xuld gete ij or iij schort pelle-axis to kepe wyth doris, and als many jakkys and ȝe may" (no.130). Margaret anticipated that Lord Moleyns, who had claimed the Paston estate at Gresham, would launch an assault in the near future. Her precautions proved necessary but insufficient. A petition sent by John I to the King reveals that Lord Moleyns did attack the manor: a thousand-strong army stormed the building while Margaret held her ground within. Despite her resistance, Margaret did not succeed in foiling her attackers who "myned down the walle of the chambre . . . and bare here oute of the yates" (no.36).

John Paston I's account establishes that his wife's part in the defense of Paston property was equal to his own (he had been expelled from the same manor by Moleyns the previous year). He depicts Margaret as an indomitable individual well able to restrain any "vnruly felechp" who might in the future threaten the household (no.74). Margaret's own letters do not contradict this portrayal, although she did weary of coping singlehandedly with such attacks. In the year following her husband's death, after John Paston II had been granted possession of Falstoff's castle at Caistre, Margaret heard rumours of more trouble. She tells her eldest son: "ye wote wele that I haue ben affrayd there be-fore this tyme whan that I had othere comfort that I haue now. And I can not wele gide ner rewle sodyour, and also thei set not be a woman as thei shuld set be a man" (no.199). Margaret's complaint is less a disavowal of her own abilities than a request for the support of "more saddere or wurchepfull persones."

Margaret Paston combined courage with self-confidence, even challenging the politically powerful. She not only sought the intervention of the shire court in the land dispute with the Duke of Suffolk, but also approached the Bishop of Norwich, Walter Lyhert, to complain about the actions of one of the Duke's agents. The agent was a rector in the Bishop's diocese and came under his jurisdiction. Margaret puts her case plainly, "desyryng hys lordshyp that he wold see a mene that a correccyon myȝt be hadde, in as moch as he was chyf justice of the peas and hys ordynare, and in asmoch as he was a prest and vndere hys correccyon that he shold haue vnderstondyng of hys dysposicyon" (no.180). The Bishop acknowledged the validity of Margaret's petition and promised to take immediate action. According to her own report, Margaret directed the course of the interview, while the Bishop, showing no surprise that a woman should represent her husband in such an appeal, remained silent until she had finished. Margery Kempe's very similar account of her interview with Thomas Arundel, Archbishop of Canterbury, confirms that the opinion of a woman could carry weight in at least some matters. In this instance, Margery Kempe rebukes the Archbishop for his unruly household: "My Lord, owyr alderes Lord almyty God hath not ȝon ȝow ȝowyr benefys & gret goodys of þe world to maynten wyth hys tretowrys. . . . ȝe schal answer for hem les þan ȝe correctyn hem or ellys put hem owt of ȝowr seruyse."[35] Archbishop Arundel listened with humility as the pious laywoman reproached him, just as Bishop Lyhert accepted as authoritative the complaint of Margaret Paston.

The Paston correspondence as a whole and Margaret's letters in particular leave the reader in no doubt that both within the immediate context of the household and in the wider society of Norfolk, Margaret Paston was an influential figure. Her didactic letters are rendered the more forceful by her understanding of the law and the politics of the court. Although most of her letters were written for an immediate purpose, whether to relay news or to request provisions, her personality, concerns and values do emerge: in her defense of Paston interests and the Paston name, Margaret shows herself to be shrewd, assertive, or aggressive as need requires. It is not inappropriate then, that this final discussion should open with a quotation not from a male authority but from one of the Paston women's own letters. Through their letters, the Paston women speak for themselves.

Notes

1. An exchange of letters can, however, take the form of a conversation rather than a dialogue. In the Middle Ages, for example, secretaries, usually members of the household, were often employed in the writing of even the most personal correspondence and they might well contribute to the substance of a letter as well as introduce (often undetectable) editorial changes into the text.

2. Virginia Woolf, *The Common Reader*, 1st ser. (London: Hogarth Press, 1925), p. 37.

3. Compare the 107 letters and documents of Margaret Paston to the correspondence and papers attributed to women in fifteenth-century collections:

The Paston letters (total: 930; by women [including Margaret]: 174): Norman Davis, ed., *Paston Letters and Papers of the Fifteenth Century* (Oxford: Oxford University Press, 1971–1976), 2 vols.

The Stonor Letters (total: 356; by women: 36): Charles L. Kingford, ed., *The Stonor Letters and Papers, 1290–1483*, Camden Society, 3d ser., 29 and 30 (London: 1919), 2 vols. and *Supplementary Stonor Letters and Papers (1314–1482)*, Camden Miscellany, 13 (London: 1923).

The Cely Letters (total: 247; by women: 2): Alison Hanham, ed., *The Cely Letters, 1472–1488*, EETS OS 273 (Oxford: Oxford University Press, 1975).

The Plumpton Correspondence (total: 241; by women: 2 [and 15 from the sixteenth century]): Thomas Stapleton, ed., *Plumpton Correspondence: A Series of Letters, chiefly Domestick (sic), written in the Reigns of Edward IV, Richard III, Henry VII and Henry VIII,* Camden Society, 4 (London: 1839).

4. The standard introduction to the Pastons is H. S. Bennett, *The Pastons and Their England: Studies in an Age of Transition*, 2nd ed. (Cambridge: Cambridge University Press, 1932). Of general interest is R. Virgoe, *Illustrated Letters of the Paston Family* (London: Macmillan, 1989). A recent historical work is Colin Richmond, *The Paston Family in the Fifteenth Century: the First Phase* (Cambridge: Cambridge University Press, 1990). Norman Davis has published a number of linguistic and philological studies of the letters: of greatest interest here is "Styles in English Prose of the Late Middle and Early Modern Period—Margaret Paston's Use of ⟨Do⟩," *Langue et Litterature* XXI (1961): 55–62.

5. All citations from the Paston correspondence are to Davis, *Paston Letters and Papers*.

6. For a brief discussion of women's property rights in the Middle Ages, see Eileen Power, *Medieval Women*, ed. M. M. Poston (Cambridge: Cambridge University Press, 1975), pp. 38–40.

7. Davis, "Styles in English Prose," p. 62.

8. An excellent study of the late medieval household is David Starkey, "The Age of the Household: Politics, Society and the Arts c.1350–c.1550" in *The Later Middle Ages,* ed. Stephen Medcalf (Methuen, 1981), pp. 225–90. Also see Kate Mertes, *The English Noble Household* (Oxford: Basil Blackwell, 1988).

9. On the education of women see Nicholas Orme, *English Schools in the Middle Ages* (London: Methuen, 1973), pp. 52–56.

10. Davis, *Paston Letters and Papers*, p. xxxvii.

11. Agnes was asked to "reporte, record & berre wyttnesse" to the variation of the will. "Record" could in this context mean oral rather than written testimony. To "declare" had an additional legal sense of clarification and interpretation. *Middle English Dictionary*, s.v. "recorden" and s.v. "declaren."

12. Orme, *English Schools in the Middle Ages*, pp. 42–43.

13. Quoted in Starkey, "The Age of the Household," 225.

14. Starkey, pp. 277–82. Starkey discusses the sixteenth-century poet Sir Thomas Wyatt.

15. Portrayals of Fortuna as smiling but changeable are not uncommon in Medieval literature: see Howard R. Patch, *The Goddess Fortuna in Mediaeval Literature* (London: Frank Cass, 1927), p. 43 and B. J. Whiting, ed. *Proverbs, Sentences, and Proverbial Phrases from English Writing Mainly Before 1500* (Cambridge, MA: Harvard University Press, 1968), F523, "Fortune is changeable."

16. John Paston III did not sign this poem and it is not certain that it is his composition. However, he is known to have written verses in Latin addressed to the Duke of Norfolk (no.393).

17. Norman Davis, "The *Litera Troili* and English Letters," *Review of English Studies* NS 16 (1965): 238.

18. Compare Dunbar's complaint, "Schir, ye have mony servitouris" which remonstrates James IV for his neglect and seeks his favour, and Hoccleve's plea for money from his patron in "La Male Regle" (note 20).

19. Norman Davis notes a resemblance between John Paston III's praise of his patron and Ector's eulogy for Sir Launcelot at the end of Malory's *The Morte Arthur*. Davis comments, "Malory finished his book in 1470, and Paston's letter is dated 2 June 1472. It seems not very likely that he could have based it directly on Malory. More probably there were other texts . . . which both he and Malory knew," "Style and Stereotype in Early English Letters," *Leeds Studies in English* NS (1967): 15.

20. "La Male Regle de T. Hoccleue" (ll. 217–18) in M. C. Seymour, *Selections from Hoccleve* (Oxford: Oxford University Press, 1981).

21. The pilgrimage to the shrine at Walshingham in Norfolk was extremely popular in the century before the Reformation.

22. John I and his eldest son also included informal verses in their correspondence (nos. 77, 270).

23. *The Franklin's Tale*, l. 793. All citations of Chaucer are from Larry D. Benson, ed., *The Riverside Chaucer*, 3rd ed. (Oxford: Oxford University Press, 1988).

24. Norman Davis describes the conventional formulae of medieval household correspondence in "The *Litera Troili* and English Letters" (note 17), 233–44 and in "A Note on *Pearl*," *Review of English Studies* NS 17 (1966): 403–5.

25. William Fulwood, *The Enimie of Idlenesse: Teaching How to Indite, Epistles* (n.p.: 1568), f.6ᵛ.

26. For an analysis of the problems of discussing colloquialisms in Middle English see D. Rygiel, "*Ancrene Wisse* and Colloquial Style: a Caveat," *Neophilologus* 65 (1981): 137–43.

27. Janel Mueller, *The Native Tongue and the Word: Developments in English Prose Style 1380–1580* (Chicago: University of Chicago Press, 1985), pp. 90–91.

28. See Suzanne Fleischman, "Philology, Linguistics, and the Discourse of the Medieval Text," *Speculum* 65, 1 (January 1990): 23.

29. Whiting, ed., *Proverbs, Sentences, and Proverbial Phrases*, B423.

30. On the oral basis of Middle English prose see Mueller, *The Native Tongue and the Word*, pp. 85–110, and Norman Davis, "The Language of the Pastons," *Proceedings of the British Academy* 40 (1954): 119–39.

31. For a detailed discussion of biblical and proverbial allusions in this passage see Norman Davis, "Style and Stereotype in Early English Letters," *Leeds Studies in English* NS (1967): 10–15.

32. Job 1:21.

33. Patrick Collinson, "Sir Nicholas Bacon and the Elizabethan *via media*," *Historical Journal* 50 (1980): 255–73. For a brief discussion of plain style in late medieval letters see Norman Davis, "Styles in English Prose of the Late Middle and Early Modern Period," *Neuphilologische Mitteilungen* 73 (1972): 165–84.

34. *Middle English Dictionary*, s.v. "maister."

35. S. B. Meech and H. E. Allen, *The Book of Margery Kempe*, EETS 212 (Oxford: Oxford University Press, 1940), p. 37.

Earl Jeffrey Richards

"*Seulette a part*"–The "Little Woman on the Sidelines" Takes Up Her Pen: The Letters of Christine de Pizan

While now best known as the author of the *Livre de la Cité des Dames* (*The Book of the City of Ladies*, 1405), the first work written by a woman in praise of women, Christine de Pizan (1365–?1431) was also a prolific letter writer.[1] During the early part of her literary career, she wrote four important verse epistles: *L'Epistre au dieu d'Amours* (*The Epistle of the God of Love*, 1399), *Le Livre du dit de Poissy* (*The Book of the Tale of Poissy*, 1400), *L'Epistre d'Othea* (*The Letter of Othea*, 1400), and *L'Epistre a Eustache Mourel* (*The Letter to Eustache Mourel* [*Deschamps*], 1404). They all seem superficially indebted to the tradition of courtly lyric, and, except for the last work, are addressed to fictional characters. Beginning with the Quarrel of the *Rose* (1401–1403), Christine shifted almost entirely to learned prose letters whose tone and style are distinctly humanist, rather than courtly, but show the influence of dictaminal models. The sheer range of Christine's epistolary writing is extraordinary: no contemporary writer produced a comparable body of letters. This range, furthermore, points to Christine's profound literary self-consciousness which explains in turn her wide-reaching experiments in epistolary form and content. Her letters, even the earliest verse epistles, innovatively synthesize three largely separate traditions: the courtly verse epistle composed in the vernacular, medieval Latin dictaminal writing, and humanist epistolography. For all their formal differences, Christine's letters reflect a growing determination to secure a place for women in the republic of letters. The clearly marked stages in this development reveal how Christine radically recasts the generic models and simultaneously redefines humanism itself.

In synthesizing these different traditions, Christine exhibited an extraordinary range of content, style and language, adapting her letters to her particular addressees and fashioning a specifically female and humanist voice. In so doing, she made a series of important, and hitherto largely unexplored, breakthroughs in both epistolary form and content. First, her starting point was to provide an alternative to the model of Héloïse's letters which, by 1400, were being cited as exemplary proof of the incompatibility of women and learning—only a woman who had overcome her female nature like Héloïse could be learned. Second, Christine's search for an alternative took her first to the verse epistle, a highly amorphous genre to begin with, which she used to explore the limits of courtliness, leading up to her *Epistre a Eustache Mourel* (1404) in which she was the first in French to experiment with the humanist *epistola metrica*. Indeed, the indistinct nature of the verse epistle in the vernacular gave Christine the opportunity to borrow from humanist letters in verse to transform what was largely a bloodless exercise in courtly clichés into a more powerful vehicle of humanist self-expression. Third, in the letters she wrote and collected between 1401 and 1403 during the debate over the *Roman de la Rose*—letters written in strict conformance with the *ars dictaminis* which address the role of Reason, the use of obscene language, and the misogynist portrayal of women in the *Roman de la Rose*—Christine was the first to introduce into the vernacular the humanistic epistolary polemic on literary questions. Fourth, Christine was the first to offer a model letter of one woman writing to other women in her *Livre des Trois Vertus* (*The Treasure of the City of Ladies, or the Book of Three Virtues*, 1405), again written following dictaminal models which she manipulated with ease as in her *Epistre a la Reine* (*Epistle to the Queen*, 1405). Fifth, in the *Lamentacion sur les maux de la guerre civile* (*Lamentation on the Evils of Civil War*, 1410), she cultivates and thematizes a specifically female voice which she had developed in her own lyric poetry to plead for social peace, a manoeuvre that marked a radical departure from the courtly *chançons royaulx*. Here the "little lonely woman" (*seulette*) of Christine's earlier verse speaks again as the *seulette a part*, literally, "little lonely woman on the sidelines." Christine took this constructed female authorial persona, with its explicit emphasis on the stereotypical diminutive and marginalized position of women, to address universal human questions in her *Epistre sur la Prison de la Vie Humaine* (*Epistle on the Prison of Human Life*, 1417).

Finding an Alternative to Héloïse's Letters and the Search for New Epistolary Forms

For Christine "writing the female voice" ultimately meant that women should speak for all humanity since men had failed in this primordial task of literary culture.[2] Men were not alone in this failure though, for Christine developed this female epistolary voice specifically as an alternative to that of Héloïse whose correspondence with Abélard she knew. I know of only a single reference to Héloïse in Christine's writings, an allusion in the letters exchanged during the Quarrel over the *Rose*, and this fact is initially surprising, since Héloïse would have been, at least on first glimpse, a perfect example for Christine to argue for the affinity of women and letters. Nor should Héloïse's affair with Abélard have been an obstacle to her being admitted in the City of Ladies. If Christine could see fit to include Semiramis, who married her own son, in the City of Ladies, she could just have easily included Héloïse there as well.

The conspicuous absence of Héloïse from Christine's writings, however, provides a key to understanding how Christine constructed a different female voice in her correspondence. Héloïse, for Christine, was the woman whom Jean de Meung had cited at the end of his long harangue against marriage in the *Roman de la Rose*—the speech of Ami in which the controversial words *coille* ("ball, testicle") and *putain* ("whore") are used. According to Ami, Héloïse was the woman who had through study overcome her female nature, a position inalterably opposed to Christine's understanding of the affinity of all humanity, including women, for study:

Héloïse wrote to him deliberately while she was still abbess: "I would rather," she noted, "and I call God to witness, be called your whore than a crowned empress." But I hardly believe, by my soul, that there has ever been such a woman since then; rather I believe that her learning permitted her to conquer and subdue the nature that she had from female behavior.

el li manda par letre expresse,
puis qu'el fu neïs abbeesse:
« . . . . .
si vodroie je mieuz, fet ele,
et Dieu a tesmoign en apele,
estre ta putain apelee
que empereriz coronee.»
Mes je croi mie, par m'ame,
c'onques puis fust nule tel fame;
si cri je que sa lestreüre
la mist a ce que la nature

que des meurs femenins avoit
vaincre et donter mieuz en savoit.
(ed. Lecoy, ll. 8785–86, 8792–8800)

Christine never explicitly criticized Héloïse, except when she wrote to
Pierre Col, the canon of Notre-Dame, that he resembled "Héloïse of the
Paraclete who said she would rather be called the *meretrix* of master Peter
Abelard than be a crowned queen" ("tu ressambles Helouye du Paraclit qui
dist que mieux ameroit estre *meretrix* appellee de maistre Pierre Abalart que
estre royne couronnee" ed. Hicks, p. 146). Nevertheless, in Christine's
judgment Héloïse was a token female for the misogynists because Héloïse
had accepted misogynist double standards in rejecting marriage and pro-
claiming her preference to be called her lover's whore. For Jean de Meung,
Héloïse's learning allowed her to overcome her own female nature, as
though a learned woman were necessary a denatured woman. The traits
that endeared Héloïse to Jean de Meung and other misogynist authors
would hardly qualify her for Christine's City of Ladies. But Héloïse's
specific significance for Christine's letter-writing is even more profound,
because no less a misogynist author than Jean de Meung had translated
Abélard's and Héloïse's correspondence and because this translation ex-
cited enormous interests in Parisian humanist circles during Christine's
career. It survives, in fact, in a single manuscript, copied by none other than
Gontier Col, the secretary of the King and one of Christine's opponents in
the Quarrel of the *Rose*. Héloïse's letters, as far as Christine was concerned,
were contaminated by the positive reception they enjoyed from Jean de
Meung and his contemporary Parisian humanist defenders. The popularity
of the French version of Héloïse's letters probably also played a role in
Christine's decision to use the vernacular herself; she had to provide an
alternative that was immediately accessible to women unlearned in Latin,
and she had to provide a form of women's writing different from that
sanctioned by misogynist clerics. The task for Christine would be to write
letters that simultaneously gave voice to women's suffering arising from
double standards (what man would want to be called his beloved's whore?),
and also exploded essentialist notions of female nature. In this regard, she is
in complete agreement with Joan W. Scott, who warned against the essen-
tialization of gender in her classic 1986 article, "Gender: A Useful Category
of Historical Discourse." There she argued that the task for women's
history was to "disrupt the notion of fixity, to discover the nature of the

debate or repression that leads to the appearance of timeless permanence in binary gender representation."[3]

The evolution of Christine's epistolary art shows how she used letter-writing, taken as a serious and formal genre, in order to break away from the artificial and brittle conventions of courtly poetry, to address current issues and questions whose answers were more than just "formally" interesting, and to demonstrate that erudition and female nature were not opposed to one another. After all, even Boccaccio, one of Christine's chief sources, dedicated his *De claris mulieribus* to a woman, Andrea Acciaiuoli, by noting that her name, Andrea, derived from the Greek word for man, and showed that she had abandoned her female nature in becoming learned. Underlying Christine's epistolary art is a radical critique, delivered in the name of a self-conscious Christian humanism, of the general abuse of literary culture to misrepresent women and of the particular sterility of courtly conventions. With Héloïse's example firmly in mind—that of how a woman should not play into the hands of misogyny—Christine chose the epistolary form to show that misogyny represented a fundamental perversion of literary tradition that must ideally be freed of bias either against one gender or in favor of the other. To this end, Christine posited the necessary fiction that literary culture was ideally universal and that when it turned hostile to women it had abandoned its own ideals. She argues in the *Livre de la Cité des Dames* that women were actively involved in literary activities from the start of human civilization, and that a woman had even invented the alphabet. Thus, literary culture should be devoted to the defense and illustration of universal standards of excellence and virtue, standards which one gender had not misappropriated to oppress the other.

The Verse Epistle: The Limits of Courtliness in a Corrupt World

Despite its enormous wealth of lyrical genres, medieval French literature offers remarkably few examples of specifically epistolary composition in verse—whence Christine's ultimate preference for prose.[4] It is useful to remember, as Giles Constable has noted, that in general the generic boundaries between prose and verse epistles were difficult to draw and that the verse epistle remained ultimately derivative of prose.[5] Though Christine first began her career by writing courtly lyric, she gradually moved to prose, both from generic and ideological necessity. In the letters exchanged during the Quarrel over the *Rose* Christine explained her choice of prose as being more appropriate to the subject, and implies that her opponents have abused the eloquence they cherish so dearly:

> Therefore, dear lord, let it not amaze you, since I was accustomed to rhyme my other writings, that this is in prose. For, as the matter requires nothing else, it is right that I follow the style of my antagonists, albeit my small wit is hardly commensurate with their fine eloquence.

> Aussi, chier seigneur, ne vous soit a merveille, pour ce que mes autres dictiéz ay acoustuméz a rimoyer, cestui estre en prose. Car comme la matiere ne le requiere autressy, est droit que je suive le stille de mes assaillans, combien que mon petit sçavoir soit pou respondant a leur belle eloquence. (ed. Hicks, p. 8)

Because Christine began her career composing verse, her subsequent choice of prose is indicative of her profound commitment to fashioning a woman's voice in the vernacular. In fact, Christine's innovative combination of verse and prose in the *Epistre d'Othea* and in the *Livre du Duc des Vrais Amants* also points to her growing dissatisfaction with verse.

For students of Christine's works, the relationship between her verse and prose has long been a thorny issue. Her verse is supposedly utterly conventional and unremarkable and her prose hopelessly long-winded and moralistic, so that it has been all too easy to dismiss Christine's works without even reading them closely. A new picture of the connection between her verse and prose, however, has begun to emerge in recent scholarship.[6] It is also not surprising, therefore, that Christine's verse epistles anticipate the criticisms of the *Roman de la Rose*'s misogyny elaborated in the prose letters that Christine composed and collected. Her critique of the courtly misrepresentation of women is consistent with the anti-courtly, humanist current of her entire work. When seen retrospectively from the standpoint of her later prose works, the criticisms of the courtly misrepresentation of women implied in her verse works are more easily recognized.

What did Christine object to in the body of courtly literature? Her hostility to courtly literature is consistent, I believe, with the criticisms of later Renaissance Elizabethan humanists in England. Her target, of course, was the portrayal of women in the *Roman de la Rose*, which alternates between the highly courtly descriptions of Guillaume de Lorris (his *jardin de Déduit* is one of the most carefully crafted portraits of a literary pleasance) to the scholastic misogynistic barbs of Jean de Meung. Christine did not miss the contrast between the courtly Guillaume and the scholastic Jean who still portrayed himself and Guillaume at the midpoint of the *Rose* as lyric poets in a line with the love poets of Antiquity, but the bottom line was that both writers, for all their differences, still misrepresent and insult women. Therefore Christine concluded about the Rose that it was a single creation, "I hold the entire work to be one edifice" ("je tiens tout ung mesme edifice").[7] Christine's relationship to courtly literature was at best an uneasy one, but as a vernacular poet she knew that her audience expected her to demonstrate her skill with courtly lyric. Her solution was to turn its conventions on their head.

She first accomplishes this transformation of courtly literature in her verse epistles. They vary enormously from the ostensibly courtly *Epistre au dieu d'Amours*[8] to the learned allegory of the *Epistre d'Othea* to the *Epistre a Eustache Mourel*, a kind of humanist *Selbstbekenntnis*. In all of these writings, Christine thematizes her position as a woman-writer and demonstrates her ability to participate fully in an unperverted tradition of literary erudition.

Christine's originality stems from this two-pronged, and fundamentally humanist—*pace* Boccaccio in *De claris mulieribus*—approach to her craft: in the name of universal culture she attacked misogyny and championed women's accomplishments throughout her entire career, and in the name of this same universalism she rejected eternally immutable differences between the sexes. For Christine, merit in literary culture could not depend on sexual or biological difference, but on moral and intellectual virtue. When she argues in her *Epistre au dieu d'Amours* that the books would be different if they had been written by women, the difference stems from women's knowledge of the injustice done to them, not from some mystical spiritual female quality into which they could mysteriously tap. She wrote:

But if women had written the books
I know truly that in fact it would be different
for they know well that they have been falsely accused.

Mais se femmes eussent li livre fait
Je sçay de vray qu'aultrement fust du fait
Car bien scevent qu'a tort sont encoulpees.
(ed. Fenster, vv. 417–19)

Similarly, she took exception when Gontier Col, one of her opponents in the Quarrel over the *Rose*, tried to disqualify her "as a woman," *comme femme*. In this same vein, she argued in the Quarrel that a literary work detrimental to the *common* good did not deserve to be praised:

> a work without great utility for the common or individual good, in deed or in example, and where there is nothing but pleasure and amusement without purpose of any other good—no matter how costly or expensive—should not be praised or exalted.

> oeuvre sans grant utilité du bien commun ou propre, en fait ou en exemple, et ou n'a fors seulement delectacion et solas sans cause d'autre bien—tout soit elle de grant coust ou travail—ne doit estre louee n'euxaussiee.[9]

The ideal solution is one of the common good, impartial to both sexes except as common members of one human community. In other ways, as I have demonstrated elsewhere, Christine appeals to androgyny in order to universalize the male-dominated clerkly tradition, epitomized most immediately for her by Jean de Meung.[10]

Rather than claiming that women's writing represented a form of writing essentially different from that of men, an untenable position for Christine in light of Héloïse's letters and their reception among her contemporaries, Christine used her letters to combat a belief in the "eternally feminine." The lyrical tradition of the *amor de lonh*—the distant, unreachable, and deathlessly beautiful woman on a pedestal—celebrates women and simultaneously dehumanizes and immobilizes them. Christine's task in her verse epistles would be to break out of the passive role assigned to women in lyric, to give them a "speaking part" instead of just the role of beautiful extra. The male speaker of medieval lyric is almost invariably caught up in his own feelings and his beloved forms the backdrop for him to show off his poetic skill, to "make a verse from absolutely nothing" ("ferei un vers de dreit rien"), as Guillaume IX claimed. Lyric thus reinforced and sanctioned the very category of the eternally feminine. Both parts of the *Roman de la Rose* illustrate the depersonalization of women in a textbook way: all attention centers on Amant and his quest of the Rose, who has a non-speaking decorative part in the work. All of the speeches and digressions of the work, whether exquisitely courtly or expository, elaborate exclusively on Amant's pursuit and on Amant's feelings, on the lyrical ego at the center of the poem. In such a lyrical setting the woman is merely a pretext for the composition. This marginalization of women in courtly lyric explains why Christine chose to cultivate the persona of "a little lonely woman on the sidelines"—*seulette a part*, the ostensibly marginalized, diminutive female of courtly lyric. She takes the depersonalized position of woman in courtly literature, exploited so cleverly in the *Roman de la Rose* to attack women, to create a poetic identity that explodes the self-absorbed narcissistic misogynist speaker of courtly lyric. She will write on subjects that make a human difference, not on merely nothing, *dreit rien.* Later in her *Dit de Poissy* she applies the conventional description of female beauty in courtly literature to males, and the picture she draws of male beauty, including buttocks, shocked nineteenth-century editors who missed the point of Christine's attempt to unmask the double standard at the heart of courtly literature.[11]

In the *Epistre au dieu d'Amours*, "a takeoff on a royal letter, this one purporting to be presented by a royal secretary at the celestial court of the God of Love,"[12] Christine uses the fictional epistolary form to attack distorted male representations of women. Here she adapted the verse epistle form specifically to argue on behalf of women in the same way that she used the letters in the Quarrel of the *Rose* to criticize its representation of women, reason and language. Moreover, Jean de Meung presented the *Roman de la Rose* as the continuation of a poetic tradition reaching back to Antiquity of lyric poets who had died in the service of Love. This tradition was what Christine denounced when she wrote that the books would be different if women had written them. Therefore the challenge for her would be to present her writing as the continuation of an ideally universalist literary tradition. In immediate practical terms, she would have to show her Parisian humanist contemporaries that she could write prose letters on a par with her Italian humanist models, "as the matter requires nothing else."

The challenge for Christine in her verse epistles was to adapt courtly lyric to her feminist arguments. Given the virtual silence of the various dictaminal manuals on verse epistles,[13] she had three possible models: the fictional collection of abandoned women writing to their lovers in Ovid's *Heroides* (letters which take women's victimization as their starting point), Eustache Deschamps's *chançons royaulx* (these letters, popular in the late fourteenth century, emphasized the subservient position of the poet vis-à-vis the unnamed prince being addressed), and Petrarch's *epistolæ metricæ* (an epistolary genre that was highly learned but also highly experimental since it lacked classical models). What will emerge from a brief review of these possible prototypes is the increasingly important impact of humanist thought on Christine's writings, and the fact that Christine's feminism is in many ways a profound form of humanism. With due apologies to Jean-Paul Sartre, for Christine, *le féminisme, c'est un humanisme.*

In the *Epistre d'Othea a Hector*, Christine's ostensible model was Ovid's *Heroides*, but in fact her more pressing concerns with allegory in the *Othea* had little to do with the Ovidian situation of abandoned women writing to the faithless male lovers. The *Othea* pioneers a highly original form with its one hundred sections in which a verse quatrain is followed by an allegorical exposition. Its most immediate source was the *Ovide moralisé* which combined ancient myth and Christian allegory, a synthesis cultivated by Boccaccio in his *Genealogia Deorum*. At the outset, Christine uses the allegorical format to reinterpret traditionally female and male spheres of action: female prophecy become the allegory of the human search for wisdom; masculine chivalry becomes the allegory of the soul struggling for salvation:

> "Othea," according to the Greek, can be taken for the wisdom of women. . . . We will take Othea to mean the virtue of prudence and wisdom. . . . And because our spirit can be impeded by the ambushes and assaults of the infernal enemy, who is its mortal adversary and often turns it away from arriving at blessedness, we can call human life upright chivalry.

> Othea selon grec peut estre pris pour sagece de femme. . . . Par Othea nous prendrons la vertue de prudence et sagece. . . . Et pour ce que [nostre esperit] peut estre empesché par les agais et assaulx de l'ennemi d'enfer, qui est son mortel adversaire et souvent le destourne de parvenir a sa beatitude, nous povons appeller la vie humaine droite chevalerie.[14]

This interpretation allegorizes traditional male and female spheres. Here Christine is not endorsing conventional gender identities, but takes them instead as the literal event in need of a deeper spiritual meaning. For all intents and purposes, Christine follows the Christian opinion that gender is a mere accident of the flesh whose meaning for salvation is trivial. The Apostle Paul had claimed that just as in Christ no one was Jew or Greek, slave or free, no one was male or female (Galatians 3:28, "non est Iudæus neque

Græcus: non est servus neque liber: non est masculus neque femina"), and Dante wrote that the transcendence of humanity in heaven transcended human speech itself (Par. i.70, "the passing beyond humanity cannot be signified in words," "trasumanar significar *in verba*/non si poria"). These examples undergird Christine's attempt to universalize a literary heritage riddled with misogyny.

In the dedication to Louis d'Orléans, Christine describes herself as an "unworthy woman" who has undertaken to set to rhyme "a letter that was sent to Hector of Troy." This dedication and the first chapter (Othea's letter to Hector itself) are couched in the most courtly language possible, and their turns of phrases and allusions to the Trojan origins of the French royal house immediately recall twelfth-century rhymed romances. For example, after calling Louis "the most lofty flower praised throughout the world" ("tres haulte flour par le monde louee" l.1), she speaks of "the ancient nobility of Trojan stock" ("d'estoc troyan ancianne noblece" l. 10). But the reader is in store for a surprise: no sooner does Christine finish her courtly dedication than she hits the reader with the first of many didactic expositions in prose:

> So that those who are not clerkly poets can understand in brief the meaning of the significance of the histories in this book, it will be seen that everywhere the images are in clouds; it should be understood that these are the figures of gods or goddesses about which the letter following in the book speaks according to the manner of the ancient poets.

> Affin que ceulz qui ne sont mie clercs poetes puissent entendre en brief la significacion des histoires de ce livre, est a savoir que par tout ou les ymages sont en nues, c'est a entendre que ce sont les gigures des dieux ou deesses de quoy la letre ensuivant ou livre parles selon la maniere de parler des ancians poetes. (pp. 152–53)

These brief examples show how the *Epistre d'Othea* characterizes the conflicting demands of a courtly verse epistle and of humanist erudition. The allegorizations of ancient mythological *exempla* that Christine offers up in the rest of the work reflect the rising influence of early humanists. Once again, Christine uses a courtly veneer in the verse sections to present essentially humanist material, a typical interweaving of courtly conventions (often exploded) and humanist content. Christine's relationship to Eustache Deschamps (1346–1406/07, born Eustache Mourel but called Deschamps from the name of his country home) in fact illustrates her ability to transform a courtly form like the *chançon royal*, the second possible model for verse letters available to her, to serve as a vehicle for an entirely new form of writing.

Christine found in Eustache Deschamps's writings the model for the *chançon royal*, a verse epistle addressed ostensibly to princes. As he describes it in his *Art de Dictier* (1392) and as his own use of the genre shows (he wrote over one hundred and forty-two of them), the *chançon royal* was essentially a ballade with a send-off or *envoi* which began with the word *Princes*. In Eustache's works, the genre could depict a specific situation or present a specific petition to a royal personage, or place words in a prince's mouth. In practice, as one would expect from a poet attached to royal courts, Eustache rarely was concrete. Direct criticisms of the prince were out of the question. When he in fact wished to refer to actual political events, he pointedly switched to Latin, as, for example, when he condemned Paris for its fickle allegiance to the French king or when he praised the actual removal of an unjust prince.[15]

Eustache's use of Latin is a pointed reminder both of the different publics that a medieval poet could address and of the limitations of courtly lyric. By composing lyric in the vernacular, a poet effectively abandoned historical referentiality, and Guillaume IX's claim about writing lyric "from absolutely nothing" (*de dreit rien*) bears repeating. Christine's choice of vernacular prose was clearly tempered by her sensitivity both to her audience and to the constraints of lyric itself. Christine's attempt to break free from these narrow confines of lyric is particularly evident in one of her ballades, which closely follows the form of the *chançons royaulx* with an *envoi* addressed to the unnamed *Princes*, but which goes far beyond the conventional send-off. It also illustrates how far she was able to experiment within the genre of verse epistles.

In the ballade "With too much boldness and presumption" ("Trop hardement et grant presumpcion"[16]), Christine juggles courtly decorum and moral indignation. She condemns as sinful those who write against the princes, but notes that a ruler should not raise a sword against the people or against those who write against the princes. Christine follows standard courtly practice in her choice of the word "sin" since, significantly, Eustache Deschamps had used the term "sin" (*pechiez*) in the one example of the *chançon royal* which he cites in the *Art de Dictier* (1393). She uses the same refrain to link the three very different sins:

> I say it for those who by distraction dare to blame princes in order to incite the people against them by stirring up grievances and dare to call them bears, lions and wolves . . . I say to whoever does it that it is a sin.

> Therefore, good French, do not claim that you have proud tyrants filled with gall; let another nation talk like that; for you do not know what a tyrant is; and you wrongly allow such writings to be disseminated. . . . It is a vile thing to compose ballades in such a style. I say to whoever does it that it is a sin.

> Mighty princes, let there be no criminal or civil vengeance in your hearts because of these writings, for whoever raises his sword against his people, I say to whoever does it that it is a sin.

> Pour ceulx le di, qui, par destraccion,
> Osent blasmer princes, pour enflamer
> Peupple contre eulx par grief commossion,
> Et les osent, ours, lyons, loups nommer
>
>   .   .   .   .   .
> Je dis que c'est pechié a qui le fait.

> Sy ne faites, bons François, mencion,
> Que vous ayés tirans fiers plains d'amer;
> Laissiez parler a autre nacion;
> Car ne sçavés qu'est tirant, et semer
> Souffrez a tort telz dis
>
>   .   .   .   .   .
>   . . . c'est chose ville
> De soustenir contre eulx si grant tort fait,
> Et de ditter balades de tel stille,
> Je dis que c'est pechié a qui le fait.

> Princes poissans, criminelle ou civille
> Vengenance pour telz diz en voz cuers n'ait;
> Car qui glaive contre son puepple affille,
> Je dis que c'est pechié a qui le fait.
> (ll. 11–14, 20–25, 27–34)

The ballade is typical of Christine's position as a mediator between rival political factions, particularly in its attempt to posit the notion of the French nation as encompassing all estates and not just the nobility. Many of her later prose epistles will assume this function in a far more explicit and immediate way. While the refrain here conveys a political message of restraint and moderation to all parties concerned, the poem on a theoretical level is an appeal to princes to govern humanely, without any concrete reference to contemporary events, since courtly literature never mentions historical happenings. This lack of referential specificity accounts for both the charm and the bloodlessness of much courtly literature. Furthermore, it allows a misogynist *clerc* to disavow responsibility for his writings since his task was only to recycle tradition with a dash of formal playfulness to prove he had learned his craft. In this ballade Christine has taken verse epistle in medieval French to its absolute limit. After this point, she can only carry on the message in prose.

Almost four years separate Christine's first three major verse epistles from her last, and these years saw the composition of Christine's prose letters in the Quarrel of the *Rose* which explicitly articulated her humanist identity. Each of these three works hints at the limitations of verse for Christine's subject matter, and all of these concerns culminate in the *Epistre a Eustache Mourel*, Christine's last verse epistle. She uses her farewell composition in this genre to articulate her own literary identity, this time in verse as she had done in the prose letters during the Quarrel. Above all, she stresses her connection to an elite tradition of learning. The general theme of the letter is a lament on the decline of contemporary letters. In an earlier golden age, she notes with sadness, the princes were learned. She begins by expressing her solidarity with Eustache's exemplary wisdom: "the sage teaches his disciples to take sages as friends if they desire to learn" ("le saige / Enseigne aux disciples a prendre / Amistieé aux saiges, se apprendre / Desirent" ll. 10–14). She appeals to an ideal community of the wise united by their love of wisdom. She pointedly explains to Eustache Deschamps that she chooses the *tu* form over *vos*, a self-conscious humanist device cogently defended by Petrarch who had borrowed it from Cicero[17]:

May it not bother you if I now take joy in speaking to you in the singular person, for I learned it from the clerical style employed by those who spend their lives in learning.

Ne te tourt se adès plaisance
Ay qu'em singulier nom je parle
A toy, car je l'ay apris par le
Stille clergial de quoy ceulx usent
Qui en science leurs temps usent.
(ed. Roy, II, p. 296, vv. 17–22)

After sketching this ideal community, Christine then stakes her claim to membership in it. Her argument is two-fold: first, she enjoys full rights and privileges in this republic of letters by virtue of the love of knowledge which she demonstrates in her writing; and second, that literary culture in her time generally finds itself in a perilous decline because of the popularity of lying and deceit, a swipe at the popularity of the *Rose*, no doubt. The implied solution is only hinted at, but Christine implies that she, as the "handmaiden of Learning" can help restore literary culture to its pristine integrity. In all of her contentions, she is careful not to view learning as the prerogative of either sex. First, she informs him that he should not scorn her as a woman:

Do not despise my female mind, so that if I fail, rather consider the great love I bear for knowledge.

Mon femenin scens ne desprises
Sy que g'i faille, ains adès prises
La grant amour qu'ay a savoir (vv. 29–31)

The next point is highly complex, for in naming Eustache her master, as Dante had called Vergil, she implies that she is his worthy disciple and successor. The reason for this identification lies, as I have argued elsewhere, in Eustache Deschamps's claim in the *Art de Dictier* that rhetoric was the science of "straight talk," of speaking wisely, concisely, exhaustively and courageously, without gratuitous flights into ambiguity ("Rhetoric is the discipline of speaking directly . . . for even the good rhetorician must speak and say what he means wisely, briefly, pointedly and boldly," "Rethorique est science de parler droictement . . . car tout bon rethoricien doit parler et dire ce qu'il veut moustrer *saigement, briefment, substancieusement* et *hardiement.*").[18] As far as Christine was concerned, Jean de Meung had done the exact opposite in the *Rose*, and thus had not only insulted women but also had betrayed rhetoric itself. Christine then addresses Eustache directly herself about the moral corruption of her age:

> Oh master! what a hard shock it is at this time to see lying and deceit so popular in cities, castles, at princely courts, as a common rule, among the nobles and the commons, among the clergy and in every court of justice.

> O maistre! quel merveille dure
> Est de veoir ou temps qui dure
> Mençonge et barat si en cours
> En cités, en chastiaulx, en cours
> De princes, par rigle commune
> En nobles gens et en commune,
> En clergie et en toute court
> De justice
> (vv. 51–58)

The solution lies in her devotion to study. When she concludes her description of the decay of letters, she notes that this epistle of hers had been "written by a little lonely woman in my study" (*escript seulette en m'estude*, v. 205), a charged identification because it recalls her famous earlier ballade, "Seulette sui et seulette veuil estre," ("I am a little lonely woman, and I want to be a little lonely woman") and because it anticipates her opening remarks in the *Cité des Dames* that she was working in her *cele*, her study, a term perhaps deliberately evocative of the *libraria cella*, the book-lined cell, of early Italian women humanists.[19] Finally, she calls herself the handmaiden of science, "Christine de Pizan, ancelle/De Science" (vv. 209–10), a phrase that alludes of course to the famous identification of the Virgin as the *ancilla Domini* (Luke 1:36). This carefully articulated devotion to learning shows that Christine first and foremost took her cue from the humanist tradition. In many passages her epistle to Eustache Deschamps reads like one of Petrarch's metrical epistles, which could in fact have served as a model for Christine.

This supposition brings us to the final possible model of verse epistles available to Christine, namely the Petrarchan *epistola metrica*. It is difficult to prove definitively that Christine had access to the three books of sixty-six metrical epistles which Petrarch wrote and collected between 1331 and 1361. Evidence from library holdings of Petrarch's works in France shows a modest circulation there of the *Epistolæ metricæ* in the late fourteenth and early fifteenth century.[20] Christine, however, does not mention Petrarch's metrical epistles; in general, in response to her French audience's taste, she mentions Boccaccio far more frequently than Petrarch throughout her work. This silence can be explained in light of Petrarch's unpopularity in France provoked by Petrarch's severe condemnation of the cultural pretensions of humanists outside of Italy, especially in France and Germany. By way of comparison, it is clear that the prose Latin letters of Christine's contemporary, the humanist Nicolas de Clamanges, are modelled on Petrarch's prose letters even though Nicolas nowhere mentions Petrarch, as Ezio Ornato has demonstrated.[21]

Given the initial improbability of Petrarch's metrical epistles having influenced Christine, I would suggest three indirect reasons which would indicate that they could have been her model.[22] First, Petrarch's metrical epistles, unlike the *chançons royaulx* of Deschamps, are addressed to actual individuals and treat specific historical events or topics, and Christine's letter to Eustache Deschamps seems to imitate this format and carefully identifies Christine's work with humanist ideals. Second, I suspect that Christine as an Italian expatriate was keenly aware of her position between France and Italy, and she would have been especially sensitive to and familiar with the poems in which Petrarch spoke of his own relationship to Italy.[23] Third, Petrarch's metrical epistle to Guido Gonzaga[24] is the only negative criticism of the *Rose* prior to Christine, who may have taken some of her motivation to criticize the *Rose* from Petrarch. In fact Christine pointedly told Gontier Col, one of her humanist opponents in the Quarrel over the *Rose*, that Dante's *Commedia* was "a hundred times better written" than the *Rose*. These three reasons, admittedly, do not supply incontrovertible proof that Petrarch's *epistolæ metricæ* were Christine's model, but taken together with the importance of so many other of Petrarch's works for Christine's writings, and given the absence of a comparable medieval French model, the probability of this conjecture seems high.

In brief, Christine used the verse epistle to explode courtly conventions, to combine it with patristic allegorical interpretation, and to infuse it with classical exempla. Even with these innovations, she ultimately moved to prose as her preferred epistolary form.

Christine's Letters on the *Roman de la Rose* and the Humanist Critique of Courtliness

The epistolary dispute on a literary topic, as several critics have noted, had first been cultivated by Christine's favorite models, the Italian humanists,[25] and in several instances her writings echo this larger humanist discussion. When, for example, in the *Cité des Dames* I.9, Christine criticizes Ovid in favor of Vergil, her comparison of the two authors recalls the subject of exchanges beginning in late 1397 between two contemporary humanists, Jean de Montreuil (1361–1418), secretary of finances under King Charles V, and Ambrogio de'Migli, an Italian then residing in Paris about whom little is known, regarding the relative merits of Ovid, Vergil and Cicero. During the course of the quarrel over the *Rose*, Jean de Montreuil, rather than invoking Ovid, specifically cited Vergil and Cicero to praise Jean de Meung.[26] Since Jean de Montreuil at this time was particularly keen in rejecting Petrarch's claim that poets or orators should not be sought outside Italy ("in Petrarca legisse . . . extra Italiam poetas aut oratores non esse querendos"[27]), he would naturally have seen in Jean de Meung's classic invocation of the *translatio studii* topos at the mid-point of the *Rose* strong counter-evidence to Petrarch.[28] Nicholas Mann has also shown that both Jean Gerson and Jean de Montreuil were enthusiastic readers of Petrarch's moralist writings, and Petrarch's *De remediis utriusque fortunæ* (*Concerning Remedies for Good and Bad Fortune*, 1354–66) would have been a possible inspiration for Christine in writing her own *Livre de la mutacion de Fortune* (*The Book of the Change of Fortune*, 1400–1404). In his metrical epistle to Guido Gonzaga from 1340, Petrarch claimed that the obvious shortcomings of the *Rose* were proof of the superiority of Italian eloquence.[29] This same argument forms the basis of Christine's critique some sixty years later concerning the *Commedia*'s superiority over the *Rose*. Petrarch seems to have been a source for much of Christine's work, inspiring her in her biography of Charles V, to draw "parallels between his qualities and those represented in episodes from ancient history, clearly a humanistic technique."[30]

In light of this reception of Petrarch's works in France, Jean de Montreuil's treatise in praise of the *Rose* and Christine's response are clearly part of a much larger humanist quarrel. Taken together, these facts strongly suggest that the letters which Christine wrote and collected during the Quarrel of the *Rose* were patterned after similar humanist epistolary exchanges.

Christine also describes her indebtedness to humanism and her critique of courtly conventions in *L'Avision-Christine* (*The Vision of Christine*, 1405). She recounts the beginning of her literary career and stresses the change of direction it took under the influence of "foreign things" which may be identified with the growing influence of Italian writers like Petrarch and Boccaccio in late fourteenth-century France:

> Then I began to compose pretty pieces, and when I first began lighter ones, and just like the artisan who makes his work more subtle the more he devotes himself to it, so too my mind, always studying different topics, became more and more imbued with alien matters, modifying my style to be much subtler and loftier.

> Adonc me pris a forgier choses jolies, a mon commencement plus legieres, et tout ainsi comme l'ouvrier qui de plus en plus son oeuvre s'asoubtille comme plus il la frequente, ainsi tousjours estudiant diverses matieres, mon sens de plus en plus s'imbuoit de choses estranges, amendant mon stile en plus grant soubtilleté et plus haulte matiere.[31]

This shift under the influence of unspecified *choses estranges* ("alien, or foreign, or strange, matters") helps clarify her attitude toward the courtly conventions current in the late fourteenth century. Under the influence of Italian humanists, especially Petrarch, Christine in fact did change the direction of her writing, and her epistolary compositions typify this shift from the gratuitously pretty and formalist play of late medieval courtly lyric to more somber, yet more lofty matters, *plus haute matiere*, articulated in an innovative, "socially committed" prose. Christine's interest in patristic authors may have had its most direct roots in the example of Italian humanists, and two of her works in particular conspicuously employ the Church Fathers: *L'Avision-Christine*, whose prologue carefully explains the working of allegory and may have taken its cue from Boccaccio's views on allegory[32], and the *Lamentacion*, which interweaves classical and patristic commonplaces on consolation. Incorporating this patristic strain into the *Lamentacion*, a letter to women of all conditions, underscores the seriousness and the originality of Christine's epistolography; she adapts a humanistic stance in the vernacular to fashion a woman's voice on matters of historical and moral consequence. These developments and the shift in emphasis they herald, while clearly evident in her later epistolary compositions, are nevertheless also present *in nuce* in the letters she wrote during the Quarrel.

How do Christine's letters in the Quarrel of the *Rose* illustrate this shift more precisely? Christine deliberately followed humanist practice when she collected the letters written during the Quarrel of the *Rose* in imitation of Petrarch who had himself consciously imitated Cicero. As Paul Oskar Kristeller observed, Petrarch begins the long line of humanists who collected their own letters and at the same time carefully polished and revised them.[33] By contrast, for example, Catherine of Siena's letters were only collected by editors culling them from the various addressees.

Christine deliberately linked her use of letters to her defense of women, and this tactic on her part marks a consistent pattern of deploying letters in a gender-specific context, of expanding the humanist approach to encompass women as well. She wrote in the dedicatory epistle:

> I am moved to send you the present letters in which, my most revered Lady . . . you may understand the diligence, desire and determination in which my small power endeavors to uphold itself with veritable defenses against several opinions contrary to integrity as well as the honor and praise of women, which several clerics and others have attempted in their poetry to cut down, something which is not permitted either to endure or to sustain.

> sui meue a vous envoyer les presens epistres, esquelles, ma tres redoubtee dame . . . pourréz entendre la diligence, desir et voulenté ou ma petite puissance s'estent a soustenir par deffenses veritables contre aucunes oppinions a honnesteté contraires, et aussi l'onneur et louenge des femmes (laquelle pluseurs clercs et autres se sont efforciéz par leurs dittiéz d'amenuisier, qui n'est chose loisible ne a souffir ne soustenir). (ed. Hicks, p. 6)

The fact that she singled out courtly lyric (*dittiéz*) is not coincidental. It marks her consistent attack on the misogyny of courtly lyric. Christine understood how easily the prettified objectification of women in courtly lyric could be dialectically transformed into misogynist attacks. As her epistolary skill would demonstrate, she refused to be a dupe of these conventions.

In the concluding letter of her collection, addressed to Gontier Col,

Christine returns to the same issues raised in the dedicatory epistle, which of course chronologically post-dated this last letter. What is striking here is that Christine pointedly rejects Col's *ad feminam* attacks on her position. He had argued that she was speaking "like a woman caught up emotionally in this subject" (*comme femme passionnee en ceste matiere*, p. 23). She rejects any attempt to undercut the validity of her arguments against the *Rose* which tie them to her biological identity "as a woman" (*comme femme*). In this regard, Christine adheres completely to the humanist tradition: what she has to say is valid in its own right as a treatise and not because it was said or written by a woman. Her epistolary art, deployed on behalf of women in the vernacular, was not meant to repeat endlessly the misogynist dialectic it unmasked. In other words, Christine was trying to restore the universality of letters to its own ideals.

For this reason, Christine's prose letters often seem to be treatises, and here the final resemblance to humanist epistolography becomes evident. As Kristeller noted regarding the form of humanist epistles, "the letter had a scholarly or philosophical content and was really nothing but a treatise to which the form of the letter gave as it were a personal tone, as the humanists like to do. In fact it is not always easy to draw the line between letters of this kind and treatises."[34] Like humanist epistles, Christine's letters address a specific, concrete occasion. Her restrained use of verse epistles will illustrate how she attempted to carry this criticism further and why, to this end, she ultimately came to prefer prose letters to verse.

Women Writing to Women: *Ars dictaminis* and the Letter of Madame de la Tour in the *Livre de Trois Vertus* (1405) and the *Epistre a la Reine* (1405)

It should now be clear that Christine's hostility to the *Rose* and to the kind of courtly love or *fin'amors* which it appeared to her to champion link her verse and prose letters. Both kinds of epistolary composition stress erudition rather than the expression of personal feeling. Here a reminder from Giles Constable bears repeating: "Whereas intimacy, spontaneity, and privacy are now considered the essence of the epistolary genre, in the Middle Ages letters were for the most part self-conscious, quasi-public literary documents, often written with an eye to future collection and publication. . . . They were therefore designed to be correct and elegant rather than original and spontaneous, and they often followed the form and content of model letters in formularity."[35] Christine pointedly cultivated an erudite style in her letters to demonstrate that a woman need not be denatured to be erudite. Christine's letters also form an important part of her critique of courtly love (*fin' amors*) and of the importance of women to defend their honor and chastity.

This point becomes especially clear in looking at the letter written by Madame de la Tour and included as a model for other women in both the *Livre des Trois Vertus* and the *Livre du Duc des Vrais Amants*. As Charity Cannon Willard suggested, Christine certainly presented the figure of the wise lady, *la sage dame*, as a counter-example to the scurrilous Duenna (*La Vieille*) of the *Rose*: "Christine's views on the subject of honor are best summed up in a letter written by Madame de la Tour (Book I, Chapter 27), a lady charged with the education of a susceptible young princess. The role of this elderly governess is particularly interesting, because she offers advice entirely opposed to the sort given to the Lover by the Old Woman in *The Romance of the Rose*."[36]

The admonishments delivered in the letter are carefully presented according to standard dictaminal models. Christine's knowledge of the *ars dictaminis* may in fact be linked to her ancestral home, for it was first in her home city of Bologna that the dictaminal handbooks were first developed.[37] Charles H. Haskins summarized the standard format expected by the dictaminal manuals:

> There should be five parts arranged in logical sequence. After the salutation—as to which the etiquette of the mediaeval scribe was very exacting, each class in society having its own terms of address and reply—came the exordium, consisting of some commonplace generality, a proverb, or a scriptural quotation, and designed to put the reader in the proper frame of mind for granting the request to follow. Then came the statement of the particular purpose of the letter (the narration), ending in a petition which commonly has the form of a deduction from the major and minor premises laid down in the exordium and narration, and finally the phrases of a conclusion.[38]

This five-part division is found in most medieval handbooks. Alberic of Monte Cassino, for example, writes, "Its parts are namely five: salutation, appeal to the reader's good will, narration, petition and conclusion" ("cuius videlicet quinque sunt partes: salutatio, beniuolentie captatio, narratio, petitio, atque conclusio").[39] As will become apparent, Christine followed this practice very closely in many of her prose letters. Her familiarity with dictaminal practice could have been a direct result of her own employment in the royal chancellory, for, as Charity Cannon Willard noted regarding a possible identification of Christine's own handwriting, Christine probably "wrote the cursive script that was used in the correspondence of the royal chancellory, and not the *lettres de forme* that in the past had generally been favored for literary manuscripts and Books of Hours."[40] This cursive script, of course, was the favored script for letters. Indeed, it would seem that Christine's close adherence to dictaminal practice, down to the form of the script that she consciously chose, reinforces all the more the theory that she had worked in the royal chancellory.

What Christine does in the *Livre des Trois Vertus* is to provide a dictaminal model for women. She explains that women counselling a young princess might not know how to advise their charge against illicit love and so provides a prototypical letter. In the original, the letter is divided as would be expected into five "paragraphs" or sections corresponding to the five prescribed dictaminal divisions of *salutatio* (ll. 21–35), *exordium* or *captatio benevolentiæ* (ll. 36–81), *narratio* (ll. 82–214), *petitio* (ll. 215–264) and *conclusio* (ll. 265–283). The uneven length of these "paragraphs" indicates how closely Christine was following the standard model. The first short "paragraph" greets the lady and apologizes for the necessity of writing. The second section provides the *exordium*, though it does not cite Scripture or a Latin author, Christine's usual ploy in her letters against the *Rose*, but these were letters after all addressed to humanists. (Adjusting her message for her audience, Christine pointedly does not use the humanist *tu* in this letter, but reverts to the courtly *vos*.) Instead, Christine diplomatically notes that highly placed princesses and noblewomen should serve as the example of virtue to all women, "the example by which other ladies, and even all women, must conduct themselves in all affairs" ("l'exemplaire par lequel les autres dames, et meismement toutes femmes, se doivent rigler en tout maintien," ed. Willard/Hicks, p. 111). This statement is what Haskins would call the major premise, whose minor premise is then provided in the third section or *narratio*. Here the *narratio* is the longest section of all as the lengths in lines given above indicate. I suspect that this section is one of the longest "paragraphs" found in all Christine's writings and that its very length attests to Christine's adherence to standard dictaminal practice. Christine presents numerous examples of model female virtue and tough-minded wisdom, very much like Madame de Sevigné writing to her daughter almost three centuries later. Christine warns the young princess tempted to stray, "do not be deceived and do not let yourself be deceived," ("ne vous y decevez ne laissiez decepvoir," p. 113). The *petitio* in this letter is disguised: rather than requesting something from the princess who is the addressee, the governess asks what will the lady's servants and others think of the lady if she falls into the trap of illicit love? Is not the lady aware of the slanderous talk to which her behavior has given rise? These questions represent veiled warnings and function in fact as a petition not to act in a certain way. The governess concludes by reiterating her good will in writing and then closes.

For all its conformity to dictaminal prescriptions, the letter of Madame de la Tour deftly conceals its own erudition, perhaps because Christine was adapting her prose to a less well-educated audience of female readers. Allison Kelly has demonstrated as well the fundamentally anti-courtly tenor of the letter.[41] It is hard to believe that it comes from the same pen as the letters on the *Rose* or the *Epistre a Eustache Mourel*. It attests on the one hand to Christine's enormous range and consummate versatility as an accomplished letter-writer, in verse, in dictaminal prose or in humanist exchanges, and on the other to the very real practical differences separating male and female spheres.

Contemporaries did not miss Christine's adherence to dictaminal models. The best demonstration of this exemplary status is that Christine's impassioned petition from October 5, 1405, to Isabeau de Bavière to mediate between the rival Dukes of Orléans and Burgundy, a text now referred to as the *Epistre a la Reine* (*Epistle to the Queen*), was included in one of the most important surviving dictaminal formularies of the late Middle Ages.[42] Christine signs the letter by apologizing for its hurried script, claiming that she had finished the letter at one o'clock in the morning and could find no scribe to copy it for her, though, of course, even this claim could be a humanist tag, for during the Quarrel of the *Rose*, Gontier Col signed one of his letters, "written hastily," *escript hastivement* (ed. Hicks, p. 11). Some critics argue on the basis of these remarks that the letter was written quickly and informally. The reception of the work as a dictaminal model and a closer examination of internal evidence disprove this claim. Besides being included in several manuscripts containing other works by Christine, it is found in All Souls Ms. 182, one of the best epistolary formularies for both medieval Latin and medieval French prose letters. The entire codex was compiled by John Stevens, an ecclesiastical judge (d. 1460). Its first half is devoted to dictaminal manuals and Latin letters, primarily Archbishop Peckham's register (*Registrum Epistolarum Fratris Iohannis Peckham*), and its second half contains an extraordinary collection of letters, largely ecclesiatical and royal in origin, from around 1400. These texts range from letters of condolence, to a manor lord's warrant, to letters by Henry of Monmouth and Richard I the Lionhearted's correspondence from Ireland.[43] The inclusion of Christine's *Epistre a la Reine* demonstrates that Christine quickly attained contemporary recognition and by a compiler of a formulary manuscript in England, no less, as an accomplished letter-writer in prose. The fact also that All Souls Ms. 182 presents both French and Latin letters confirms once again the importance of the medieval Latin dictiminal tradition in evaluating Christine's works.

The letter itself exemplifies a variation on the standard five-part dictaminal model, for it consists of an extended series of narrations coupled with petitions to the Queen. This kind of variation was termed a *commutatio partium* by Alberic of Monte Cassino. The narrations cite three examples of women who had acted decisively to mediate political rivalries and whom Christine had mentioned in the *Cité des Dames*, finished earlier in the same year of 1405: Esther (II.32.1), Veturia (II.34.1) and Blanche of Castille (I.13.2). The deliberate choice of an exemplary woman from Scripture, from a classical author and from contemporary French history corresponds to Christine's attempt in the *Cité des Dames* to demonstrate the continuity of women's accomplishment throughout history in answer to Boccaccio's claim in *De claris mulieribus* that there were no *claræ* in Christian history. This interweaving of Hebrew, classical, and Christian history was a hallmark of humanism even if Boccaccio's attitude in *De claris mulieribus* must serve as the exception that confirms the rule. Equally consistent with humanist practice is Christine's use of a concrete historical occasion to write a short treatise on women's mediating role in politics. What is also remarkable about the letter to Isabeau is that Christine addresses the Queen with the courtly *vos*, whereas in letters to royal patrons written later, Christine employed the preferred humanist form of address, *tu*. Isabeau is addressed nine times in the course of the letter, usually with the formula, "most high lady" ("tres haute dame") or "most revered lady" ("tres redoubtee dame"). These titles enhance the epistle's courtly veneer, a practice completely consistent with Christine's earlier epistolary habits. Thus the letter to Isabeau reveals Christine synthesizing dictaminal, humanist, and courtly models to the best possible advantage as part of a carefully elaborated argument on behalf of women. Furthermore, it was done in a way that contemporaries were quick to recognize as a model of dictaminal art.

"A Little Lonely Woman on the Sidelines": The Female Voice in Christine's Later Letters

Christine's skill at combining courtly, dictaminal, and humanist traditions in her letter-writing permitted her what amounts to an "open letter" to the royal princes, the *Lamentacion sur les maux de la guerre civile* (*Lamentation on the Evils of Civil War*, 1410). Here she comments more directly than she had earlier on current events from an explicitly "female" perspective. Christine, of course, very carefully constructs the female *persona* which she then dramatically "produces" in a veritable *mise en scène*. In an allusion both to her most famous lyric poem on her widowhood, "I am a little lonely woman and I want to be a little lonely woman," ("seulete suis, et seulete veuil estre") and to the end of her letter to Eustache Deschamps, "escript seullete en m'estude," she presents herself at the beginning of the *Lamentacion* as a "little lonely woman on the sidelines," *seulette à part*. After addressing the various princes and the Queen herself in a manner not unlike the *chançons royaulx* of Eustache Deschamps, she passes in review the evils of civil war from classical sources. She signs off as a "poor voice crying out in this kingdom," ("povre voix criant en ce royaume"), with the biblical allusion to Luke 3:4 *vox clamantis in deserto* foremost in mind. As Margarete Zimmermann pointed out, "This lamenting female voice of the *Lamentacion* subsequently turns into both a 'voice crying in the desert' and the voice of an incisive Cassandra."[44] What Christine does in the *Lamentacion* now appears entirely consistent with her earlier practice: the synthesis of lyrical conventions (calling herself *seulette* and addressing the princes), classical references, and biblical *exempla* has become the trademark of Christine's mature epistolography.

On January 20, 1417, Christine completed her last major epistolary work, the *Epistre sur la Prison de Vie Humaine* (*The Epistle on the Prison of Human Life*), which was addressed to Marie of Berry, Duchess of Bourbon and Auvergne, though Christine is aiming at a larger audience, as she had in the *Lamentacion*. The body of the letter again demonstrates Christine's skill at interweaving biblical, patristic, and classical sources, yet as Charity Cannon Willard noted, "The true inspiration for Christine's letter, however, was the humanistic tradition of writing letters to give advice to princes, princesses, and other leaders of society."[45] This humanistic trait is the common thread running through all of Christine's epistolary art. It is also tied to Christine's drawing attention to her situation as a woman writing a letter to another woman, a situation she had thematized on several previous occasions. Christine takes pains to explain her position carefully. Though she speaks specifically to Marie, Christine turns to a vastly larger audience, namely all afflicted women. This acute sense of her public reflects Christine's self-conscious cultivation of her specifically female voice:

> I will speak to all women in like manner, in fulfilling my duty by means of writing, according to my bare wit and knowledge, to recollect for you the appropriate reasons taken and drawn both from received stories as from the Holy Scriptures which can and must move you to restrain and stop the shedding of tears.

> Je parleray a toutes semblablement, en faisant mon devoir, par moien d'escripture, selon mon petit savoir et congnoissance, de te ramentevoir aucunes raisons a propos prises et puisiees tant en hystoires approuvees comme es Saintes Escriptures, qui te pevent et doivent mouvoir a restraindre et delaissier l'effusion de lermes.[46]

The striking rhetorical situation of the letter as a consolation for all women—not a first, for in the *Livre de la Paix* Christine had also written a letter addressed to all people—dovetails with Christine's humanistic intention. Here, unlike her writing in the *Epistre a la Reine*, she addresses Marie of Berry with the humanist *tu*, and even explains her reasons:

> Before I proceed any further in this matter, I humbly beg your human grace that there is nothing bad if I speak to you in the singular, that is, with *tu*, just as I spoke earlier in my short writings and letters to your most noble father, the Duke of Berry—may his soul be in heaven— and to many other princes and princesses, following in this part the style of poets and orators.

> Avant que plus oultre je procede en ceste matiere, suppli humblement ton humaine debonnaireté, que n'ait a mal se en singulier je parle a toy, c'est assavoir par tu, ainsi comme meismement autrefois ay parlé en mes petites escriptures et epistres a ton trés noble pere, l'excellent duc de Berry—dont l'ame soit au ciel—et a maints autres princes et princesses, suivant le stille en ceste partie des poëtes et orateurs. (pp. 4–6)

With one stroke of the pen Christine has successfully brought her entire career as a letter-writer to bear on her appeal to Marie and all women suffering the loss of their loved ones. Her most important epistolary compositions—the *Epistre a Eustache Mourel* with its mention of "clerical style" (*stille clergial*), the *Epistre a la Reine* (in which she kept to *vos*) and the *Lamentacion* (in which she switched to *tu* for the Queen and princes)—are all present here in order to aid her in her task of consolation. This single use of *tu* evokes Christine's most fundamental positions in the literary culture of her day and lends her consolation a powerful force and dignity. All of this she accomplishes within the standard dictaminal requirements of the *captatio benevolentiæ*. The remainder of her long letter is studded with erudition. It combines, again in Christine's trademark fashion, classical, biblical, and patristic sources, and relatively few allusions to contemporary events. Christine's intent was to console from the heights of the Lucretian *serena templa sapientum* rather than to dwell too much on this vale of tears, this prison of human life.

With this final epistle, Christine's letter-writing becomes even more public than it had been hitherto. For while illustrating with textbook perfection her knowledge of the conventions of dictaminal literature, the *Epistre sur la Prison de Vie Humaine* also demonstrates her ready ease with the theological and philosophical issues of her age, generously and fluently supported by patristic sources. In this letter, as in her previous works, she incorporates rhetorical elements borrowed from courtly lyric, dictaminal handbooks, and humanist epistolography in order to recast classical models with an eye to revealing that a woman can plead effectively on behalf of all humanity. Perhaps her synthesis is in fact more effective than those found in male writers whose misogyny limited their vision. Christine speaks indeed as a little lonely woman in her study, *seullete en m'estude*, but with her message of consolation she speaks not only to all women, but also to all men. The power behind this synthesis was preeminently humanist, for it was the power of erudition, of learning, of study, and this power was ideally open to all.

Notes

1. The first overall survey of Christine as a letter-writer is found in Marie-Josèphe Pinet, *Christine de Pisan, 1364–1431: Étude biographique et littéraire* (Paris: Champion, 1927), pp. 263–80. Although in many ways uneven, Pinet's study wrestled with the question of Christine's models for verse epistles without considering

the rising influence of Italian humanism in France during Christine's day, a question which is absolutely central in interpreting Christine's verse and prose epistles.

2. When Elizabeth C. Goldsmith proposes a "gender-genre" connection between women and letter-writing in her collection of essays, *Writing the Female Voice: Essays on Epistolary Literature* (Boston: Northeastern University Press, 1989), she does not assume that there is an essential female voice but only a constructed one. The women writers scrutinized in *Writing the Female Voice* often manipulated and subverted the conventions of epistolary form, but unlike Christine de Pizan they seldom strove, it seems, to break free of the most fundamental construction in the genre itself, namely the dialectic of gender. The best survey of literature on Héloïse and related problems is Barbara Newman, "Authority, Authenticity, and the Repression of Heloise," *Journal of Medieval and Renaissance Studies* 22, 2 (Spring 1992): 121–57.

3. Joan W. Scott, "Gender: A Useful Category of Historical Analysis," *American Historical Review* 91 (1986): 1068.

4. For prose letters, see M. Dominica Legge, *Anglo-Norman Letters and Petitions from All Souls ms. 182* (Oxford: Blackwell, 1941), who prints the *Epistre a la Reine* (pp. 144–50). As far as verse epistles are concerned, one must look at ballades with *envois* and the *lettres royales* of Deschamps but these works are a far cry from Christine's verse letters. See the illuminating remarks of Mario Marti, "L'epistolario comme «genere» e un problema editoriale," in *Studi e problemi di critica testuale* (Convegno di Studi di Filogia italiana nel Centenario della Commissione per i Testi di Lingua, 7–9 Aprile 1960), ed. Raffaele Spongano (Bologna: Commissione per Testi di Lingua, 1961), pp. 203–8.

5. "Is the poetic *salut*, for instance, which developed out of the epistolary salutation as defined in the handbooks of letter-writing, an epistolary poem or a poetic epistle?" Giles Constable, *Letters and Letter-Collections*, Typologies des Sources du Moyen Âge occidental, fasc. 17 (Turnhout: Brepols, 1976), p. 12.

6. The essays in *The Reception of Christine de Pizan from the Fifteenth Through the Nineteenth Century, Visitors to the City*, ed. Glenda McLeod (Lewiston, ME: E. Mellen, 1991), *Reinterpreting Christine de Pizan*, ed. E. J. Richards et al. (Athens: University of Georgia Press, 1992) and *Gender, Genre and Politics, Essays on Christine de Pizan*, (Boulder, CO: Westview Press, 1992) constitute an enormous advance in Christine scholarship in this regard.

7. *Le Débat sur le Roman de la Rose*, ed. Eric Hicks (Paris: Champion, 1977), p. 135.

8. The best synopsis and analysis of the *Epistre au dieu d'Amours* is Thelma Fenster's introduction to her recent edition and translation: *Poems of Cupid, God of Love: Christine de Pizan's "Epistre au dieu d'Amours" and "Dit de la Rose," Thomas Hoccleve's "The Letter of Cupid,"* ed. Thelma S. Fenster and Mary Carpenter Erler (Leiden: E. J. Brill, 1990), pp. 3–19. All citations are from this edition.

9. Hicks, ed., *Le Débat*, p. 57.

10. Richards, "Feminism as Universalism: Virginia Woolf's *Orlando* and Christine de Pizan's *Livre de la Mutacion de Fortune*: Sexual Metamorphosis, Gender Difference and the Republic of Letters," *Romance Languages Annual* (Purdue University) 2 (1991): 146–52.

11. See Barbara K. Altmann's skillful analysis of this phenomenon, "Reopening the Case: Machaut's Judgement Poems as a Source in Christine de Pizan," in *Reinterpreting Christine de Pizan*, pp. 137–56.

12. Charity Cannon Willard, *Christine de Pizan: Her Life and Works* (New York: Persea, 1984), p. 47.

13. The basic dictaminal manuals are found in Ludwig Rockinger, *Briefsteller und Formelbücher des eilften bis vierzehnten Jahrhunderts* (Munich, 1863; reprinted, New York: Franklin, 1961) and the best bibliography on medieval letter-writing is contained in James Murphy, *Medieval Rhetoric, A Select Bibliography*, 2nd ed. (Toronto: University of Toronto Press, 1989). Dictaminal writers concede the existence of metrical letters, but devote their attention almost exclusively to prose. After noting the existence of dictaminal composition in meter, in rhythm and in prose, Alberic of Monte Cassino wrote, "But since the only proposition of our intention is to treat prose, we will follow more attentively what it is and how it must be done" ("Verum quoniam de prosaico solum intentionis nostre propositum est pertractare, quid ipsum sit et qualiter fieri debeat attentius prosequamur" ed. Rockinger, v.1, p. 9). Hugo of Bologna, for example, wrote "we know indeed two kinds of dictaminal writing, the first of course is prose and the second is called metrical" ("duo quidem dictaminum genera nouimus, unum videlict prosaicum, alterum quod vocatur metricum" ed. Rockinger, v. 1, p. 54) and then turned straight to prose without wasting another word on verse. This silence makes the question of Christine's models for verse epistles all the more acute.

14. The *Epistre d'Othea* is cited here from Halina Loukopoulos, "Classical Mythology in the Works of Christine de Pisan with an Edition of 'L'Epistre d'Othea' from the Manuscript Harley 4431," Ph.D. dissertation, Wayne State University, 1977, pp. 155–57.

15. Poem No. 1332, *Oeuvres complètes d'Eustache Deschamps*, ed. Gaston Raynaud (Paris: Didot, 1891), vol. 7, pp. 102f: "O sinful city of the French, Paris, mother of sinners, twice rebellious against your kings" ("O pecatrix civitas Francorum, Parisius, mater peccatorum, Bis rebellis contra tuo reges"). In Poem 1335 (v. 7, p. 107), Eustache explains that power is justly transferred "when a prince does not wish to judge the truth, but when injury to an innocent party comes to naught" ("quando princeps non vult veritatem/Judicari, sed anichilatur/Injuria contra innocentem").

16. "Autres Ballades, no. XLIX, in *Oeuvres poétiques de Christine de Pisan*, ed. Maurice Roy (Paris: Didot, 1882), v. 1, pp. 263–64.

17. See J. D. Burnley, "Christine de Pizan and the so-called *style clergial*," *Modern Language Quarterly* 81 (1986): 1–6.

18. See my discussion of these points in my essay "Christine de Pizan, the Conventions of Courtly Diction and Italian Humanism," in *Reinterpreting Christine de Pizan*, pp. 250–71.

19. See Margaret L. King, "Book-Lined Cells: Woman and Humanism in the Early Italian Renaissance," in *Beyond Their Sex: Learned Women of the European Past*, ed. Patricia H. Labalme (New York: New York University Press, 1980), pp. 66–90.

20. The metrical epistles are found in *Poesie minori del Petrarca*, ed. Domenico de Rosetti (Milan: Dalla Società tipografica de' classici italiani, 1829–1834), vol. 2, *Epistolarum tomus* (1831). In Elisabeth Pellegrin's survey, "Manuscrits de Pétrarque dans les bibliothèques de France," *Italia medioevale e umanistica* 4 (1961): 341–31; 6

(1963): 271–379, there is evidence for the circulation of individual metrical epistles, especially the *Epistola ad Italiam* (III, 24), see pp. 364, 366, 393–94, 397–98. Of course such evidence is suggestive only. Ezio Ornato in his study, "La prima fortuna di Petrarca in Francia, I: Le letture petrarchesche di Jean de Montreuil," *Studi francesi* 5 (1961): 201–17; II: Il contributo del Petrarca alla formazione culturale di Jean de Montreuil," *Studi francesi* 6 (1962): 401–14, doubted that Jean de Montreuil could have known all of Petrarch's *Familiares*, but demonstrates that he definitely knew select letters, specifically *Familiares*, XXIV, 3. He concludes on a general note, p. 413: "We have seen, moreover, how Jean de Montreuil's attention turned not only to moral philosophy, but also, indissolubly, to [Petrarch], the master in the field of rhetoric and the *ars dictandi*" ("Abbiamo visto, inoltre, come l'attenzione di Jean de Montreuil si rivolgesse non solo al filosofo morale, ma anche, in indissolubile unione, al maestro nel campo della retorica e dell'*ars dictandi*"). See also Nicholas Mann, "La fortune de Pétrarque en France: Recherches sur le «De Remediis»," *Studi francesi* 13 (1969): 3–13; "Petrarch's Role as Moralist in Fifteenth-Century France," in *Humanism in France at the End of the Middle Ages and in the Early Renaissance*, ed. A. H. T. Levi (New York: Barnes and Noble, 1970), pp. 6–28; "La prima fortuna del Petrarca in Inghilterra," in *Il Petrarca ad Arquà* (Atti del Convegno di Studi nel VI. centenario [1370–1374], Arquà Petrarca 6–8 novembre 1970), ed. Giuseppe Billanovich and Giuseppe Frasso (Padua, 1975), 279–89.

21. Ezio Ornato, *Jean Muret et ses amis Nicholas de Clamanges et Jean de Montreuil. Contribution à l'étude des rapports entre les humanistes de Paris et ceux d'Avignon (1394–1420)* (Geneva: Droz, 1969).

22. For more information on the *Epistolæ metricæ*, see Enrico Bianchi, "Le «Epistole metriche» del Petrarca," *Annali della R. Scuola normale superiora di Pisa* ser. 2, vol. 9 (1940): 251–66 and Ernest A. Wilkins, *The «Epistolæ metricæ» of Petrarch, A Manual* (Rome: Edizioni di Storia e letteratura, 1956).

23. In particular, the poems on this theme are: III.9, "Dulce iter in patriam" ("The way back to one's homeland is sweet") and the apostrophe to Italy which he wrote on returning from Avignon in 1351, III.22, "Salve, cara Deo tellus sanctissima" ("Hail, most holy land, dear to God").

24. III.30, "Itala quam reliquias superet facundia linguas" ("How Italian eloquence conquers all other languages").

25. Alexander Peter Saccaro, *Französischer Humanismus des 14. und 15. Jahrhunderts* (Munich: Fink, 1975), pp. 81–89; Pierre-Yves Badel, *Le Roman de la Rose au XIVᵉ siècle, Étude de la réception de l'oeuvre* (Geneva: Droz, 1980), pp. 462–63; Willard, *Christine de Pizan* (note 12), pp. 91–92, 197.

26. ed. Hicks, pp. 38–39 (Vergilian citation to support Jean de Meung and his defenders); pp. 42–43 (citation of Cicero's story of Leontium, the woman who criticized Theophrastus, to whom Jean de Montreuil compares Christine, who in turn cites the story of Leontium in the *Cité des Dames*, I.30.3, as an example of female impartiality correcting tainted auctoritas: "Leontium . . . dared, for impartial and serious reasons, to correct and attach the philosopher Theophrastus").

27. Jean de Montreuil, *Opera*, ed. Ezio Ornato, v. 1: *Epistolario* (Turin, 1963), p. 136, cited in Saccaro, *Französischer Humanismus*, p. 154.

28. See Karl D. Uitti, "Remarks on Old French Narrative: Courtly Love and Poetic Form (II)," *Romance Philology* 28 (1974): 190–99.

29. Cf. my study, *Dante and the "Roman de la Rose": An Investigation into the Vernacular Narrative Context of the "Commedia"*, Beiheft zur Zeitschrift für romanische Philologie, Bd. 184 (Tübingen: Max Niemeyer Verlag, 1981), pp. 62–64, 71–73.

30. Willard, *Christine de Pizan*, p. 118.

31. *L'Avision Christine*, ed. Mary Louise Towner (Washington DC: Catholic University of America, 1932), p. 164.

32. See Christine Reno's remarks on Christine's use of allegory, "The Preface to the *Avision-Christine* in ex-Phillipps 128," in *Reinterpreting Christine de Pizan* (note 6), pp. 207–227; and Rosalind Brown-Grant, "*L'Avision-Christine*: Autobiographical Narrative or Mirror for the Prince?" in *Politics, Gender, and Genre* (note 6), pp. 95–112.

33. Kristeller, "The Scholar and His Public in the Late Middle Ages and the Renaissance," in *Medieval Aspects of Renaissance Learning*, ed. and trans. Edward P. Mahoney (Durham, NC: Duke University Press, 1974), p. 15.

34. Ibid., pp. 12–13.

35. Constable, *Letters and Letter-Collections* (note 5), p. 11.

36. Charity Cannon Willard, "Christine de Pizan's Advice to Woman," in Christine de Pizan, *A Medieval Woman's Mirror of Honor, The Treasury of the City of Ladies*, trans. Charity Cannon Willard (New York: Persea, 1989), p. 38.

37. The best and still useful introduction is Charles H. Haskins, "The Early *Ars dictandi* in Italy," in his *Studies in Medieval Culture* (Oxford: Clarendon Press, 1929; reprint, New York: Ungar, 1958), pp. 170–92. Franz-Josef Schmale noted that the influence of the Bolognese tradition was particularly strong in France, in the school of Orléans; see his "Die Bologneser Schule der Ars dictaminis," *Deutsches Archiv für die Erforschung des Mittelalters* 13 (1957): 16–34.

38. Haskins, "Early *Ars dictandi*," pp. 2–3.

39. "Alberici Cassinensis rationes dictandi," in Rockinger ed., v. 1, p. 10.

40. Willard, *Christine de Pizan*, p. 47.

41. Allison Kelly, "Christine de Pizan and Antoine de la Sale: The Dangers of Love in Theory and Fiction," in *Reinterpreting Christine de Pizan* (note 16), pp. 173–86.

42. The best edition is by Angus Kennedy, "Christine de Pizan's *Epistre à la reine* (1405)," *Revue des Langues Romanes* 92 (1988): 253–64. It has also been edited by Josette A. Wisman: Christine de Pizan, *The Epistle of the Prison of Human Life, with an Epistle to the Queen of France and Lament on the Evils of the Civil War*, ed. and trans. Josette A. Wisman (New York: Garland, 1984).

43. Besides drawing on Legge's somewhat short introduction—she took on the editorial project after the death of its original editor—the discussion here is indebted to H. G. Richardson's lengthy review of Legge's work in the *English Historical Review* 58 (1943): 222–30.

44. Margarete Zimmermann, "*Vox femina, vox politica*: The 'Lamentations sur les maux de la France' (1410)" (trans. E. J. Richards), in *Politics, Gender and Genre* (note 6), pp. 119–20.

45. Williard, *Christine de Pizan*, p. 197.

46. Cited from Wisman, ed. (note 42), p. 4; translation is my own.

Ulrike Wiethaus

"If I had an Iron Body": Femininity and Religion in the Letters of Maria de Hout

"She is neither one nor two. She cannot strictly speaking be determined as one person or two. She renders any definition inadequate. Moreover, she has no proper name."

Luce Irigaray, *This Sex Which is Not One*

The Context of the Letters

Little is known of the life of the Beguine Maria de Hout, also known as Maria of Osterwyk or Maria de Ligno (d. September 30, 1547).[1] She spent most of her life in a community of Beguines in Osterwyk and enjoyed the reputation of a holy woman and spiritual teacher. She composed devotional treatises and spiritual letters to fellow sisters and other religious. Her close contacts with a group of well-educated compatriot Carthusians in Cologne ensured the survival and circulation of these texts. Attracted by her renown and the exemplary lives of her fellow Beguines, the Carthusian scholar Gerhard Kalckbrenner (d. 1562), prior of the intellectually vibrant Carthusian monastery of St. Barbara in Cologne, visited her, chose her as spiritual advisor, and subsequently worked toward the publication of her treatise *Der rechte Wech zo d'Euangelischer volkomenheit* (*The Right Way to Evangelical Perfection*). Maria's surviving epistolary collection of fourteen letters, the focus of this essay, stems from around 1531, the time of her first contact with Kalckbrenner.[2] Other prominent members of St. Barbara who took an interest in Maria were Peter Blomevenna (1466–1536), like Kalckbrenner and Maria born in the Low Countries, and Johannes Landsberger (ca. 1490–1539). Maria was also known to the remarkable Jesuit Peter Canisius (1521–97), a pupil of Nikolaus Esch (1507–1578). Esch had donated a little house to the Beguines in Osterwyk in 1539.[3]

Drawing immediate spiritual inspiration from Maria and other similarly pious lay people, the Carthusians passionately promoted the publication of the writings of German mystics of the preceding centuries. For example, Landsberger, an ascetical writer in his own right, published Gertrud the Great's (1256–c. 1302) *Legatus divinae pietatis* (*Messenger of Divine Love*). Blomevenna wrote several polemical anti-Reformation treatises, edited and published the works of the Franciscan mystic Heinrich Herp of Brabant (d. 1477), and collaborated in the publication of the works of Dionysius of Rickel (d. 1471), an eminent Carthusian theologian and mystic, who was born in Limburg. Peter Canisius brought to print the first edition of the works of Johannes Tauler (c. 1300–1361).

As I will elaborate below, the much older Maria represented a source of inspiration to these men. A motherly muse, blessed with a "special tenderness" that united her with God, she could draw them nearer to the divine.[4] She was revered as a living example of the mystical traditions that the German circle of Carthusian and Jesuit scholars attempted to preserve and continue. Maria literally *embodied* the intellectual and cultural aspirations of the Catholic reformers.

Maria did not invent or freely chose *embodiment* as a form of religious self-expression; it already existed as a stereotyped role model for religious women. As in the case of women mystics of the Middle Ages in general, Maria's gender and the resulting lack of access to theological training excluded her from the world of the Latin-speaking *literati* and rational discourse. In order to be heard publicly, a woman mystic was forced to find alternative modes of authoritative communication of her ideas. One of these modes is vernacular language, and women mystics such as Hadewijch (second quarter of the thirteenth century) or Mechthild of Magdeburg (c. 1208–1282/97) have been credited with advancing the vernacular to new heights.[5] As the cases of Hadewijch, Catherine of Siena (1347–1380), and other women mystics show, the use of the vernacular and an oftentimes concomitant criticism of academic learnedness not only posed a threat to the ecclesiastical order but also attracted a loyal following among the laity. The following quotation describes what must have been a typical scenario in many lay settings. The woman mystic depicted in this excerpt, Maria de Cazalla, was eventually arrested by the Inquisition in 1532.

> . . . there were a lot of people there, and it seemed as if they were all women . . . I think that there were more than twenty women because the kitchen was big and it was full. Maria de Cazalla read from a book, and then spoke, and everyone was silent as if they were listening to a sermon.[6]

The second mode of communication cultivated by women mystics is the visionary discourse. In the twelfth century, it tended to stress prophetic content over ecstatic states (as in the case of Hildegard of Bingen, 1098–1179), but as women were increasingly manoeuvred to the margins of the Church, their prophetic messages became submerged in the display of standardized ecstatic physical phenomena and ascetical feats. Maria of Osterwyk is a typical example of this trend: her mystical *lifestyle*, that is, her practice and embodiment of spiritual values, is regarded as her central message. Her writing is ancillary and illustrative.

Late in Maria's life, efforts were made to bring her and two of her Beguine sisters, Ida and Eva, to St. Barbara in Cologne. To the Carthusians in Cologne, Beguines were a common sight, since they were well represented in the city in the fifteenth and early sixteenth centuries. Unfortunately, the city government, who saw the Beguines as a threat to the guilds, succeeded in restricting their economic activities and well-being.[7] Maria arrived in Cologne in 1545, but she died only two years later. Ida and Eva left the city immediately after her death. It is known that Ida became a recluse in the Beguinage in Diest under the guidance of Nikolaus Esch.[8]

The lifestyle of the Beguines was first documented by Jacques de Vitry (1180–1254) at the beginning of the thirteenth century in the diocese of Liège, when significant numbers of women began to live together under a vow of chastity and without a monastic rule. In his fight against heretical movements, Jacques de Vitry recorded as exemplary the life of Marie d'Oignies (1177–1213), who is generally regarded as the first "official" Beguine. As in the case of Maria of Osterwyk and her spiritual protégé Kalckbrenner, the relationship between Marie d'Oignies and Jacques de Vitry was one of spiritual friendship and curious symbiosis.[9] As Paul Mommaers pointed out, the disparity between a "learned man" (*literatus*) and an "unlettered woman" (*rustica, idiota*) who despite or because of her alleged theological illiteracy was judged to be closer to God and thus capable of inspiring her male admirer(s), turned into a well-worn topos that disguised the fact that many of the women were theologically educated and sophisticated thinkers.[10] As such, this stereotype supported a patriarchally convenient myth of the gendered distribution of intellectual prowess associated with masculinity and spiritual inspiration and loving care which became identified with femininity. This set-up allowed for an unequal exchange of desired services. Men received spiritual counsel and faithful devotion despite their long absences as itinerant preachers (lay religious women were in close contact with Dominicans and Franciscans). With the help of their male friends, women, on the other hand, derived some measure of legitimization by the patriarchal establishment. A pattern of cross-sex relations evolved that we still see in existence in Maria of Osterwyk's epistles. In the paradigmatic case of Jacques de Vitry and Marie d'Oignies, Jacques legitimized Marie's chosen lifestyle on the basis of his high social position as ecclesiastical administrator, whereas Marie d'Oignies spiritually nurtured Jacques and supported his church-political manoeuvers by posing as a living model of his ideals.

Historically, these intriguing cross-sex friendships were made possible by the institution of confessorship, which allowed for a more intimate exchange between religious men and women. As we will see, however, the often touching intimacy between women and their confessors could also turn into a mirror of oppressive patriarchal power relations. At the beginning of their movement, Beguines were able to choose their spiritual guides among the Dominicans and the Franciscans and could exercise substantial freedom in selecting a particular friar.[11] These acts of self-determination did not last for long, however. The bulls issued at the general council in Vienna in 1311/12, *Ad nostrum* and *Cum de quibusdam*, mark the decline of ecclesiastical tolerance of Beguines, and a subsequent tightening of the Church's control over their lives.[12] As Maria's letters indicate, it is not any more the relation to her confessor, but the contract between herself and Kalckbrenner to become his spiritual "mother," that repeated this long established pattern of cross-sex friendship. Their relationship seems to have been based on mutual attraction and freely given and received affection. And, as Maria writes to Kalckbrenner, this affection was understood to have been granted by God.

> From God emanates the goodness of God and [it] has stirred you to surrender to me as a child, and [has stirred] me that I should esteem you as my son, since you are pressed to my heart so I can pray for you.
>
> . . . want got kompt die gutheitt gotz und hait uch dair tzo erweckt, dat ir hait myr uch gegeven vur ein kynt, und ich sal uch halden vur myn son, want ir sydt myr an mynn hertz gedruckt umb vur uch tzo bidden. (letter 6)

In the following pages, I will explore Maria's sense of female self and the ensuing opportunities to exert power as they unfold in her letters.

Unlike her treatises, the letters offer a fascinating combination of personal and theoretical reflections on the making of a saintly woman against the background of relationships and power structures outlined above.

Three Audiences, Three Selves

The fourteen letters that have survived are addressed to three different audiences: there are those written to other women, those written to her spiritual "sons" or protégés, and those specifically addressed to her confessor. All letters are primarily intended to function as spiritual instructions and reflections. Yet, as in the case of another famous Beguine from the thirteenth century, Hadewijch, they are interspersed with touching personal information. In varying degrees, the letters assert their authority from the patriarchally shaped notion of feminine spirituality mentioned above.

Maria's comments on her personal life selectively deal with her claim to sainthood, that is, her skill at what I call "female mystical embodiment." Maria appears to have fully identified with the part she was asked to play. Within that role, however, she retains a measure of authority and independence. The letters indicate that in the circle of her fellow Beguines, Maria's voice is her own. Vis-à-vis her Carthusian sponsors and protégés, the richness of her personality is narrowed down to a maternal *persona*. The dark underside of her public self-representation, however, emerges in the relationship to her confessor. The following excerpts illustrate the range of Maria's movements within the circumference of her role in the Carthusian community. In one letter, written in Leuven, November 9, 1546, by the Jesuit P. Cornelius Vischaven to the Jesuit P. Leonhard Kessel in Cologne, Kessel is instructed how to behave in the presence of Maria, whom he intends to visit.

> I ask you for one thing in a brotherly spirit. When you visit Maria, obey this precautionary rule, since I believe that I know her fairly well: do you wish to progress in spiritual matters, you must not argue with her by emphasizing your own insight or your own judgment, or by contradicting her. If mystics find such [a conversation partner], they immediately fall silent and subjugate themselves . . .

> Um das eine moechte ich in bruederlicher Gesinnung Dich bitten. Wenn Du auch zu Maria kommst, so halte Dich an diese Vorsichts-

massregel,—ich glaube naemlich, dass ich sie einigermassen kenne: Wollt Ihr in geistlichen Dingen Fortschritte machen, duerft Ihr nicht mit ihr streiten, indem Ihr Eure Einsicht oder Euer eigenes Urteil betont, oder indem Ihr widersprecht. Wenn naemlich Mystiker einen solchen finden, schweigen sie sofort und unterwerfen sich. . . .[13]

Clearly, Maria's strategy in dealing with these scholars is to refuse their mode of discourse, a refusal we note also in the cases of Hadewijch and Catherine of Siena.[14] Hadewijch scolds and pokes fun at scholastic learnedness; Catherine takes pride in the vernacular. Maria, however, withdraws into silence when her views are challenged or rejected. Like a mystical Cheshire cat, she disappears, and only a display of humility remains of her presence. What reads on the surface as proper female behavior—humble submission to a male—is in truth an adroit manoeuver to control the situation. For her visitors, Maria's "humility" thus could become extremely frustrating. They could only "advance in spiritual matters" if they left their assertive behavior behind and assumed the role of receptive listeners. That Maria consciously employed this strategy seems to be indicated in one of her letters to Kalckbrenner. Here she discusses what led to her spiritual success as a teacher:

. . . because I always gained more through praying than through speaking, and I led them with examples [i.e., exemplary behavior], and I yielded to them as if I [intended to] flatter them.

dan ich gewan altzyt meer mit bidden dan mit sprechen, und ich gienge yn ouch mit exempelen vur, und ich buegede mich under sie recht off ich mit yn gesmeicht hedde.(letter 7)

She knows what results this yielding and flattering, this spiritual guidance in silence did bring: ". . . yet in the end, I gained victory nonetheless" (". . . aver tzom lesten verwan ich noch," ibid).

However, even with her spiritual pupils, her skills as manipulator engender only limited freedoms. Her remarkable request to be allowed to read heretical books, negotiated by Petrus Canisius in 1547, was rejected. Unfortunately, the correspondence does not yield any information as to the titles, authors, and contents of the books. Canisius writes, "There is good hope that dispensation will be granted regarding the portable altar, but not that permission will be given to read heretical books" ("Gute Hoffnung besteht zwar, dass bezueglich des Tragaltares Dispens erteilt wird, nicht aber, dass die Erlaubnis gegeben wird, ketzerische Bücher zu lesen").[15]

This quotation poignantly illustrates Maria's male-approved role. She is allowed and encouraged to participate in religious activities that require embodiment (in this case, the Eucharistic rite) and that are securely controlled by a male clergy. Yet to think and to participate in theological discussions is prohibited, although Maria's extraordinary qualification as a woman who is close to God is widely acknowledged. Her request to read controversial books poses a challenge to male-established orthodoxy and tests the invisible limits of gendered territory in the late medieval Church.

Unlike her treatises, Maria's letters clearly display the sutures between the staging of a mystical persona and the spiritual teachings that undergird her self-presentation. How do her spiritual instructions reflect her sense of self and her audience's expectations of her? The mystico-theological system that informed Maria's religiosity is neither bridal nor mother mysticism, although images from both traditions contribute to her religious lexicon. It is rooted in the ancient mystical tradition of the *via negationis* or *via negativa*, the flight into *nothingness* and the deconstruction of a self, the self-emptying that in the eyes of the believer becomes an opening for the divine. Among Beguine writings, we find this self-emptying already in the texts of Marguerite Porete (she died at the stake in 1310), who was one of the major sources for Meister Eckhart's (c. 1260–1328) teachings. For Marguerite Porete and Meister Eckhart, the *via negationis* led to a radical sense of freedom and a breathtaking vision of the nobility of human existence through divinization, that is, through the gradual understanding of the soul's identity with the divine. In Meister Eckhart's words, "the eye with which I see God is the same eye with which God sees me; my eye and God's eye are only one eye and one seeing and one knowing and one love."[16]

Self-emptying was also the tenet of the *Devotio Moderna*, a spiritual lay movement that resembled in some ways the Beguines' lifestyle and was particularly active in the Low Countries. In the writings and practices of this group, however, it stopped short of the radical liberating notion of divinization that can be found in Marguerite Porete. In its ideal form, it stood for full identification with the suffering human Jesus, and a rejection of all that was perceived as worldy and vain. In the movement of the Devotio Moderna, this process is marked by a language of control, self-discipline, and even violence.[17] Thomas à Kempis (1379/80–1471), for example, exhorts his fellow brothers and sisters, to "strive for this, pray for this, desire this, to be stripped of all selfishness and naked to follow the naked Jesus, to die to self and live forever."[18] The constitution of the brother-houses in Deventer and Zwolle is even more explicit.

> Since the final end of religion consists in purity of heart, without which we shall see perfection in vain, let it be our daily aim to purge our poisoned hearts from sin, so that in the first place we may learn to know ourselves, pass judgment upon the vices and passions of our minds, and endeavor with all our strength to eradicate them; despise temporal gain, crush selfish desires, aid others in overcoming sin, and concentrate our energy on the acquisition of true virtues, such as humility, love, chastity, patience, and obedience.[19]

When translated into the relationship between male and female followers of the Devotio Moderna movement, this path of inner transformation was used by the brothers as a more or less conscious rationalization to subordinate the sisters. Women's unconditional obedience to male authority was depicted as a practice in humility and self-emptying. In fairness to the movement, however, it has to be said that both men and women exercised strict self-criticism (*scrupulositas*).

Maria's concept of self-emptying and humility vascillates between the two poles represented by Marguerite Porete and Meister Eckhart on the one hand and the Devotio Moderna movement on the other. Whereas the former developed the liberating aspects of this path, which promptly placed them into the camp of medieval dissent, the latter group propagated a spirituality of humility that served to oppress its female members, but also ensured its survival in the embattled landscape of lay religious movements.

On a psycho-spiritual level, practicing the *via negativa* can allow for inner growth and clearer spiritual perception. Maria often experienced her self-emptying as empowering and liberating from social constraints. To cite an example: in a letter to another sister and her mother superior ("min werdige moder"), she takes stock of her spiritual growth. She writes,

> . . . it is not possible for me that I should always conduct myself in such a manner that it may be well pleasing to human beings, even if I could thus win or lose heaven and earth. . . . my Lord, my God is worth everything to me, and he alone has power over me. I fear no created being anymore.

> . . . id is myr niet muglich, dass ich mich altzyt also halden solde, dat idt dem mynschen wail behagen soilde, al mucht ich hemel und erdt dair mit wynnen off verliesen. . . . myn her myn got isses mir allet wert,

und hei hait allein macht over mich. Ich vorchte gein creatuir merr. (letter 4)

Implicit in this growth experience is an (at least partial) deconstruction of power relations. Whereas the ideal of humility and passivity served to reinforce patriarchy in secular contexts and in the rigidly organized communities of the Devotio Moderna, it had an equalizing effect in the more freely structured relations between Maria and her Carthusian supporters. In the letter by Vischaven quoted above, Maria's mode of discourse and the acknowledgment of her spiritual leadership is generated by the acceptance of the centrality of humility. In letter 7, addressed to Kalckbrenner, Maria again first assumes a posture of humble submission, but only to quickly retrieve in two-fold measure the seemingly surrendered authority.

Disconcertedly, she demands the following from Kalckbrenner: "Also know, my dear son and my heart, I am writing it now once and for all that you should never again ask me, but command me [to do] what you want" ("Vort wist myn lieve son an myn hertz, Ich scryff uch eins vur al, dat ir mich nit meer en biddet, dan gebiedet wat ir wilt"). A few lines below this remark she "notifies and orders" two other Carthusians in her role as spiritual advisor. The German scholar Wilhelm Oehl, who edited her letters, could not help but label this incident as "very remarkable"; to him, Maria carried on like the fierce Hildegard of Bingen (1098–1179) in her jeremiads addressed to men of the Church.[20]

Drastically juxtaposed to these displays of freedom is Maria's relationship to her confessor. Contrary to the attitude displayed in her letters to her "sisters" and "sons," the author now practices humility to the point of masochism. She writes,

I am in your hands. If it pleases the Lord and you, you may condemn me and spurn me, you and all created beings. Exercise your revenge on me.

Ich stain in uren henden believet den Heren und uch yr mueget mich verduemen und verwerpen, yr und alle creatuyren doet wraich over mich. (letter 9)

Maria appears to have internalized the sadistic elements of a spirituality of humility and suffering to such a degree that she actively reproduces what oppresses her:

For this I ask you, punish me and don't spare me, because my soul hungers for suffering and punishment like the body longs for bread. And let me suffer and lament, beg and scream.

Dair umb bid ich uch, straeft mich und spart mich niet, want myn siel hungert na lyden and straffen, als der lycham na dez broede, und laist mich lyden und clagen, bidden und schryen. (letter 10)

As contemporary observers, we must ask whether this type of cross-sex relationship is not the unavoidable outcome of a spirituality that from its very beginning stresses the value of *obedience* and couples it with the practice of humility. Approximately a hundred years before Maria writes her letters, the Carthusian Marguerite d'Oingt (d. 1310) relates to the divine in a way that structurally resembles Maria's attitude toward her confessor. Here is a representative excerpt from the *Meditations* (*Pagina Meditationum*) by Marguerite d'Oingt, in which female obedience is still associated with mutual loving acceptance.

Sweet Lord, inscribe into my heart that which you want me to do. Inscribe into it your law, inscribe into it your orders so that nothing will be deleted. Sweet Lord, I know well that I am subject to laziness and lethargy more than I should, but my spirit is moved to do your will. Sweet Lord, . . . I delight in your desire and love. . . .

Domine dulcis, scribe in corde meo illud quod vis ut faciam. Scribe ibi tuam legem, scribe ibi tua mandata ut numquam deleantur. Domine dulcis, ego bene scio quod caro mea est tota plena pigricia et sompnolentia, sed spiritua meus promptus est facere voluntatem tuam. Domine dulcis, . . . delector in desiderio et in amore tui. . . .[21]

In a feminist reading, Maria's posture toward her confessor thus appears neither displaced nor truly idolatrous (in both cases, women revere masculinity as divine), yet it renders the added violent self-depreciation more disturbing. How does this imbalance of power affect Maria's self-expressiveness? Not surprisingly, Maria's confessor functions as a counterforce and censoring agency to her own emerging voice. Thinking of him, she is silenced for good:

. . . Since wherever I go or stay, you are always in my mind [lit. you always stand before my eyes]. If I say something, I must think: what if my spiritual father heard this, would I dare say it then, too? And then, I have to keep quiet.

. . . Want wair ich gain off stain altzyt staet ir mir vur ougen, als ich yet sprech so moiss ich dencken off dit myn geistlich vader hoirde, solde ich dat dan ouch doeren sagen und dan moiss ich swygen. (letter 9)

To conclude, the spiritual ideal of humility and self-emptying does not exist in a social vacuum. As the letters demonstrate, it is linked to the hierarchy of power with which Maria is confronted. Compared to the Dominican and Franciscan confessors of Beguines of earlier centuries, Maria's confessor represents fully institutionalized ecclesiastical power and consequently, she acts the most obediently and self-destructively toward him. This set-up is reminiscent of the cross-sex dynamics in the Devotio Moderna communities, both on the level of spiritual theory and on the level of spiritual praxis.

Maria's male supporters and protégés rank below the confessor, and as a consequence, the relationship between them and Maria is one of greater freedom and equality. As noted above, this is mirrored in Maria's more ambidextrous use of humility, which she often seems to turn into a means to an end. The self-images associated with humility in her correspondence to the Carthusians are paradoxical; they both uplift and denigrate. In the same breath, Maria thus can assert that the attention showered on her makes her feel like a "goddess," and yet she should shed "bloody tears," "crawl into the earth" and "shred her heart to pieces" in shame about her shortcomings (letter 7).

Let us move now to her letters to fellow Beguines and consider in greater detail what kind of femininity emerges from this web of strategies in regard to all three audiences: the Carthusians, her confessor, and her fellow sisters.

"She is Neither One nor Two": Staging the Feminine

The five letters written to fellow sisters are dynamic, strongly autobiographical and self-reflective. They are characterized by little formal introduction or discussion of status. In the beginning of letter 1, the reasons for such informality are clearly spelled out.

> Out of my love [for you], I inform you about my state of affairs in simple humility, [and] because I cannot hide anything before you, because you know me well, and I know well that you take this [knowledge] from God.

> Ich laissen uch uss lieffden wissen myne saichen in sympeler oit-moedichkeit, want ich vur uch niet verbergen kan, want ir mich wail kennet, und ich weiss wail dat yr idt van Got nemet. (letter 1)

In all the letters to other women she describes her inner changes, her struggles, her victories, her sense of freedom through self-annihilation (the practice of the *via negativa*), and her joy of being of use to others. She notes in letter 1:

> Oh sister, would you only know how bare, poor and unattached I am within myself, you would be amazed. But I overflow [with riches] for my fellow creatures to bring them to God. It makes me happy when someone asks something of me, since then the Lord is acting through me, the unworthy worm.

> Och suster wust ir wie bloiss, arm un ledich ich van binnen stae, yr sult uch verwunderen, mer overfloedich tzo minen evenminschen, umb die tzo got tzo brengenn, des mach ich mich verblyden, als d'etwas van mich begert, want dan wirkt der heer durch mich unwerdich wormgen.

The pleasure and sense of mastery that Maria has acquired through years of arduous spiritual struggle emerge in the following two quotations, which are exemplary for the whole collection of Maria's same-sex correspondence. "Oh, oh sister, I do not know of any greater joy than [that] which the Lord gives to me unworthy creature" ("Och och suster ich en weiss niet off d'vrede groisser mucht syn, dan d'Her mich unwerdig creaturen gieft," letter 2). In letter 4 she notes, "Know that I am very content now. Because the Lord has it well arranged. He granted me numerous preventive acts of grace to help me with all sufferings" ("Wisset dat ich nu soe wail zu vrede byn. Want d'here had id wail gefuicht he hait myr sommige gevurkomende gratie gegeven, umb dair mit durch alle lyden tzo helffen").

Maria's relationship with her sisters appears to be warm, uncomplicated, and mutually supportive. She writes, "When you share your spiritual and physical goods with me, you become imprinted into my heart, and I must help you supplicate" ("Want yr ure geistlich und lichaemlich guyt mir mitdeilt, so werdet ir mir in myn hertz gedruckt, dat ich uch mois helffen bidden," letter 1). In this group of women, femininity is not a self-conscious issue. Maria refers to women, including herself, in the neutral theological term *creatur*, created being, except for the address formulae at the beginning of a letter, where she indicates the status of the recipient ("Myn werdige moder"; "myne suster"). In contrast to her male correspondents, Maria's female audience permits her to probe her spiritual experiences more objectively. She can openly point to her achievements and yet commiserate about how hard it has been to gain them. " . . . and I am content with everything as God arranges it. But it has cost me a martyr's life to arrive at this [attitude]" ("und bin al tzo freden wie idt got fuecht. Mer eir ich hietzo komen bin dat heit myr ein mertelers leven gekost," letter 2). Most remarkably perhaps, she can express the unmitigated joy and contentment that her religious lifestyle affords her. Such expressions of pleasure are noticeably absent in her letters to men. In her correspondence with other women, femininity thus appears to be an unselfconscious and unpretentious *mode of communication* that allows for a degree of self-disclosure and frankness lacking in cross-sex discourse.

Not surprisingly, the most visible difference between the letters to other Beguines and those to her spiritual "sons" in terms of style is a greater emphasis on form and status in the latter. In the letters to men, Maria as a sometimes struggling, sometimes triumphant human being disappears behind the mask of spiritual counselor and self-effacing maternal figure. She expresses her motherly concern in bodily metaphors. Referring to the Carthusian community, Maria writes, "and I embrace them close to my heart in the name of God as if they were my own children, and I had carried them under my heart" ("und ich untfange sy in die plaetze van got an myn hertz also off idt myn eigen kynder weren, unnd ich sy an min hertz gedragen hedde," letter 7). Her commitment to the men is psycho-physical. It suggests Maria's identification with Christ's self-sacrifice on one hand and the feminine birthing process and suckling of an infant on the other:

"And I shall help you faithfully with supplications in everything that I am able to in God; I will not spare myself, neither flesh nor blood" ("Und ich sal uch getreuwelich helpen bidden, na allet dat ich in got vermag, dae en wil ich mich niet yn sparen, vleisch noch bloit," letter 5). In the same letter, she explicitly refers to Mary's motherhood as a paradigm for her relations to the men. "Furthermore note, dear father, [that] I ask you to be my father [and] take me as your daughter as the heavenly father has chosen Mary. And [he] gave her his only son. In this symbolic way, your son N. is assigned to me" ("Vorst wist lieve vader ich bidden uch wilt doch myn vad' syen wilt mich nemen vur ure dochter gelich der himelsche vader Mariam erkoren hadde. Und gaff Yr synen einigen so, soe is mir in ein gelichenis ure son, N, tzo gefuegt").

Contrary to the letters to the Beguines, but in line with her role as maternal figure, she de-emphasizes her skills as speaker and writer in the correspondence with the Carthusians. Nonetheless, the letters are very articulate and lively. Maria the author is now replaced by Maria the mother; throughout this set of letters, she stresses her talent as spiritual mediator between her "sons" and the divine. When with her sisters, she gives bountifully of *herself* in the form of common-sense advice and encouragement. This generosity assumes a supernatural quality, however, when she faces her sponsors and protégés. Maria hints repeatedly at miracles that have happened to her. In letters 6 and 7, two such miracles are reported. They function to reinforce her ties to the Carthusian community, and to console its members. In the first supernatural event, she receives the grace of knowing that God wants her to adopt Kalckbrenner as her son. On St. Peter's day, around 2 a.m., she awakes with the intense feeling that God literally presses Kalckbrenner on her heart.

Wonder upon wonder, and grace upon grace. The goodness of God emanates from God and has you awakened to be given to me as a child, and I shall regard you as my son, because you are pressed to my heart so that I shall pray for you. [This has happened] with such immense grace that my heart hurt so much that I was forced to get up and walk around a little . . . Therefore rejoice and find out what God wishes to do through you.

Wonder boven wonder, und gratie boven gratie, want got kompt die gutheitt gotz und hait uch dair two erweckt, dat ir hait myr uch gegeven vur ein kynt, und ich sal uch halden vur myn son, want ir sydt myr an mynn hertz gedruckt umb vur uch tzo bidden mit so groisser gratien dat myn hertz myr also wee dede, dat ich up moist stain und vergain mich etwas . . . Darumb erfreuwet uch und syet zo wat got durch uch wircken will. (letter 6)

From the Carthusians' perspective, Maria of Osterwyk's maternal care is literally a psycho-spiritual fantasy come true, since the identities of the Virgin Mary and Maria as motherly figure merge. Among Carthusians the figure of the Virgin looms large: the order chose her as a patron, and much of their spiritual identity is centered on Marian piety.[22] As in the case of the relationship between Maria and her confessor, we note a peculiar fusion of spiritual beings with real persons, and observe how the dynamics between the image of a supernatural being (God; the Virgin Mary) and a human person mold the actual relations between humans. In the first instance, a male divine being prefigures the role of confessor; in the second, a female semi-divine figure shapes a gamut of role-expectations and behaviors for Maria and her protégés. In both instances, the identification with a divine character transfers power to the human counterpart, but it is Maria, not the men, who suffers the inherent contradictions and paradoxes of such a set-up.

The second of Maria's miracles is part of the standard repertoire of Christian mystics, a physical mimesis that recurred frequently in Maria's life: the experience of the physical pains of the suffering Christ. This event usually takes place at night, Maria points out, when the monks in Cologne celebrate the Matins service. This synchronicity is intentional, it appears, and serves to strengthen the ties between Maria and her students. The miracle is mediumistic in nature; Maria "has to give herself over to be led by God." She describes it as follows.

And tell your brothers that they shall think of me sometimes at night as they are conducting the Matins service, singing and praying; then I have to give myself over to God to be led. Since nowadays, I awake at one o'clock at night, and experience wretched pain in my head, hands, feet, and heart. And especially my feet, they sting as if they were on fire. And my head is stung as if by thorns, day and night, as if a hat of thorns were pressed on my head. These pains resemble no others, so that water runs from my eyes, and they hurt so much that I often do not want to open or move them.

Und wilt ure mitbrueders sagen dat sy somtzytz an mich denken, in d'nacht als sy stayn in d'metten als sy syngen und bidden, dan moiss ich mich selven minen got zo voren geven. Want nu duck alle nacht werden ich wacker umbtrynt ein ure, und werden so iemerligen gepynigt in myn heufft, handen, voessen und hertz. Und besunder myn voesse gelich off sy vol furs weren, so doerstechen sy mich. Und myn heufft is nacht und dach off idt vol doernen stich, gelich off ein hoet van doernen in myn heufft gedruckt wer. Disse pyneen hait gen gelich, dat myr dat wasser duck tzo den ougen ussleufft ind' sy doin myr so wee dat ich dieselve duck niet wal upslain off ruren mach. (letter 7)

Absorbed in her maternal concern for the brothers, Maria's voice is beginning to fade away and becomes problematic to herself. "So know, my chosen father and son, whose souls I dearly love, that you won't get angry at me writing in such an audacious manner. I wrote as well as may be, just as it came to me unworthy one" ("Alsus wissent min userkoiren vad' und son, wilcher sielen ich lieff hain, en wilt doch he in niet entsticht syn, dat ich uch so aventuerlich schriven. ich hain uch slecht und recht geschreven, wie id mir unwerdich durchlauffen is," letter 6).

For the men, the rewards of Maria's display of maternal femininity are her unequivocal loyalty, her care and nurture. The promise of such affection is fusion with the divine. As Maria is one with God via her embodied spirituality, so the sons will become one with God through Maria's assistance; she carries them up to God (letter 7). Psychologically speaking, this mother-father-son scenario reflects private as much as larger social conflicts. For the loyal Catholic Carthusians, it symbolically appears to resolve the Oedipal conflict that is played out so savagely during the Reformation period: the Protestant sons break away from the authority of the fathers, and the Catholic/Carthusian sons stage the part of reconciliation with paternal-papal authority through the intervention of the mother. And the psycho-social dimension appears to mesh with the intellectual: the Carthusians' vivid interest in rekindling the mystical tradition of the past and active participation in the fight against Protestantism is mirrored on a personal level in their search for mystical union through Maria.

Maria of Osterwyk wins and loses in this set-up. She loses the spectrum of self-expressiveness displayed in the letters to her sisters and her voice becomes maimed, but she gains the pleasures of affectionate motherhood and filial reverence. Addressing the Carthusians' admiration for her, she comments, "it seems to me that all the good hearts are poured out just as if I were a goddess" ("mich dunckt dat alle die gude hertzen ussgesturtzt syn, recht off ich ein godynne weer," letter 7).

The shadow side of Maria's spiritual role as holy woman emerges in the presence of her confessor. I have already indicated the nature of this relationship above. Self-inflicted suffering, a secondary motif in the letters to her spiritual sons, now moves into the forefront. Following the pre-scribed power distribution, Maria presents herself as an unworthy sinner, a child rather than a mother or co-equal. Her own voice as human being is muted: she compares herself to animals. ". . . and I can think now that I am with the beasts, sucking in the earth" (". . . und mach nu dencken dat ich mit den beesten byn suygende in d'erden," letter 8). Following the rhetoric of women mystics before her, she attempts to reconcile her success as spiri-tual teacher with the confessor's expectation of self-accusation by stressing again and again that God speaks through her despite her will and despite her unworthiness. From a twentieth-century perspective, Maria's self ap-pears here to be radically diminished, especially so when compared to the letters to her fellow sisters. Maria's previously cited affirmation that she stopped fearing any creature is diametrically opposed to the posture of self-depreciation and passivity that she assumes toward her confessor. Alluding to Christ's last words on the cross, she invites her confessor to rule over her. "Within myself, I don't know more than a child, thinking neither higher nor lower than 'O father, what do you want that I do and suffer?'" ("Ich en weiss in mich niet meer dan ein kynt hoeger off ned' tzo dencken, dan o vad' wat wilstu dat ich doe und lyde," letter 8).

The relationship to her confessor, measured by perimeters of guilt and self-accusation, turns her body into a symbol of these emotionally tense attitudes. She wishes it to function like a machine, without flesh and blood and a life of its own. Using the vivid imagery that is so typical of her style, she writes, "Oh my, oh my, if I had an iron body, how courageously would I risk myself" ("Och och off ich hedde einen yseren lychaem wie kuenlich wolde ich mich selver wagen," letter 10). Yet her body is not an iron machine, and it can also be not maternal, strong and mobile as in the image where she flies to God, carrying all her "sons" in her arms. The female body displayed to the male gaze of a confessor is a body in pain: ". . . if you would see the tears that I cry and hear the screams to God that he will provide for it in you, because I cannot follow you quite the way you want it—this should move you to pity" (". . . want siegt yr die traenen die ich schrey, und dat roiffen tzo got dat he idt in uch versien wille dat ich uch so recht niet kan gevolgen als ir wult idt sold uch erbarmen," letter 10). In the end, the life-affirming optimism that we find in the letters directed at other audiences gives way to morose dejection: "Oh death, death—when will you come, since I only long to be with my beloved and the world is a heavy cross to carry and I am a burden [lit., cross] for it as well" ("O doit, doit wanner salstu komen, want mir allein verlangt tzo syn bi minem lieffhaver und die werld is mir ein swair cruytz und ich bin ir ein cruitz" letter 11).

"It Will All be Well in Time"

There are three female personae contained in Maria de Hout's letters. Seen together, they reflect the dilemma of a woman intent on carving a niche for herself in late medieval Christianity. We find a spontaneous, unselfconscious, and confidently articulate woman in the letters to the Beguines; a maternal spiritual guide who tries to balance humility with authority in the letters to the Carthusians; and finally, in the correspondence with her confessor, an abject sinner on the course to self-destruction.

Maria writes these roles into being with the help of a genre that demands conscious self-representation of the author and an awareness of the expectations of her audience. Which one of the three roles Maria assumes is authentic? Luce Irigaray, quoted in the beginning of this essay, would answer that the posing of this question assumes the existence of a uniform sense of self that is a masculine and, when applied to women, a patriarchal and therefore oppressive assumption. From this perspective, all three roles are true, yet they are informed differently by patriarchy. In her relationship to her confessor, Maria is least able to experience and describe herself with self-love and pride. It is here that Irigaray's description of the fragmented woman who is alienated from herself rings true. In Irigaray's words,

> The rejection, the exclusion of a female imaginary undoubtedly places woman in a position where she can experience herself only fragmentarily as waste or as excess in the little structured margins of a dominant ideology, this mirror entrusted by the (masculine) "subject" with the task of reflecting and redoubling himself. The role of "femininity" is prescribed moreover by the masculine specula(riza)tion and corresponds only slightly to woman's desire, which is recuperated only secretly, in hiding, and in a disturbing and unpardonable manner.[23]

The relationship to her "sons" allows for the return of imagining the pleasures of femininity as motherhood, where the heart becomes a womb, and the body life-giving and pleasure-giving. Yet this imagining of a feminine self is curtailed by male expectation: the female body has to exist with a truncated head, the feeling without much thought. The gendered distribution of access to education forestalls a full development of the maternal persona. That leaves us with the letters to other women, perhaps not incidentally the smallest set of epistolary texts preserved by the Carthusians. Here Maria develops a vision of an egalitarian community and a sharing and living together that is hopeful and peaceful. She writes to them in letter 1:

> And I shall help carrying the crosses of all of you. And what the Lord gives me that is yours; and I give you what is mine, and what belongs to you is mine. And so I hope that we shall once become one spirit. And be of help to your fellow sisters, and tell them that they must take strong courage and walk in the fear of God. Should [things] be hard for them [lit., sour], it will all be well in time.

> und ich sal urer alre crutz helpen dragen. Und dat der Heer mi gyfft, dat is ure und ich geeff uch dat myne, und dat ure is myn. Und also hoffen is, dat wir noch altzo samen einen geist sullenn werden, und staet uren mitsusteren tzer hant, und sagt ure yn dat sye einen starckenn moit gryffen, und in der vorten gotz wandelen, al wurdet yn wat suyr, idt sall all wailkomen mit der tzit.

This vision rings utopian. The question of why it could only be developed in a circle of trusted women friends might well be Maria's most provocative contribution to an exploration of medieval women's letters.

I wish to thank Merlyn Mowrey, Gillian T. W. Ahlgren, and Karen Cherewatuk (in her rôle as friend, not editor) for their extensive and thorough reading of an earlier draft of this essay. Patricia Ranft's thoughts on the institution of confession were helpful and stimulating. All translations from Maria's letters and the translation from Marguerite d'Oingt's text are mine.

Notes

1. Wilhelm Oehl, *Deutsche Mystikerbriefe des Mittelalters 1100–1500* (Darmstadt: Wissenschaftliche Buchgesellschaft Darmstadt, 1972), p. 682.

2. The following primary sources have been used in interpreting Maria of Osterwyk's letters: J. B. Kettenmeyer, "Uit de Briefwisseling van Eene Brabantsche

Mystieke uit de 16e Eeuw. Tekstbijlage," *Ons geestelijk erf* (1927): 370–95; the manuscript Wf. 1164.113 Theol. 8(1) in Wolfenbuettel, Herzog August Bibliothek; Oehl, *Mystikerbriefe*, pp. 692–720.

3. Oehl, 683, 836–840.

4. Letter by Kalckbrenner to Arnold von Tungeren, 1531 in Oehl, p. 719, "in sonderlicher Innigkeit mit Gott vereinigt."

5. See the essay in this volume by Karen Scott on Catherine of Siena and oral culture; on Mechthild, Hadewijch, and women mystics' contribution to the vernacular in general, see Herbert Grundmann, *Religiöse Bewegungen im Mittelalter* (Hildesheim: Georg Olms Verlagsbuchhandlung Hildesheim, 1961), pp. 439–76. On the beginnings of the association of women's piety and the body, see Caroline Walker Bynum, *Holy Feast and Holy Fast: The Significance of Food to Medieval Women* (Berkeley: University of California Press, 1987).

6. Quoted in Geraldine McKendrick and Angus MacKay, "Visionaries and Affective Spirituality During the First Half of the Sixteenth Century," in *Cultural Encounters. The Impact of the Inquisition in Spain and the New World*, ed. Mary Elizabeth Perry and Anne J. Cruz (Berkeley: University of California Press, 1991), pp. 93–105, quote p. 100.

7. Edith Ennen, *Frauen im Mittelalter* (Munich: C. H. Beck, 1988), pp. 174–76. See also Herbert Grundmann, "Zur Geschichte der Beginen im 13. Jahrhundert," in *Ausgewählte Aufsätze* (Stuttgart: Anton Hiersemann, 1976), pp. 201–22, esp. 207–9.

8. Oehl, *Mystikerbriefe*, p. 686.

9. See Carol Neel, "The Origins of the Beguines," *Signs* 14, 2 (1989): 321–41.

10. See Paul Mommaers, "Hadewijch: A Feminist in Conflict," *Louvain Studies* 13, 1 (1988): 58–81, esp. pp. 70–74. It is also telling to discover that, since its foundation in 1372, the Carthusian library in Erfurt collected the writings of women mystics under the rubric of revelations and not with theological or mystical treatises. See Erich Kleineidam, "Die Spiritualität der Kartäuser im Spiegel der Erfurter Kartäuser-Bibliothek," in *Die Kartäuser*, ed. Marijan Zadnikar and Adam Wienand (Cologne: Wienand Verlag, 1983), p. 198.

11. Florence Koorn, "Women Without Vows: The Case of the Beguines and the Sisters of the Common Life in the Northern Netherlands," in *Women and Men in Spiritual Culture, XIV–XVII Centuries*, ed. Elisja Schulte van Kessel ('s Gravenhage: Staatsutgeverij, 1984), pp. 135–47.

12. See M. D. Lambert, *Medieval Heresy, Popular Movements from Bogomil to Hus* (London: Edward Arnold Ltd., 1977), pp. 178–81; Grundmann, *Religiöse Bewegungen*, pp. 531ff; Richard Kieckhefer, *Repression of Heresy in Medieval Germany* (Philadelphia: University of Pennsylvania Press, 1979), pp. 19–53, with special emphasis on ecclesiastical politics. For a general discussion of the decline of the Beguines which also pays attention to economic factors and to the shift in ecclesiastical rhetoric regarding lay piety, see Jean-Claude Schmitt, *Mort d'une heresie* (Paris: Mouton Éditeur, 1978).

13. Oehl, *Mystikerbriefe*, p. 720.

14. See Paul Mommaers, "Hadewijch: A Feminist in Conflict" and Karen Scott in this volume, pp. 107–8.

15. Oehl, 720.

16. Quoted in Alois Maria Haas, "Schools of Late Medieval Mysticism," in *Christian Spirituality: High Middle Ages and Reformation*, ed. Jill Raitt (New York: Crossroad, 1987), pp. 140–76, quote p. 150.

17. For a survey and transcript of central texts in the Devotio Moderna movement, see John van Engen, *Devotio Moderna: Basic Writings* (New York: Paulist Press, 1988).

18. Quoted in Otto Gruendler, "Devotio Moderna," *Christian Spirituality*, 176–93, p. 183. The quotation is taken from Thomas à Kempis (1380–1471), *The Imitation of Christ*. (London: Penguin Books), p. 86.

19. Gruendler, "Devotio Moderna," p. 187. The quotation is taken from the constitutions of the brotherhouses in Deventer and Zwolle, written in 1414.

20. Oehl, *Mystikerbriefe*, pp. 836–837.

21. Quoted in Roland Maisonneuve, "L'Experience mystique et visionnaire de Marguerite d'Oingt (d. 1310), moniale chartreuse," in *Kartäusermystik und -Mystiker*, vol. 1, ed. James Hogg (Salzburg: Institüt für Anglistik und Amerikanistik, 1981), pp. 81–103, quote p. 85.

22. For medieval examples of the Carthusians' devotion to the Virgin, see *Die Kartäuser in Österreich*, vol. 2, ed. James Hogg (Salzburg: Institut für Anglistik und Amerikanistik, 1981).

23. Luce Irigaray, "This Sex Which Is Not One," in *New French Feminisms*, ed. Elaine Marks and Isabelle de Courtrivon (Amherst: University of Massachusetts Press, 1980), pp. 99–107, quote p. 104.

Bibliography

Alberic of Monte Cassino. *Alberici Cassinensis rationes dictandi. Briefsteller und Formelbücher des elften bis vierzehnten Jahrhunderts.* Ed. Ludwig Rockinger. 2 Vols. Munich: 1863; reprint New York: Franklin, 1961.

Altman, Janet Gurkin. *Epistolarity: Approaches to a Form.* Columbus: Ohio State University Press, 1982.

Altmann, Barbara K. "Reopening the Case: Machaut's Judgement Poems as a Source in Christine de Pizan." In Richards, ed., *Reinterpreting Christine de Pizan,* 137–56.

Anodal, Gabriella. *Il linguaggio cateriniano.* Siena: Edizioni Cantagalli, 1983.

Astell, Ann. *The Song of Songs in the Middle Ages.* Ithaca, NY: Cornell University Press, 1990.

Augustine. *De Genesi ad litteram.* Vol. 34 of J. P. Migne, ed., *Patrologia Latina.* Paris: Garnier, 1887, cols. 245–486.

Ausonius. "Parentalia." *Ausonius I.* Trans. Hugh G. Evelyn White. Loeb Classical Library. Cambridge, MA: Harvard University Press, 1961.

Badel, Pierre-Yves. *Le Roman de la Rose au XIVe siècle, Étude de la réception de l'oeuvre.* Geneva: Droz, 1980.

Baudonivia. "Vita Sanctae Radegundis." *Monumenta Germaniae Historica: Scriptores Rerum Merovingicarum.* Ed. Bruno Krusch. Vol. 2. Hanover: Weidmann, 1888, 377–95.

Bell, Rudolph M. *Holy Anorexia.* Chicago: University of Chicago Press, 1985.

Bennett, H. S. *The Pastons and Their England: Studies in an Age of Transition,* 2nd ed. Cambridge: Cambridge University Press, 1932.

Benson, Larry D., ed. *The Riverside Chaucer,* 3rd ed. Oxford: Oxford University Press, 1988.

Benton, John F. "Fraud, Fiction, and Borrowing in the Correspondence of Abélard and Héloïse." In *Pierre Abélard—Pierre le Vénérable,* pp. 469–512.

———. "A Reconsideration of the Authenticity of the Correspondence of Abelard and Heloise." In Thomas, *Petrus Abaelardus,* pp. 41–52.

Beowulf and Judith. Ed. Elliot van Kirk Dobbie. Anglo-Saxon Poetic Record, Vol. 4. New York: Columbia University Press, 1953.

Bianchi, Enrico. "Le «Epistole metriche» del Petrarca." *Annali della R. Scuola normale superiora di Pisa.* Ser. 1, Vol. 9 (1940): 251–66.

Boniface. "Des Briefe des Heligen Bonifatius und Lullus." Ed. Michael Tangl. *Monumenta Germaniae Historica: Epistolae Selectae.* Vol. 1. Berlin: Weidmann, 1955.

Brabant, Margaret, ed. *Gender, Genre, and Politics: Essays on Christine de Pizan.* Boulder, CO: Westview Press, 1992.

Brundage, James. "Sexual Equality in Medieval Canon Law." In *Medieval Women and the Sources of Medieval History*. Ed. Joel T. Rosenthal. Athens: University of Georgia Press, 1990, pp. 66–79.

Burke, Peter. "The Uses of Literacy in Early Modern Italy." In Burke, *Historical Anthropology of Early Modern Italy: Essays on Perception and Communication*. Cambridge: Cambridge University Press, 1987, pp. 110–132.

Burnley, J. D. "Christine de Pizan and the so-called *style clergial*." *Modern Language Quarterly* 81 (1986): 1–6.

Bynum, Caroline Walker. *Holy Feast and Holy Fast: The Significance of Food to Medieval Women*. Berkeley and Los Angeles: University of California Press, 1987.

Caesaria. "Epistola ad Richildam et Radegundim." *Patrologia Latina. Supplementum*. Vol. 4. Paris: Garnier 1969, cols. 1404–09.

Caffarini, Thomas. *Il Processo Castellano*. Ed. M.-H. Laurent. Fontes Vitae S. Catharinae Senensis Historici. Vol. 9. Milan: Bocca, 1942.

———. *Libellus de Supplemento: Legenda prolixe virginis Beate Catharine de Senis*. Ed. Giuliana Cavallini and Imelda Foralosso. Rome: Edizioni cateriniane, 1974.

Cardini, Franco. "Alfabetismo e livelli di cultura nell'età communale." *Quaderni storici* 13 (1978): 488–522.

Catherine of Siena. *Il Dialogo della divina provvidenza ovvero Libro della divina dottrina*. Ed. Giuliana Cavallini. Rome: Edizioni cateriniane, 1980.

———. *The Dialogue*. Trans. Suzanne Noffke. New York: Paulist Press, 1980.

———. *Epistolario*. Ed. Eugenio Dupré Theseider. Rome: Tipografia del Senato, 1940.

———. *Le Lettere di S. Caterina de Siena*. Ed. Piero Misciattelli. 6 Vols. Florence: Giunti, 1960.

———. *Le Orazioni*. Ed. Giuliana Cavallini. Rome: Edizioni cateriniane, 1978.

———. *L'Opere di Santa Caterina de Siena, nuovamente pubblicate da Girolamo Gigli*. Siena: Bonetti, 1707–1726.

———. *The Letters of Catherine of Siena*. Trans. Suzanne Noffke. Medieval and Renaissance Texts and Studies. Binghamton, NY: Center for Medieval and Early Renaissance Studies, 1988.

Catullus. *Catullus Tibullus and Pervigilium Veneris*. Trans. F. W. Cornish. Loeb Classical Library. Cambridge, MA: Harvard University Press, 1976.

Charrier, Charlotte. *Héloïse dans l'histoire et dans la legende*. Paris: Champion, 1933.

Cherewatuk, Karen. "Germanic Echoes in Latin Verse: The Voice of the Lamenting Woman in Radegund's Poetry," forthcoming, *Allegorica*.

Christine de Pizan. *The Book of the City of Ladies*. Trans. Earl Jeffrey Richards. London: Pan Books, 1983.

———. *The Epistle of the Prison of Human Life, with an Epistle to the Queen of France and Lament on the Evils of Civil War*. Ed. Josette Wisman. New York: Garland, 1984.

———. *Epistre d'Othea*. In Halina Loukopoulos, *Classical Mythology in the Works of Christine de Pisan with an Edition of "L'Epistre Othea" from the Manuscript Harley 4431*. Ph.D. dissertation, Wayne State University, 1977.

———. *"Epistre à la Reine* (1405)." Ed. Angus Kennedy, *Revue des Langues Romanes* 92 (1988): 253–64.

———. *L'Avision Christine*. Ed. Mary Louise Towner. Washington DC: Catholic University of America Press, 1932.

———. *Le Débat sur le Roman de la Rose*. Ed. Eric Hicks. Paris: Champion, 1977.

———. *Oeuvres poétiques de Christine de Pisan*. Ed. Maurice Roy. 3 Vols. Paris: Didot, 1886–96.

Clark, Anne L. *Elizabeth of Schönau: A Twelfth-Century Visonary*. Philadelphia: University of Pennsylvania Press, 1992.

Classen, Albrecht. "Female Epistolary Literature from Antiquity to the Present: An Introduction." *Studia Neophilologia* 60 (1988): 3–13.

———. "From *Nonnenbuch* to Epistolarity: Elsbeth Stagel as a Late Medieval Woman Writer." In *Medieval German Literature. Proceedings from the 23rd International Congress on Medieval Studies, Kalamazoo, Michigan, May 5–8, 1988*. Ed. Albrecht Classen. Göppingen: Kümmerle Verlag, 1989, 147–170.

Coakley, John Wayland. "The Representation of Sanctity in Late Medieval Hagiography: The Evidence from *Lives* of Saints of the Dominican Order." Th.D. Dissertation, Harvard University, 1980.

Collinson, Patrick. "Sir Nicholas Bacon and the Elizabethan *via media*." *Historical Journal* 50 (1980): 255–73.

Colloques. See *Pierre Abélard—Pierre le Vénérable*.

Colombini, Giovanni. *Le Lettere di Giovanni Colombini*. Ed. Dino Fantozzi. Lanciano, n.d.

Constable, Giles. *Letters and Letter Collections*. Typologie des sources du Moyen Âge occidental, fasc. 17. Turnhout: Brepols, 1976.

Crossley-Holland, Kevin, trans. and ed. *The Anglo-Saxon World*. New York: Oxford University Press, 1982.

Curtius, Ernst. *European Literature and the Latin Middle Ages*. Trans. Willard Trask. Bollingen Series 36. Princeton, NJ: Princeton University Press, 1973.

Datini, Margherita. "Le Lettere di Margherita Datini a Francesco di Marco." Ed. Valeria Rosati. *Archivio storico pratese* XLX (1974): 4–93.

Davis, Norman. "The Language of the Pastons." *Proceedings of the British Academy* 40 (1954): 119–39.

———. "Styles in English Prose of the Late Middle and Early Modern Period— Margaret Paston's Use of ⟨Do⟩." *Langue et Litterature* XXI (1961): 55–62.

———. "The *Litera Troili* and English Letters." *Review of English Studies* n.s. 16 (1965): 233–44.

———. "A Note on *Pearl*." *Review of English Studies* n.s. 17 (1966): 403–5.

———. "Style and Stereotype in Early English Letters." *Leeds Studies in English* 1 (1967): 7–17.

———. "Styles in English Prose of the Late Middle and Early Modern Period." *Neuphilologische Mitteilungen* 73 (1972): 165–84.

———, ed. *Paston Letters and Papers of the Fifteenth Century*. 2 Vols. Oxford: Oxford University Press, 1971–1976.

DeBlasi, Nicola. "La lettera mercantile tra formulario appreso e lingua d'uso." *Quaderni di retorica e poetica* 1 (1985): 39–47.

DeJean, Joan. *Fictions of Sappho, 1546–1937*. Chicago: University of Chicago Press, 1987.

Delhaye, Philippe. "Le Dossier anti-matrimoniale de l'*Aversus Jovinianum* et son influence sur quelques écrits latines du XIIe siècle." *Mediaeval Studies* 12 (1951): 65–86.

Deschamps, Eustache. *Oeuvres complètes d'Eustache Deschamps*. Ed. Gaston Raynaud. Paris: Didot, 1891.

Dhuoda. *Dhuoda: Manuel pour mon fils*. Ed. Pierre Riché. Sources Chrétiennes 225. Paris: Éditions du Cerf, 1975.

Dionisotti, Carlo. *Gli umanisti e il volqare fra quattro e cinquecento*. Florence: F. Le Monnier, 1968.

Doni, Anton Franceso. *La Libraria*. Ed. Vanni Bramanti. Milan: Longanesi, 1972.

Drane, Augusta Theodosia. *The History of St. Catherine of Siena and Her Companions*. London: Longmans, Green, 1915.

Dronke, Peter. *Abelard and Heloise in Medieval Testimonies*. W. P. Kerr Memorial Lecture no. 26. Glasgow: University of Glasgow Press, 1976.

———. "Francesca et Héloïse." *Comparative Literature* 27 (1975): 113–25.

———. "Heloise's *Problemata* and Letters." In Thomas, ed., *Petrus Abaelardus*, 53–74.

———. *The Medieval Lyric*. Cambridge: Cambridge University Press, 1977.

———. *Poetic Individuality in the Middle Ages: New Departures in Poetry 1000–1150*. Oxford: Clarendon Press, 1970.

———. *Women Writers of the Middle Ages: A Critical Study of Texts from Perpetua (†203) to Marguerite Porete (†1310)*. Cambridge: Cambridge University Press, 1984.

Duby, Georges. "Private Power, Public Power." In Duby, ed., *Revelations of the Medieval World*. Vol. 2 of *A History of Private Life*.

———, ed. With Philippe Ariès. *Revelations of the Medieval World*. Trans. Arthur Goldhammer. 2 vols. Cambridge, MA: Harvard University Press, 1988.

Duckett, Eleanor. *Women and Their Letters in the Early Middle Ages*. Baltimore: Barton-Gillet Company, 1965.

Egeria. *Egeria: Diary of a Pilgrimage*. Ed. and trans. George E. Gingras. Ancient Christian Writers no. 35. New York: Newman Press, 1970.

Ennen, Edith. *Frauen im Mittelalter*. Munich: C. H. Beck'sche Verlagsbuchhandlung, 1988.

The Exeter Book. Ed. George Philip Krapp and Elliott van Kird Dobbie. Anglo-Saxon Poetic Record. Vol. 3. New York: Columbia University Press, 1936.

Fawtier, Robert. "Catheriniana." *Mélanges d'archéologie et d'histoire* 34 (1914): 31–32.

———. *Sainte Catherine de Sienne. Essai de critique des sources*. 2 Vols. Paris: Éditions de Boccard, 1930.

Fell, Christine. "Some Implications of the Boniface Correspondence." In *New Readings on Women in Old English Literature*. Ed. Helen Damico and Alexandra Hennessey Olsen. Bloomington: Indiana University Press, 1990, pp. 29–43.

Fenster, Thelma S and Mary Carpenter Erler, eds. *Poems of Cupid, God of Love: Christine de Pizan's "Epistre au dieu d'amours" and "Dit de la Rose," Thomas Hoccleve's "The Letter of Cupid."* Leiden: E. J. Brill, 1990.

Ferguson, Chris. "Autobiography as Therapy: Guibert de Nogent, Peter Abelard, and the Making of Medieval Autobiography." *Journal of Medieval and Renaissance Studies* 13 (1983): 187–212.

Ferrante, Joan. "Public Postures and Private Maneuvers: Roles Medieval Women Play." In *Women and Power in the Middle Ages*. Ed. Mary Erle and Maryanne Kowaleski. Athens: University of Georgia Press, 1988, pp. 213–29.

Flanagan, Sabina. *Hildegard of Bingen, 1098–1179: A Visionary Life*. New York: Routledge, 1990.

Fleischman, Suzanne. "Philology, Linguistics, and the Discourse of the Medieval Text." *Speculum* 65 (1990): 19–37.

Fulwood, William. *The Enimie of Idlenesse: Teaching How to Indite Epistles*. n.p.: 1568.

Georgianna, Linda. "Any Corner of Heaven: Heloise's Critique of Monasticism." *Medieval Studies* 49 (1987): 221–53.

Getto, Giovanni. *Saggio letterario su S. Caterina da Siena*. Florence: G. C. Sansoni, 1939.

Gilson, Étienne. *Héloïse et Abélard*. 2nd ed. Paris: Librairie Philosophique J. Vrin, 1948.

Goldsmith, Elizabeth C., ed. "Introduction." *Writing the Female Voice: Essays on Epistolary Literature*. Boston: Northeastern University Press, 1989.

Grant-Brown, Rosalind. "*L'Avision-Christine*: Autobiographical Narrative or Mirror for the Prince?" In Brabant, ed., *Gender, Genre, and Politics*, pp. 95–112.

Greenspan, Kate. *Magdalena of Freiburg: Selections*. Brookline Village, MA: Focus Library of Medieval Women, forthcoming.

Grender, Paul F. *Schooling in Renaissance Italy: Literacy and Learning, 1300–1600*. Baltimore: Johns Hopkins University Press, 1989.

Gregory of Tours. *Historia Francorum*. Ed. W. Arndt. *Monumenta Germaniae Historica: Scriptores Rerum Merovingicarum*. Tomus I, part I. Hanover: Weidmann, 1885, 1–450.

———. *History of the Franks*. Trans. O. M. Dalton. 2 Vols. Oxford: Clarendon Press, 1927.

———. *Liber in gloria confessorum*. Ed. B. Krusch. *Monumenta Germaniae Historica: Scriptores Rerum Merogingicarum*. Tomus I, part I. Hanover: Weidmann, 1885, 744–820.

Gruendler, Otto. "Devotio Moderna." In *Christian Spirituality: High Middle Ages and Reformation*. Ed. Jill Raitt. New York, 1987, 176–93.

Grundmann, Herbert. *Movimenti religiosi nel Medioevo*. Bologna: Il Mulino, 1974.

———. *Religiöse Bewegungen im Mittelalter*. Hildesheim: Georg Olms Verlagsbuchhandlung, 1961.

———. "Zur Geschichte der Beginen im 13. Jahrhundert." In *Ausgewaehlte Aufsätze*. Stuttgart: Anton Hiersemann, 1976, 201–22.

Haas, Alois Maria. "Schools of Late Medieval Mysticism." In *Christian Spirituality: High Middle Ages and Reformation*. Ed. Jill Raitt. New York: Crossroad, 1987, 140–176.

Hadewijch. *Hadewijch, the Complete Works*. Trans. Columba Hart. New York: Paulist Press, 1980.

Hanham, Alison, ed. *The Cely Letters, 1472–1488*. EETS o.s. 273. Oxford: Oxford University Press, 1975.

Harris, Joseph. "Elegy in Old English and Old Norse: A Problem in Literary History." In *Old English Elegies*. Ed. Martin Green. Rutherford, NJ: Fairleigh Dickinson University Press, 1983, 46–56.

Haskins, Charles H. "The Early *Ars dictandi* in Italy." In his *Studies in Medieval Culture*. Oxford: Clarendon, 1929; rpt. New York: Ungar, 1958, 170–92.

Heilbrun, Carolyn G. *Writing a Woman's Life*. New York: Ballantine Books, 1988.

Herwegen, Hildegons. "Les collaborateurs de Sainte Hildegarde." *Revue bénédictine* 21 (1904): 192–203, 302–15, 381–403.

Hildegard of Bingen. *Epistolarium*. Ed. L. van Acker. Vol. 91 of *Corpus Christianorum Continuatio Medievalis*. Turnhout: Brepols, 1991.

———. *Scivias*. Trans. Columba Hart and Jane Bishop. New York: Paulist Press, 1990.

———. Selections. Vol. 197 of *Patrologia Latina*. Ed. J. P. Migne. Paris, Garnier, 1855.

———. Selections. Vol. 8 of *Analecta Sacra*. Ed. J. Pitra. Westmead, England: Gregg Press, 1966.

———. *Illuminations of Hildegard of Bingen*. Ed. Matthew Fox. Santa Fe, NM: Bear & Co., 1985.

Hogg, James, ed. *Die Kartäuser in Österreich*. 2 Vols. Salzburg: Institüt für Anglistik und Amerikanistik, 1981.

Horace. *Odes and Epodes*. Tr. C. E. Bennett. Loeb Classical Library. Cambridge, MA: Harvard University Press, 1968.

Irigaray, Luce. "This Sex Which Is Not One." In *New French Feminisms*. Ed. Elaine Marks and Isabelle de Courtrivon. Amherst: University of Massachusetts Press, 1980, 99–107.

Jacobson, Howard. *Ovid's "Heroides."* Princeton, NJ: Princeton University Press, 1974.

Jaeger, C. S. "The Prologue to the *Historia calamitatum* and the Authenticity Question." *Euphorion* 74 (1980): 1–15.

Jean de Montreuil. *Opera*. Ed. Ezio Ornato. Turin: G. Giappichelli, 1963.

Kamuf, Peggy. "Marriage Contracts: The Letters of Heloise and Abelard." In Kamuf, *Fictions of Feminine Desire: Disclosures of Heloise*. Lincoln: University of Nebraska Press, 1982.

Kauffman, Linda. *Discourses of Desire: Gender, Genre, and Epistolary Fiction*. Ithaca, NY: Cornell University Press, 1986.

Kelly, Allison. "Christine de Pizan and Antoine de la Sale: The Dangers of Love in Theory and Fiction." In Richards, ed., *Reinterpreting Christine de Pizan*, 173–86.

Kieckhefer, Richard. *Repression of Heresy in Medieval Germany*. Philadelphia: University of Pennsylvania Press, 1979.

———. *Unquiet Souls: Fourteenth Century Saints and Their Religious Milieu*. Chicago: University of Chicago Press, 1984.

King, Margaret L. "Book-Lined Cells: Woman and Humanism in the Early Italian Renaissance." In *Beyond Their Sex: Learned Women of the European Past*. Ed. Patricia H. Labalme. New York: New York University Press, 1980, 66–90.

———. *Women of the Renaissance*. Chicago: University of Chicago Press, 1991.

King, Margaret L. and Albert Rabil, Jr., eds. *Her Immaculate Hand: Selected Works by and about Women Humanists of Quatrocento Italy*. Medieval and Renaissance Texts and Studies. Binghamton, NY: Center for Medieval and Early Renaissance Studies, 1983.

Kingford, Charles L., ed. *The Stonor Letters and Papers, 1290–1483*. 2 Vols. London: Camden Society, 1919.

———. *Supplementary Stonor Letters and Papers (1314–1482)*. London: Camden Society, 1923.

Klapisch-Zuber, Christiane. *Women, Family, and Ritual in Renaissance Italy*. Trans. Lydia Cochrane. Chicago: University of Chicago Press, 1985.

Kleineidam, Erich. "Die Spiritualität der Karäuser im Spiegel der Erfurter Karäuser-Bibliothek." In *Die Kartäuser*. Ed. Marijan Zadnikar and Adam Wienand. Cologne: Wienand Verlag, 1983, pp. 185–202.

Knowles, David. *The Evolution of Medieval Thought*. New York: Vintage, 1962.

Koorn, Florence. "Women Without Vows. The Case of the Beguines and the Sisters of the Common Life in the Northern Netherlands." In *Women and Men in Spiritual Culture, XIV–XVII Centuries*. Ed. Elisja Schulte van Kessel. 's Gravenhage: Staatsutgeverij, 1984, 135–147.

Kraft, Kent. *The Eye Sees More than the Heart Knows*. Ph.D. dissertation. University of Wisconsin, 1977.

Kristeller, Paul Oskar. "The Scholar and His Public in the Late Middle Ages and the Renaissance." In *Medieval Aspects of Renaissance Learning*. Ed. and trans. Edward P. Mahoney. Durham, NC: Duke University Press, 1974.

Labarge, Margaret Wade. *The Small Sound of a Trumpet: Women in Medieval Life*. Boston: Beacon Press, 1986.

Lalanne, Ludovic. "Quelques doutes sur l'authenticité de la correspondance amoureuse d'Héloïse et d'Abélard." *La Correspondance Littéraire* 1 (1856): 27–83.

Lambert, Malcolm. *Medieval Heresy: Popular Movements from Bogomil to Hus*. London: Edward Arnold, 1977.

Leclercq, Jean. "Modern Psychology and the Interpretation of Medieval Texts." *Speculum* 47 (1973): 476–90.

Legge, M. Dominica. *Anglo-Norman Letters and Petitions from All Souls MS. 182*. Oxford: Blackwell, 1941.

Levasti, Arrigo. *S. Caterina da Siena*. Turin: U.T.E.T., 1947, pp. 414–500.

Lippert, W. "Zur Geschichte der hl. Radegunde von Thüringen." *Geschichte und Altertumkunde* 7 (1890): 16–38.

Luscombe, D. E. "The *Letters* of Heloise and Abelard since 'Cluny 1972.'" In Thomas, *Petrus Abaelardus*, pp. 19–40.

———, ed. *Peter Abelard's "Ethics." An Edition with Introduction*. Oxford: Clarendon Press, 1971.

Maisonneuve, Roland. "L'Expérience mystique et visionnaire de Marguerite d'Oingt (d. 1310), moniale chartreuse." In Hogg, ed., *Kartäusermystik und -Mystiker*, pp. 81–103.

Makowski, Elizabeth. "The Conjugal Debt and Medieval Canon Law." *Journal of Medieval History* 3 (1977): 99–114.

Mann, Nicholas. "La Fortune de Pétrarque en France: Recherches sur le «De Remediis»." *Studi francesi* 13 (1969): 3–13.

——. "La prima fortuna del Petrarca in Inghilterra." In *Il Petrarca ad Arquà: Atti del Convegno di Studi nel VI. centenario (1370–1374)*. Arquà Petrarca, 6–8 novembre 1970. Ed. Giuseppe Billanovich and Giuseppe Frasso. Padua: Antenore, 1975, 279–289.

——. "Petrarch's Role as Moralist in Fifteenth-Century France." In *Humanism in France at the End of the Middle Ages and in the Early Renaissance*. Ed. A. H. T. Levi. New York: Barnes and Noble, 1970, 6–28.

Maria of Osterwyk. Wolfenbuettel. Herzog August Biblithek. MS. Wf. 1164, 113 Theol. 8 (1).

——. Ed. J. B. Kettenmeyer. "Uit de Briefwisseling van Eene Brabantsche Mystieke uit de 16e Euw. Tekstbijlage." In *Ons geestelijk erf* (1927): 370–95.

Marti, Mario. "Il epistolario comme «genere» e un problema editoriale." In *Studi e problemi di critica testuale*. Convegno di Studi di Filologia italiana nel Centenario della Commissione per i Testi di Lingua, 7–9 Aprile 1960. Ed. Raffaele Spongano. Bologna: Commissione per Testi di Lingua, 1961, pp. 203–8.

Martial. *Epigrams I*. Trans. Walter C. A. Ker. Loeb Classical Library. Cambridge, MA: Harvard University Press, 1961.

Matter, E. Ann. *The Voice of My Beloved: The Song of Songs in Western Medieval Christianity*. Philadelphia: University of Pennsylvania Press, 1990.

McCarthy, Maria Caritas S.H.C.J. *The Rule for Nuns of St. Caesarius of Arles: A Translation with a Critical Introduction*. Washington, DC: Catholic University of America Press, 1960.

McKendrick, Geraldine and Angus MacKay. "Visionaries and Affective Spirituality during the First Half of the Sixteenth Century." In *Cultural Encounters. The Impact of the Inquisition in Spain and the New World*. Ed. Mary Elizabeth Perry and Anne J. Cruz. Berkeley and Los Angeles: University of California Press, 1991, 93–105.

McLaughlin, Mary. "Abelard as Autobiographer." *Speculum* 42 (1967): 463–88.

——. "Peter Abelard and the Dignity of Women: Twelfth Century "Feminism" in Theory and Practice." In *Pierre Abélard—Pierre le Vénérable*, pp. 287–334.

McLeod, Glenda, ed. *The Reception of Christine de Pizan from the Fifteenth Through the Nineteenth Century: Visitors to the City*. Lewiston, ME: E. Mellen, 1991.

McNamara, Jo Ann. "A Legacy of Miracles: Hagiography and Nunneries in Merovingian Gaul." In *Women of the Medieval World: Essays in Honor of John H. Mundy*. Ed. Julius Kirshner and Suzanne Fonay Wemple. Oxford: B. Blackwell, 1985, 36–52.

——. *A New Song: Celibate Women in the First Three Christian Centuries*. Women and History, no. 6/7. New York: Haworth Press and the Institute for Research in History, 1983.

Meech, S. B., and H. E. Allen. *The Book of Margery Kempe*. EETS 212. Oxford: Oxford University Press, 1940.

Mertes, Kate. *The English Noble Household*. Oxford: Blackwell, 1988.

Meerseman, Giles. "Gil amici spirituali di S. Caterina a Roma alla luce del primo manifesto urbanista." *Bulletino Senese di Storia Patria* 69 (1962): 83–123.

Mommaers, Paul. "Hadewijch: A Feminist in Conflict." *Louvain Studies* 13 (1988): 58–81.

Monfrin, Jacques. "Le Problème de l'authenticité de la correspondance d'Abélard et d'Héloïse." In *Pierre Abélard—Pierre le Vénérable*, pp. 409–24.

Muckle, J. T. "The Personal Letters Between Abelard and Heloise." *Mediaeval Studies* 15 (1953): 47–84.

———. "The Letter of Heloise on Religious Life and Abelard's First Reply." *Mediaeval Studies* 17 (1955): 240–81.

Mueller, Janel. *The Native Tongue and the World: Developments in English Prose Style 1380–1580*. Chicago: University of Chicago Press, 1985.

Murphy, Gerard, trans. and ed. *Early Irish Lyrics*. Oxford: Clarendon Press, 1956.

Murphy, James J. *Medieval Rhetoric: A Select Bibliography*, 2nd ed. Toronto: University of Toronto Press, 1989.

———. *Rhetoric in the Middle Ages. A History of Rhetorical Theory from St. Augustine to the Renaissance*. Berkeley and Los Angeles: University of California Press, 1974.

Neel, Carol. "The Origins of the Beguines." *Signs* 14 (1989): 321–41.

Newman, Barbara. "Authority, Authenticity, and the Repression of Heloise." *Journal of Medieval and Renaissance Studies* 22, 2 (Spring 1992): 121–57.

———. "Hildegard of Bingen: Visions and Validation." *Church History* 54 (1985): 163–75.

———. *Sister of Wisdom: St. Hildegard's Theology of the Feminine*. Berkeley and Los Angeles: University of California Press, 1987.

Nisard, Charles. "Des poésies de sainte Radegonde attribués jusqu'ici à Fortunat." *Revue historique* 37 (1888): 1–6.

Noonan, John T. "Marital Affection in the Canonist." *Studia Gratiana* 12 (1967): 479–509.

Oehl, Wilhelm, ed. *Deutsche Mystikerbriefe des Mittelalters 1100–1500*. Munich-Vienna: Georg Muller, 1931, reprint Darmstadt: Wissenschaftliche Buchgesellschaft, 1972.

Orme, Nicholas. *English Schools in the Middle Ages*. London: Methuen, 1973.

Ornato, Ezio. "La prima fortuna di Petrarca in Francia, I: Le Letture petrarchesche di Jean de Montreuil." *Studi francesi* 5 (1961): 201–17; "II: Il contributo del Petrarca alla formazione culturale di Jean de Montreuil." *Studi francesi* 6 (1962): 401–14.

———. *Jean Muret et ses amis Nicholas de Clamanges et Jean de Montreuil. Contribution à l'étude des rapports entre les humanistes de Paris et ceux d'Avignon (1394–1420)* Geneva: Droz, 1969.

Ovid. *Heroides and Amores*. Trans. Grant Showerman. Loeb Classical Library. Cambridge, MA: Harvard University Press, 1977.

———. *Tristia, Ex ponto*. Trans. Arthur Leslie Wheller. Loeb Classical Library. Cambridge, MA: Harvard University Press, 1959.

Papi, Anna Benvenuti. "Penitenza e santità femminile in ambiente cateriniano e bernardiniano." In *Atti del simposio internazionale cateriniano-bernardiniano, Siena, 17–20 aprile 1980*. Ed. Domenico Maffel and Paolo Nardi. Siena: Accademia senese degli intronati, 1982.

Patch, Howard. *The Goddess Fortuna in Mediaeval Literature*. London: Frank Case, 1927.

Peers, E. Allison, tr. *The Life of Teresa of Jesus: The Autobiography of St. Teresa of Avila*. Garden City, NY: Image Books, 1960.

Pellegrin, Elisabeth. "Manuscrits de Pétrarque dans les bibliothèques de France." *Italia medioevale e umanistica* 4 (1961): 341–431; 6 (1963): 271–379.

Petrarch. *Poesi minore del Petrarca*. Ed. Domenico de Rossetti, Milan: Dalla Societá tipogration dé classici italiani, 1829–1834.

Petroff, Elisabeth Alvida. *Medieval Women's Visionary Literature*. Oxford: Oxford University Press, 1986.

Pierre Abélard—Pierre le Vénérable: Les courants philosophiques, littéraires et artistiques en occident au milieu du XII siécle. No editor. Colloques Internationaux du Centre National de la Recherche Scientifique, no. 546. Paris: Éditions du Centre National de la Recherche Scientifique, 1975.

Pinet, Marie-Josèphe. *Christine de Pisan, 1364–1431: étude biographique et littéraire*. Paris: Champion, 1927.

Polak, E. J. "Dictamen." *Dictionary of the Middle Ages*. Ed. Joseph R. Strayer. Vol. 4. New York: Charles Scribner, 1984, 173–177.

Power, Eileen. *Medieval Women*. Ed. M. M. Postan. Cambridge: Cambridge University Press, 1973.

Propertius. *Propertius*. Tr. H. E. Butler. Loeb Classical Library. Cambridge, MA: Harvard University Press, 1962.

Quondam, Amadeo. "Dal 'Formulario' al 'Formulario': cento anni di 'Libri di lettere.'" *Le "carte messaggiere." Retorica e modelli di comunicazione epistolare: per un indice dei libri di lettere del Cinquecento*. Rome: Bulzoni, 1981, 13–156.

Rabil, Albert, Jr. *Laura Cereta: Quattrocento Humanist*. Medieval and Renaissance Texts and Studies. Binghamton, NY: Center for Medieval and Early Renaissance Studies, 1981.

Radegund. "De excidio Thoringiae," "Ad Iustinum et Sophiam Augustos," and "Ad Artachin." *Monumenta Germaniae Historica: Auctores Antiquissimorum*. Ed. Friedrich Leo. Vol. 4, part 1. "Opera Poetica Venanti Fortunati, Appendix Carminum." Berlin: Weidmann, 1881, 271–75.

Radice, Betty, tr. *The Letters of Abelard and Heloise*. Baltimore: Penguin, 1974.

Raymond of Capua. *Legenda Major* or *De S. Catharina, Senensi virgine de Poenitentia S. Dominici*. In *Acta Sanctorum Aprilis*, vol. 3. Antwerp: M. Cnobarvm, 1675, pp. 853–959.

———. *The Life of Catherine of Siena*. Trans. Conleth Kearns. Wilmington, DE: Michael Glazer, 1980.

Régnier-Bholer, Danielle. "Imagining the Self: Exploring Literature." In Duby, ed., *Revelations of the Medieval World*, pp. 311–94.

Reno, Christine. "The Preface to the Avision—Christine in ex-Phillipps 128." In Richards, ed., *Reinterpreting Christine de Pizan*, pp. 207–27.

Rey, E. "De l'authenticité de deux poèmes de Fortunat attribués à tort à Ste. Radegonde." *Revue de philologie* 30 (1906): 124–38.

Richards, E. J. "Christine de Pizan, the Conventions of Courtly Diction and Italian Humanism." In Richards, ed., *Reinterpreting Christine de Pizan*, pp. 250–271.

——. *Dante and the "Roman de la Rose": An Investigation into the Vernacular Narrative Context of the "Commedia."* Beiheft zur Zeitschrift für romanische Philologie, Bd. 184. Tübingen: Max Niemeyer Verlag, 1981.

——. "Feminism as Universalism: Virginia Woolf's *Orlando* and Christine de Pizan's *Livre de la Mutacion de Fortune*: Sexual Metamorphosis, Gender Difference and the Republic of Letters." *Romance Languages Annual* 2 (1991): 146–52.

——, ed. with Joan Williamson, Nadia Margolis, and Christine Reno. *Reinterpreting Christine de Pizan*. Athens: University of Georgia Press, 1992.

Richardson, H. G. Untitled review of M. Dominica Legge, *Anglo-Norman Letters and Petitions from All Souls MS. 182. English Historical Review* 58 (1943): 222–30.

Richmond, Colin. *The Paston Family in the Fifteenth Century: The First Phase.* Cambridge: Cambridge University Press, 1990.

Robertson, D. W., Jr. *Abelard and Heloise*. New York: Dial Press, 1972.

Rockinger, Ludwig. *Briefsteller und Formelbücher des eilften bis vierzehnten Jahrhunderts*. Munich, 1863; rpt., New York: Franklin, 1961.

Rupprich, Hans. ed. *Der Briefwechsel des Conrad Celtis*. Munich: C. H. Beck'sche Verlagsbuchhandlung, 1934.

Rygiel, D. "*Ancrene Wisse* and Colloquial Style: A Caveat." *Neophilologus* 65 (1981): 137–43.

Saccaro, Alexander Peter. *Französischer Humanismus des 14. und 15. Jahrhunderts.* Munich: Fink, 1975.

Sapegno, N. *Il Trecento*. Milan: Vallardi, 1966.

Schmale, Franz-Josef. "Die Bologneser Schule der Ars dictaminis." *Deutsches Archiv für die Erforschung des Mittelalters* 13 (1957): 16–34.

Schmeidler, Bernhard. "Der Briefwechsel zwischen Abälard und Héloïse: eine Fälschung." *Archiv für Kulturgeschichte* 11 (1913): 1–30.

——. "Der Briefwechsel zwischen Abaelard und Heloise dennoch eine literarische Fiction Abelards." Revue benedictine 52 (1940): 85–95.

Schmitt, Jean-Claude. *Mort d'une heresie*. Paris: Mouton Éditeur, 1978.

Schrader, Monika and Führkötter, Adelgundis *Die Echtheit des Schrifttums der heiligen Hildegard von Bingen. Quellenkritische Untersuchungen*. Cologne: Böhlau, 1956.

Schulenberg, Jane Tibbetts. "Female Sanctity: Public and Private Roles, ca. 500–1100." In *Women and Power in the Middle Ages*. Ed. Mary Erler and Maryanne Kowaleski. Athens: University of Georgia Press, 1988, pp. 102–25.

Schweickart, Patrocinio. "Reading Ourselves: Toward a Feminist Theory of Reading." In *Gender and Reading: Essays on Readers, Texts, and Contexts*. Ed. Elizabeth A. Flynn and Patrocinio P. Schweickart. Baltimore: Johns Hopkins University Press, 1986, 31–57.

Scott, Joan W. "Gender: A Useful Category of Historical Analysis." *American Historical Review* 91 (1986): 1053–75.

Scott, Karen. "Catherine of Siena, *Apostola*." *Church History*. Forthcoming.

——. "La practica della tolleranza religiosa da parte di S. Caterina." *Nuovi Studi Cateriniani* 3 (1987): 5–26.

——. "La tolleranza religiosa nel pensiero di Santa Caterina da Siena." *Nuovi studi cateriniani* 2 (1985): 97–111.

———. "Not Only With Words, But With Deeds: The Role of Speech in Catherine of Siena's Understanding of Her Mission." Doctoral dissertation, University of California, Berkeley, 1989.

Seymour, M. C., ed. *Selections from Hoccleve*. Oxford: Oxford University Press, 1981.

Southern, R. W. "The Letters of Abelard and Heloise." In Southern, *Medieval Humanism and Other Studies*. New York: Harper and Row, 1970, pp. 86–104.

Spacks, Patricia. *Imagining a Self*. Cambridge, MA: Harvard University Press, 1976.

Spitzer, Leo. "The Epic Style of the Pilgrim Aetheria." *Comparative Literature* 1 (1949): 225–48.

Stapleton, Thomas, ed. *Plumpton Correspondence: A Series of Letters, chiefly Domestick, written in the Reigns of Edward IV, Richard III, Henry VII and Henry VIII.* London: Camden Society, 1839.

Starkey, David. "The Age of the Household: Politics, Society and the Arts c. 1350–c. 1550." In *The Later Middle Ages*. Ed. Stephen Medcalf. London: Methuen, 1981, pp. 225–90.

Statius. "Silvae." *Silvae, Thebaid I–IV*. Tr. J. H. Mozley. Loeb Classical Library. Cambridge, MA: Harvard University Press, 1967.

Stuard, Susan. "The Dominion of Gender: Women's Fortunes in the High Middle Ages." In *Becoming Visible: Women in European History*. Ed. Renate Bridenthal, Claudia Koonz, and Susan Stuard. Boston: Houghton Mifflin: 1987, pp. 153–75.

Szövérfly, Josef. *Weltliche Dichtungen des lateinischen Mittelalters*. Berlin: Erich Schmidt, 1970.

Tangl, Michael, ed. "Die Briefe des Heiligen Bonifatius und Lullus." *Monumenta Germaniae Historica: Epistolae Selectae* 1. Berlin: Wiedmann, 1955.

Tanquerey, F. J., ed. *Recueil de lettres Anglo-Francaises (1265–1399)*. Paris: Champion, 1916.

Thiebaux, Marcelle. *The Writings of Medieval Women*. New York: Garland, 1987.

Thomas, Rudolf, ed. *Petrus Abaelardus, 1079–1142: Person, Werk und Wirkung*. Trierer Theologische Studien 38. Trier: Paulinus, 1980. Cited in Notes as *Trier 1980*.

Uitti, Karl D. "Remarks on Old French Narrative: Courtly Love and Poetic Form (II)." *Romance Philology* 28 (1974): 190–99.

Van Acker, L. "Der Briefwechsel der heiligen Hildegard von Bingen. Vorbemerkungen zu einer kritischen Edition." *Revue bénédictine* 98 (1988): 141–68 and 99 (1989): 118–54.

Van Engen, John. *Devotio Moderna. Basic Writings*. New York: Paulist Press, 1988.

Vauchez, André. "La sainteté mystique en Occident au temps des papes d'Avignon et du Grand Schisme." In *Genèse et débuts du Grand Schisme d'Occident: Avignon, 25–28 septembre 1978*. Paris: Éditions du Centre National de la Recherche Historique, 1980, pp. 361–68.

———. "Les représentations de la sainteté d'après les procès de canonization mediévaux (XIII–XVe siècles)." *Convegno internazionale. Agiografia nell-occidente cristiano, secoli XIII–XV, Roma (1–2 marzo 2979)*. Rome: Accademia nazionale del lincei, 1980.

Venantius Fortunatus. "Vitae Sanctae Radegundis." *Monumenta Germaniae Historica: Auctores Antiquissimorum.* Ed. Bruno Krusch. Vol. 4, part 2, "Opera Pedestria Venanti Fortunati." Berlin: Weidmann, 1885, 38–49.

Verducci, Florence. *Ovid's Toyshop of the Heart: Epistulae Herodium.* Princeton, NJ: Princeton University Press, 1985.

Virgil. *Eclogues, Georgics, Aeneid I–VI.* Trans. H. Rushton Fairclough. Loeb Classical Library. Cambridge, MA: Harvard University Press, 1965.

Virgoe, R. *Illustrated Letters of the Paston Family.* London: Macmillan, 1989.

von Moos, Peter. "Cornelia und Heloise." *Latomus* 34 (1975): 1024–59.

———. "Le Silence d'Héloïse et les idéologies modernes." In *Pierre Abélard—Pierre le Vénérable,* pp. 425–68.

———. "Post festum—Was kommt nach der Authentizitätsdebatte über die Briefe Abaelards und Heloises?" In Thomas, ed., *Petrus Abaelardus,* pp. 75–101.

Wentzlaff-Eggebert, Friedrich-W. and Erika. *Deutsche Literatur im späten Mittelalter, 1250–1450.* 2 Vols. Hamburg: Rowohlt Verlag, 1971.

Wemple, Suzanne Fonay. *Women in Frankish Society: Marriage and the Cloister, 500–900.* Philadelphia: University of Pennsylvania Press, 1981.

Whiting, B. J., ed. *Proverbs, Sentences, and Proverbial Phrases from English Writing Mainly Before 1500.* Cambridge, MA: Harvard University Press, 1968.

Wilkins, David. "Woman as Artist and Patron in the Middle Ages and the Renaissance." In *The Roles and Images of Women in the Middle Ages and the Renaissance.* Ed. Douglas Radcliff-Umstead. Pittsburgh: University of Pittsburgh Press, 1975, pp. 107–31.

Wilkins, Ernest A. *The «Epistolæ metricæ» of Petrarch, A Manual.* Rome: Edizioni di Storia e Litteratura, 1956.

Willard, Charity Cannon. "Christine de Pizan's Advice to Woman." In Christine de Pizan, *A Medieval Woman's Mirror of Honor, The Treasury of the City of Ladies.* Ed. Charity Cannon Willard. New York: Persea, 1989.

———. *Christine de Pizan, Her Life and Works.* New York: Persea, 1984.

Williams, Sir Ifor, trans. *The Burning Tree.* Dublin: Institute for Advanced Studies, 1954.

Wilson, Katharina M. *Women Writers of the Renaissance and Reformation.* Athens: University of Georgia Press, 1987.

Wilson, Katharina M. and Elizabeth M. Makowski. *Wykked Wyves and the Woes of Marriage: Misogamous Literature from Juvenal to Chaucer.* SUNY Series in Medieval Literature, no. 1. Albany: State University of New York Press, 1990.

Wilson-Kastner, Patricia. "Egeria." In *A Lost Tradition: Women Writers of the Early Church.* Ed. Patricia Wilson-Kastner, Ann Millin, Rosemary Rader, and Jeremiah Reedy. Washington, DC: University Press of America, 71–134.

Woolf, Virginia. *The Common Reader.* 1st ser. London: Hogarth Press, 1925.

Yates, Frances. *The Art of Memory.* Chicago: University of Chicago Press, 1966.

Zarri, Gabriella. "Le sante vive. Per una tipologia della santità femminile nel primo Cinquecanto." *Annali dell-Istituto storico italo-germanico in Trento* 6 (1980): 408–419.

Zdekauer, Lodovico. *Lettere familiari del Rinascimento senese (1409–1525)*. Siena: L. Lazzeri, 1897.

———. *Lettere volgari del Rinascimento senese*. Siena: L. Lazzeri, 1897.

Zimmermann, Margarete. "*Vox femina, vox politica*: The 'Lamentations sur les maux de la France' (1410)." Trans. E. J. Richards. In Brabant, ed., *Gender, Genre, and Politics*, 119–120.

Index

Abélard, 2, 8, 64–86, 122, 141; attempt to
control Héloïse, 68; attitude toward love
affair, 69; *Ethica*, 85 n.26; *Historia Calamitatum*, 64–65, 67–70, 83 n.7, 85 n.26; use
of Song of Songs imagery, 74. *See also*
Abélard and Héloïse, letters of; Héloïse
Abélard and Héloïse, letters of, 64–86; authenticity, 64, 82 n.2; autobiography in,
64–65; letter 1 (Héloïse), 65–70, 72–73, 77,
83 n.7; letter 2 (Abélard), 68, 70–71, 76;
letter 3 (Héloïse), 67, 70–74, 77–79; letter
4 (Abélard), 74–75, 79, 81; letter 5
(Héloïse), 65–66, 73, 75–82, 84 n.22; letter
6 (Abélard), 84 n.22; metaphor in, 71, 74–
76, 78, 85 n.28; salutations in, 65, 70–72,
74, 76–77; use of spatial metaphor, 66, 71,
74–75, 81, 83 n.11. *See also* Abélard; Héloïse
Acciaiuoli, Andrea, 143
Academia della Crusa, 89
Ad nostrum, 174
"Ad Radegundem" (Fortunatus), 25
Adversus Jovinianum (St. Jerome), 68
Aeneid (Virgil), 27, 29
"affliction topos," 14
Agnes, Abbess, 23
Ahlgren, Gillian T. W., 2, 15, 189
Alberic of Monte Cassino, 5, 160, 163, 168 n.13
Alcuin, 7
Alice la Desperance, 9
Alice of Winchester, 9
allegory, use of, 148, 155, 157; Christine de
Pizan, 170 n.32
Allen, H. E., 138 n.35
All Souls Ms. 182, 162–63
Altman, Janet Gurkin, 4
Altmann, Barbara K., 168 n.11
Amalasuntha, Queen, 7
Ambrogio de'Migli, 156
Amores (Ovid), 30
Analecta Sacra (Pitra), 61 n.13
Anastasia, Empress, 7

Anastasius, Pope, 53, 62 n.41
androgyny, 146
Anglo-Saxon poetry. *See* elegy, Germanic
Arnold, Archbishop of Mainz, 50
ars dictaminis/ars dictandi, 4–6, 12–13, 127,
140, 159–64, 169 n.20
ars rhetorica, 131
Artachis, 20, 26, 38–40
Art de Dictier (Deschamps), 150–51, 153
Arundel, Thomas, Archbishop of Canterbury, 135–36
Astell, Ann, 85 n.29
Athiers, 22
Augustine, Saint, 8, 60 n.7, 62 n.30, 69, 76,
84 n.22, 94
Augustinian visionary epistemology, 48, 60
n.7
aureolus liber de nuptiis (Theophrastus), 68
Ausonius, 29
authority, 3, 9, 15–16, 40, 48, 50, 100; divine,
46–54, 58–60; woman's, in Paston household, 133–36
Avignon, France, 87–88, 103, 116 n.17

Bacon, Sir Nicholas, 133
ballade, 150, 152, 154, 167 n.4
Balthard, 7
barbara, 33, 39
Baudonivia, 20–24, 26, 41 n.2, 42 nn.6, 7–9,
43 n.12
Beguine(s), 3, 9, 13, 15, 171, 173–75, 181, 183–
84, 188, 190 n.12
Bell, Rudolph M., 115 n.14
benevolentiae captatio. See *captatio benevolentiæ*
Bennett, H. S., 137 n.4
Benton, John, 82 n.2
Beowulf, "Song of Finnesburg," 37
Bernard of Clairvaux, 11, 47–48, 52, 85 n.29;
correspondence with Hildegard, 47–48,
52

Contributors

GILLIAN T. W. AHLGREN is Assistant Professor of Theology at Xavier University. She earned her Ph.D. in History of Christianity from the University of Chicago in 1991. She has published articles on Teresa of Avila and is currently studying women and the Spanish Inquisition.

KAREN CHEREWATUK, Associate Professor of English at St. Olaf College, received her Ph.D. from Cornell University in 1986. She has published articles on medieval romance and on the Latin letters of medieval women. She is currently working on Sir Thomas Malory and chivalric culture.

GLENDA MCLEOD received her Ph.D. in Comparative Literature from the University of Georgia in 1987 and now teaches at Gainesville College. She has published *Virtue and Venom: Catalogs of Women from Antiquity to the Renaissance* and articles on medieval and baroque women writers. At present she is working on a translation of Christine de Pizan's *Avision-Christine*.

EARL JEFFREY RICHARDS, Professor of French at Tulane University, is the author of *Dante and the "Roman de la Rose"* and *Medievalism, Modernism and Humanism: A Research Bibliography on the Reception of the Works of Ernst Robert Curtius*. He has translated Christine de Pizan's *Book of the City of Ladies* and edited *Reinterpreting Christine de Pizan*. His study on national images in European literature from the Middle Ages through the eighteenth century is forthcoming.

KAREN SCOTT is Assistant Professor of History at DePaul University. She received her Ph.D. from the University of California at Berkeley in 1989. She has published articles on Catherine of Siena and on medieval women and spirituality.

DIANE WATT'S article in this volume builds on her 1989 M.A. dissertation from the University of Bristol, entitled "Gender Distinctions in the Paston Letters." While at Balliol College, she was Snell Exhibitioner for 1990–1991. She received her D.Phil. from the University of Oxford in 1992 for a thesis on "Women Prophets and Visionaries in the Late Middle Ages and Early Modern Period."

ULRIKE WIETHAUS received her Ph.D. from Temple University in 1986. She has written *Ecstatic Transformation*, an interdisciplinary study of mystical experience, and edited *Maps of Flesh and Light*, a collection of essays on medieval women's religious experiences. In addition she has published articles on medieval women's and contemporary feminist spirituality. She teaches Religion at Wake Forest University.

University of Pennsylvania Press
MIDDLE AGES SERIES
Edward Peters, General Editor

F. R. P. Akehurst, trans. *The* Coutumes de Beauvaisis *of Philippe de Beaumanoir*. 1992.

Peter L. Allen. *The Art of Love: Amatory Fiction from Ovid to the* Romance of the Rose. 1992.

David Anderson. *Before the Knight's Tale: Imitation of Classical Epic in Boccaccio's* Teseida. 1988.

Benjamin Arnold. *Count and Bishop in Medieval Germany: A Study of Regional Power, 1100–1350*. 1991

Mark C. Bartusis. *The Late Byzantine Army: Arms and Society, 1204–1453*. 1992.

J. M. W. Bean. *From Lord to Patron: Lordship in Late Medieval England*. 1990

Uta-Renate Blumenthal. *The Investiture Controversy: Church and Monarchy from the Ninth to the Twelfth Century*. 1988

Daniel Bornstein, trans. *Dino Compagni's* Chronicle *of Florence*. 1986

Maureen Barry McCann Boulton. *The Song in the Story: Lyric Insertions in French Narrative Fiction, 1200–1400*. 1993.

Betsy Bowden. *Chaucer Aloud: The Varieties of Textual Interpretation*. 1987

James William Brodman. *Ransoming Captives in Crusader Spain: The Order of Merced on the Christian-Islamic Frontier*. 1986

Kevin Brownlee and Sylvia Huot, eds. *Rethinking the* Romance of the Rose: *Text, Image, Reception*. 1992

Matilda Tomaryn Bruckner. *Shaping Romance: Interpretation, Truth, and Closure in Twelfth-Century French Fictions*. 1993.

Otto Brunner (Howard Kaminsky and James Van Horn Melton, eds. and trans.). Land *and Lordship: Structures of Governance in Medieval Austria*. 1992

Robert I. Burns, S.J., ed. *Emperor of Culture: Alfonso X the Learned of Castile and His Thirteenth-Century Renaissance*. 1990

David Burr. *Olivi and Franciscan Poverty: The Origins of the* Usus Pauper *Controversy*. 1989

Thomas Cable. *The English Alliterative Tradition*. 1991

Anthony K. Cassell and Victoria Kirkham, eds. and trans. *Diana's Hunt/Caccia di Diana: Boccaccio's First Fiction*. 1991

Brigitte Cazelles. *The Lady as Saint: A Collection of French Hagiographic Romances of the Thirteenth Century*. 1991

John C. Cavadini. *The Last Christology of the West: Adoptionism in Spain and Gaul, 785–820*. 1993

Karen Cherewatuk and Ulrike Wiethaus, eds. *Dear Sister: Medieval Women and the Epistolary Genre*. 1993

Anne L. Clark. *Elisabeth of Schönau: A Twelfth-Century Visionary*. 1992

Willene B. Clark and Meradith T. McMunn, eds. *Beasts and Birds of the Middle Ages: The Bestiary and Its Legacy.* 1989

Richard C. Dales. *The Scientific Achievement of the Middle Ages.* 1973

Charles T. Davis. *Dante's Italy and Other Essays.* 1984

Katherine Fischer Drew, trans. *The Burgundian Code.* 1972

Katherine Fischer Drew, trans. *The Laws of the Salian Franks.* 1991

Katherine Fischer Drew, trans. *The Lombard Laws.* 1973

Nancy Edwards. *The Archaeology of Early Medieval Ireland.* 1990

Margaret J. Ehrhart. *The Judgment of the Trojan Prince Paris in Medieval Literature.* 1987

Richard K. Emmerson and Ronald B. Herzman. *The Apocalyptic Imagination in Medieval Literature.* 1992

Felipe Fernández-Armesto. *Before Columbus: Exploration and Colonization from the Mediterranean to the Atlantic, 1229–1492.* 1987

Robert D. Fulk. *A History of Old English Meter.* 1992

Patrick J. Geary. *Aristocracy in Provence: The Rhône Basin at the Dawn of the Carolingian Age.* 1985

Peter Heath. *Allegory and Philosophy in Avicenna (Ibn Sînâ), with a Translation of the Book of the Prophet Muḥammad's Ascent to Heaven.* 1992

J. N. Hillgarth, ed. *Christianity and Paganism, 350–750: The Conversion of Western Europe.* 1986

Richard C. Hoffmann. *Land, Liberties, and Lordship in a Late Medieval Countryside: Agrarian Structures and Change in the Duchy of Wrocław.* 1990

Robert Hollander. *Boccaccio's Last Fiction: Il Corbaccio.* 1988

Edward B. Irving, Jr. *Rereading* Beowulf. 1989

C. Stephen Jaeger. *The Origins of Courtliness: Civilizing Trends and the Formation of Courtly Ideals, 939–1210.* 1985

William Chester Jordan. *The French Monarchy and the Jews: From Philip Augustus to the Last Capetians.* 1989

William Chester Jordan. *From Servitude to Freedom: Manumission in the Sénonais in the Thirteenth Century.* 1986

Ellen E. Kittell. *From Ad Hoc to Routine: A Case Study in Medieval Bureaucracy.* 1991

Alan C. Kors and Edward Peters, eds. *Witchcraft in Europe, 1100–1700: A Documentary History.* 1972

Barbara M. Kreutz. *Before the Normans: Southern Italy in the Ninth and Tenth Centuries.* 1992

E. Ann Matter. *The Voice of My Beloved: The Song of Songs in Western Medieval Christianity.* 1990

María Rosa Menocal. *The Arabic Role in Medieval Literary History.* 1987

A. J. Minnis. *Medieval Theory of Authorship.* 1988

Lawrence Nees. *A Tainted Mantle: Hercules and the Classical Tradition at the Carolingian Court.* 1991

Lynn H. Nelson, trans. *The Chronicle of San Juan de la Peña: A Fourteenth-Century Official History of the Crown of Aragon.* 1991

Charlotte A. Newman. *The Anglo-Norman Nobility in the Reign of Henry I: The Second Generation.* 1988

Joseph F. O'Callaghan. *The Cortes of Castile-León, 1188–1350.* 1989

Joseph F. O'Callaghan. *The Learned King: The Reign of Alfonso X of Castile*. 1993.

William D. Paden, ed. *The Voice of the Trobairitz: Perspectives on the Women Trou-badours*. 1989

Edward Peters. *The Magician, the Witch, and the Law*. 1982

Edward Peters, ed. *Christian Society and the Crusades, 1198–1229: Sources in Transla-tion, including The* Capture of Damietta *by Oliver of Paderborn*. 1971`

Edward Peters, ed. *The First Crusade: The* Chronicle of Fulcher of Chartres *and Other Source Materials*. 1971

Edward Peters, ed. *Heresy and Authority in Medieval Europe*. 1980

James M. Powell. *Albertanus of Brescia: The Pursuit of Happiness in the Early Thir-teenth Century*. 1992

James M. Powell. *Anatomy of a Crusade, 1213–1221*. 1986

Jean Renart (Patricia Terry and Nancy Vine Durling, trans.) *The Romance of the Rose or Guillaume de Dole*. 1993

Michael Resler, trans. Erec *by Hartmann von Aue*. 1987

Pierre Riché (Michael Idomir Allen, trans.). *The Carolingians: A Family Who Forged Europe*. 1993

Pierre Riché (Jo Ann McNamara, trans.). *Daily Life in the World of Charlemagne*. 1978

Jonathan Riley-Smith. *The First Crusade and the Idea of Crusading*. 1986

Joel T. Rosenthal. *Patriarchy and Families of Privilege in Fifteenth-Century England*. 1991

Steven D. Sargent, ed. and trans. *On the Threshold of Exact Science: Selected Writings of Anneliese Maier on Late Medieval Natural Philosophy*. 1982

Sarah Stanbury. *Seeing the* Gawain-*Poet: Description and the Act of Perception*. 1992

Thomas C. Stillinger. *The Song of Troilus: Lyric Authority in the Medieval Book*. 1992

Susan Mosher Stuard. *A State of Deference: Ragusa/Dubrovnik in the Medieval Centuries*. 1992

Susan Mosher Stuard, ed. *Women in Medieval History and Historiography*. 1987

Susan Mosher Stuard, ed. *Women in Medieval Society*. 1976

Jonathan Sumption. *The Hundred Years War: Trial by Battle*. 1992

Ronald E. Surtz. *The Guitar of God: Gender, Power, and Authority in the Visionary World of Mother Juana de la Cruz (1481–1534)*. 1990

Patricia Terry, trans. *Poems of the Elder Edda*. 1990

Hugh M. Thomas. *Vassals, Heiresses, Crusaders, and Thugs: The Gentry of Angevin Yorkshire, 1154–1216*. 1993

Frank Tobin. *Meister Eckhart: Thought and Language*. 1986

Ralph V. Turner. *Men Raised from the Dust: Administrative Service and Upward Mobility in Angevin England*. 1988

Harry Turtledove, trans. *The* Chronicle *of Theophanes: An English Translation of* Anni Mundi *6095–6305 (A.D. 602–813)*. 1982

Mary F. Wack. *Lovesickness in the Middle Ages: The* Viaticum *and Its Commentaries*. 1990

Benedicta Ward. *Miracles and the Medieval Mind: Theory, Record, and Event, 1000–1215*. 1982

Suzanne Fonay Wemple. *Women in Frankish Society: Marriage and the Cloister, 500–900*. 1981

Jan M. Ziolkowski. *Talking Animals: Medieval Latin Beast Poetry, A.D. 750–1150*. 1993

This book has been set in Linotron Galliard. Galliard was designed for Mergenthaler in 1978 by Matthew Carter. Galliard retains many of the features of a sixteenth-century typeface cut by Robert Granjon but has some modifications that give it a more contemporary look.

Printed on acid free-paper.